The Science of Spirit

Beyond the Bleep

A Personal Journal

O. Frank Turner
With
Joyce Turner, Theresa Nash, Älta Turner

Mesa

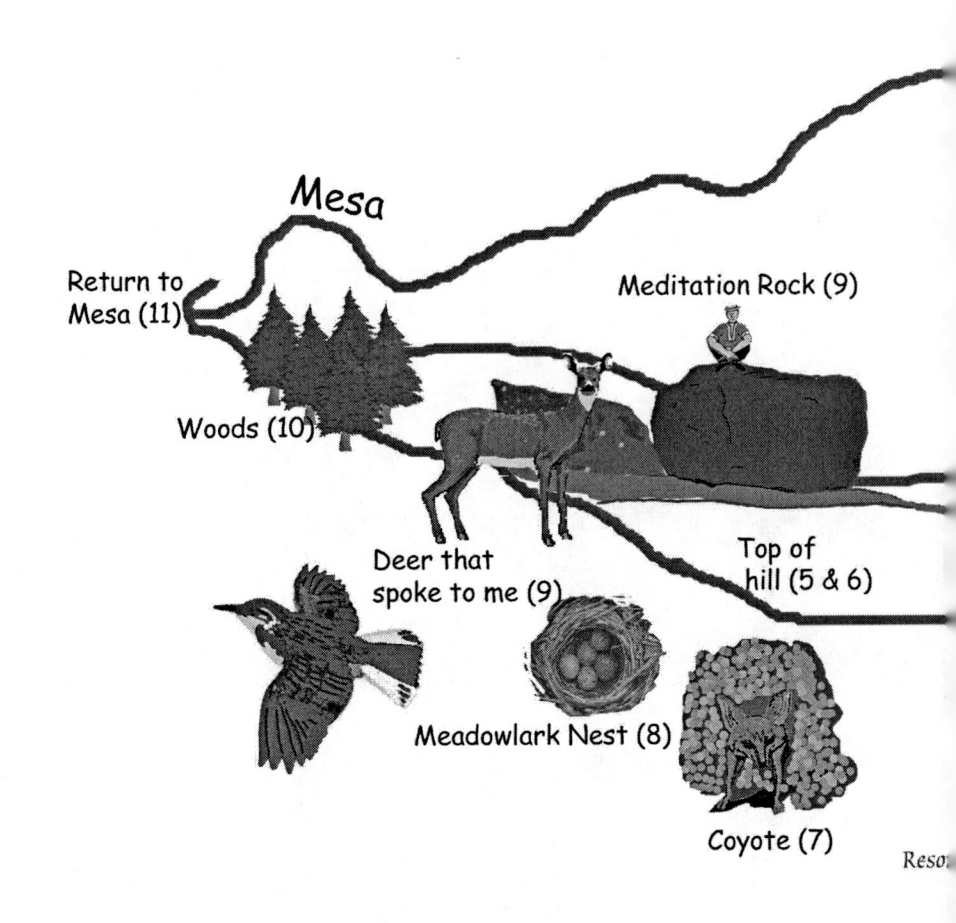

Return to Mesa (11)

Meditation Rock (9)

Woods (10)

Deer that spoke to me (9)

Top of hill (5 & 6)

Meadowlark Nest (8)

Coyote (7)

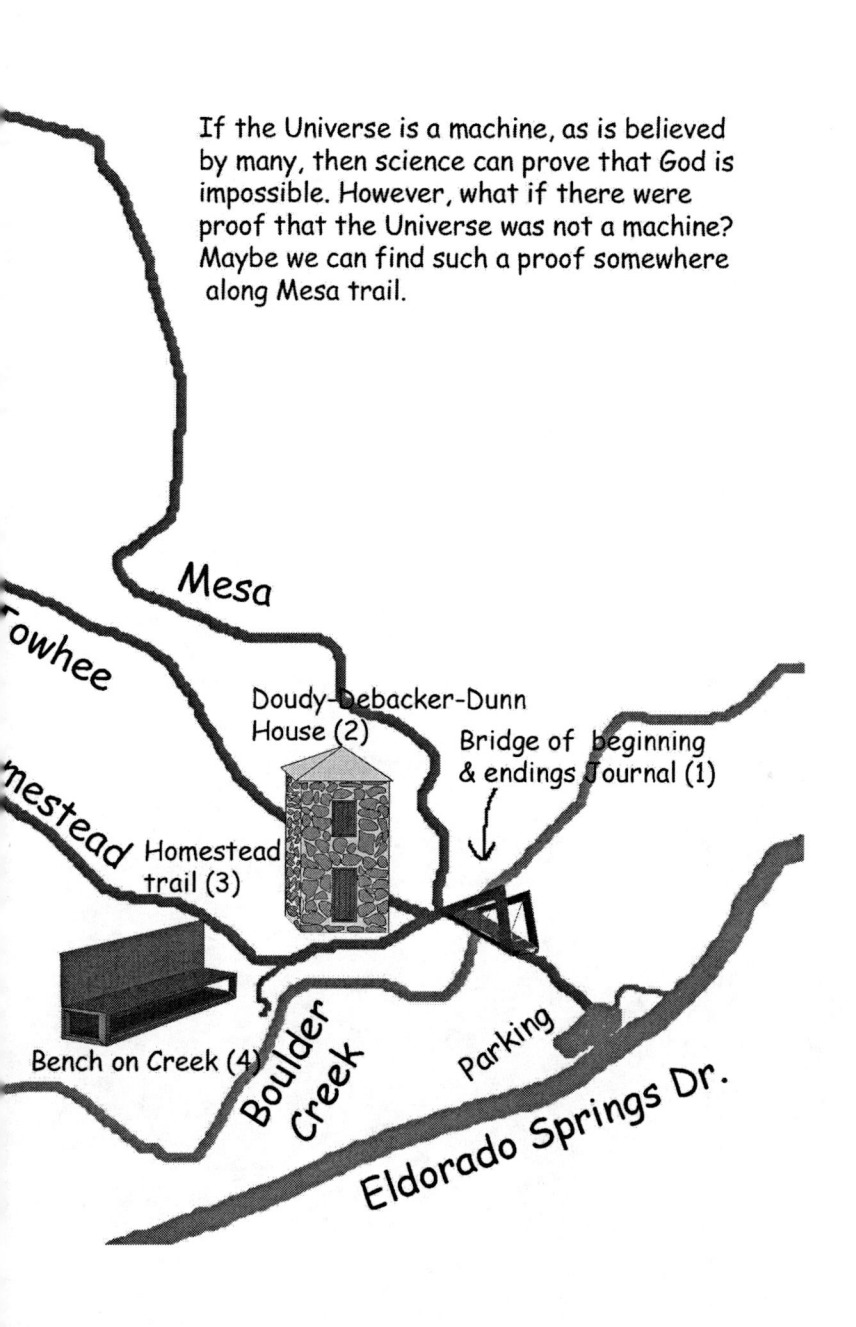

If the Universe is a machine, as is believed by many, then science can prove that God is impossible. However, what if there were proof that the Universe was not a machine? Maybe we can find such a proof somewhere along Mesa trail.

Mesa

Towhee

Homestead

Doudy-Debacker-Dunn House (2)

Bridge of beginning & endings Journal (1)

Homestead trail (3)

Bench on Creek (4)

Boulder Creek

Parking

Eldorado Springs Dr.

Copyright 2003 by Resonant Harmony

All rights reserved. No portion of this book may be reproduced in any form or by any means without written permission of the Publisher.

Turner, O. Frank
The Science of Spirit - Beyond the Bleep

Includes bibliographical references and index.

Second Edition: ISBN: 1-932344-95-0
First Edition: ISBN 0-9729112-0-0

1. Metaphysics– Ontology   2. Philosophy – Idealism   3. Science & Religion

Cover background drawing of early quasar. Downloaded from NASA public owned images. NASA in no way endorses this book.

Manufactured in the United States of America

Thornton Publishing, Inc.
17011 Lincoln Ave. #408
Parker, Colorado 80134

www.ThorntonPublishing.com
www.BooksToBelieveIn.com

Contact the author at:
The Science of Spirit
8758 W. 86th Dr.
Westminster, Colorado 80005-1521
www.ofrank.com
ofrank@ofrank.com

Dedications

To my mother
Nola Pearl Turner
Growing up I believed
that my dad had the most
influence in shaping
my personality, and it was
very significant. But in the
end, I believe it was my Mom.

In memory of my
daughter
Terina Louise
who influenced my
paradigm shift.

Writing a book is not an individual act. The author is just the leader of the team, and he/she is just the instrument of the one consciousness. Special thanks has to go to Irene Shelton who was the first to change some of my bad grammar problems. My wife Joyce spent time correcting my spelling and talking through the concepts and had an important influence on the form this book took. Also, thanks to my daughter Alta Turner and Theresa Nash for many hours of input and editing.

Special thanks goes to Michael L. Hearing, a professor, professional editor, and writer who did the last edit. There are a couple of last minute additions he did not see.

And I wish to thank so very much my reviewers
Mikki Earle
Julia Heskett
Becky Robinson
And last but not least:
I wish to thank my Coach, Carole Billingham, who pushed me to write.

Table of Contents

CONTENT

The Voice Celestial …………………………………....8

Introduction …………………………………….....11

The Call To Truth ……………………………....…...16

The Eye That Sees The World Out There …..….......…….38

The Five Assumptions of Science …………………..62

Cracks in the Machine …………………………….... 86

Part Two Introduction ……………….....…………......108

The Ghost in the Machine …………………….…....113

The Machine: She Came Undone …………....….......131

What Spirit is Made Of ……………………….....156

Genesis 1.1 Twenty-First-Century version …..…....... 181

Non-Local Mind …..………………………….....…....207

The New-Non-Machine…………………....………......217

It Is Either Love Or Nothingness ……………….…... 234

The Science of Spirit

The Voice Celestial

My Battle Cry Is Truth...................	15
Perhaps I Am Myself The Sphinx.........	37
If There Be God.........................	61
Then Suddenly The Air Was Stirred......	85
At Last You See!.......................	112
So Free Yourself From The Illusions....	130
One Does Not Stand Alone............	155
I Know Now Whom Thou Art...........	180
The Great Enigma	206
Then Look Once More	216
There Are Times When Logic...........	233
The Search Is Ended..................	252

"The Voice Celestial" is a 350-page story poem written by Ernest Holmes and his brother Fenwicke Holmes. The poem is the story of Ernest Holmes quest for the truth. Ernest Holmes was a metaphysical philosopher whose works began in the 1920s. He died sometime in the 1960's.

The Farer or Wayfarer in the poem is anybody seeking truth. The Presence or Voice Celestial becomes audible to all who develop the inner ear. The Scribe or Observer is reporting the conversation between the Farer and Presence. The Masters of the Ages appear to the Farer in his higher state of consciousness.

The poems story was hauntingly similar to mine, so I picked one poem that would foreshadow each chapter.

Foreword

By Älta Turner

I grew up in the house of science. My mother was a bit more agnostic, but she didn't discuss her beliefs; whereas my father's favorite pasttime was discussing the latest developments in his science. Some of my best memories are of sitting around the breakfast table talking about the latest discoveries in Science News. My upbringing was very rational and logical, yet democratic - typical of a psychologists child. Luckily, I was taught to be open to others' beliefs, because despite his careful training I was a true believer in the mystical side of life.

It came as a surprise to me when I read that my father first had the revelationary moment leading to this book in 1998. I'd seen it coming for a long time. I attribute it to when he started reading about quantum physics in the late 80's, but the first sign appeared to me while I was at University in the early 90's. I'd told my dad that I thought I'd had an out of body experience. Usually he would say something like, "Oh that's just the way your brain was perceiving information." Instead he said, "Do you think it could have been parallel worlds overlapping? Maybe meeting up during that brief moment?" He asked me as if I might know the answer to that question. The point was that he didn't brush off my statement. He tried to understand it, which to me is the key to this book.

When I was a kid, I would sometimes ask my dad to help me with my math problems. He would then sit down and start drawing, measuring and calculating, and sure enough coming up with the answer. I, nevertheless, was unsatisfied. It drove me crazy that he couldn't just put the numbers into the formulas. I needed to show my teacher the step by step process that I was taught. No wonder that my father didn't do well in school. He never could just fill in the blanks; he had to understand it. I got great grades in math, but I never understood what any of it was about. I just accepted.

The Science of Spirit

My father set out to solve a mystery, perhaps The mystery. He couldn't rely on faith to explain the mystical experiences that he was no longer willing to ignore. He had to find the scientific explanation, and now he's written this book.

I didn't really know what the book was about, but I fell instantly in love. I read it as I was trained, with a skeptical, scientific and rational eye. I tried to see it from the doubters point of view, and still I was overwhelmingly impressed. Yet, the most important thing to me was that it felt right. I hope everyone has experienced that feeling. The one where you're about to embark on something new and it feels like what you were meant to do. Or the feeling one gets from a revelation, or the answer to a long sought out question. That's what this book was for me.

My hope is that every doubter and skeptic reading these pages will follow the logical conclusions to the end, and perhaps have revelations of their own. But most of all I hope that it just feels right.

Älta Turner
T Denmark
2001

Introduction

"Who am I? What am I about? Is what I do important? Am I important? Where did I come from?" When we were young, these were the most critical questions of the day. Then some of us fell into jobs, and others, being more selective, went to college. In the end, we all found ourselves in the workaday world, and life went rolling on. But these questions still linger in the background. Some of us have tried to answer them by turning to religion or spirituality, and some have turned to science.

But this creates a dichotomy. Western religion and western science are diametrically opposed. It then becomes a balancing act to hold the two together. Some resolve this problem by totally rejecting one or the other, but this is just an intellectual exercise. We know in our hearts that both science and religion have their places. So what are we to do?

This is the story of my personal quest to answer these questions. I was raised as a minister's son, but I turned to science for the answers. After all, religion is based on faith while science has math and experimental proof on its side! I felt that I had no choice but to reject the existence of God or Spirit. For the laws of thermodynamics forbid the exchange of energy between a spiritual world and a material one. This meant to me that God or Spirit cannot exist. A law is a law and unbreakable, right? Science can show us how we came into being from a small particle; therefore, there is no need for God. This was my Reality Box.

"Reality Box?" you ask. "What is a Reality Box?"

A Reality Box is a set of assumptions that everyone holds about what the world is really about. These assumptions then dictate what beliefs a person can have. Because only certain beliefs can follow from certain assumptions, it is as if they are all together in a box. Our reality then, the way we see the world, comes directly from our box of assumptions and beliefs: our Reality Box. Everything begins with an assumption— even the interpretation of mathematical and scientific data. This is inescapable.

There is an old story about a truck that gets tightly wedged under a low overpass. A number of top engineers are sent out to figure out a way to get the truck unstuck. After a good hour or two of taking measurements, the engineers are at an impasse. One engineer argues for cutting out a section of the overpass; another disagrees and thinks it best to cut down the truck.

In the midst of all this arguing, a little boy begins tugging on one of the engineer's pants leg. "Excuse me," says the little boy.

"Yes! What do you want?" replies the engineer in an irritated voice.

"Well," asks the little boy, "why don't you just let the air out of the tires?"

I have not ascertained whether this story is really true, but it does illustrate how our Reality Boxes affect our day-to-day lives. The point here is not to put down the engineers or science, but to show how our inescapable human way of thinking often gets in the way of a better understanding of life. The engineers were just looking at the problem from different point of view (a very limited one) than the little boy was— that is, using a different Reality Box.

We, too, miss a lot because of our point of view. And this is where I was as I moved into the 1990's. An atheist with a burning need to find the truth and with a growing realization that science's Reality Box was inadequate.

There is a truism believed to come from Native American culture that goes like this: "You cannot judge a person until you have walked a mile in his moccasins." I am going to allow you to walk in my shoes by retracing the evolution of my thinking. So, the first chapter will begin with my childhood and my early learning and thinking— my first Reality Box. Finally, I hope to paint a picture of a New World with a different reality. A wonderful reality based on scientific knowledge, intuitive understanding, and wisdom.

Welcome

> Hi, and Welcome to our Journey. My name is Ben Zen. I will be your teacher and guide. Let's begin.

My battle cry is Truth,
My banner shall be faith. I think I can.
But where shall I begin?
I first of all must turn to mountain peaks
Of personalities and what they saw
Before men canonized and communized
And cracked the sacred crystal;
To Vedic hymns that sang of the Creation;
To Egypt, sacred keeper of the flame;
To Hebrew prophets, to Moses and the Law;
To Zendavesta, prayer-book of the Parsees,
Transcribed by Zoroaster from the gods;
Or wise Lao-tzu with his Tao old,
Whose wisdom, Lost to China, sealed her doom.

I shall essay to sample all the ore
Of ev'ry land and age but most of all
Extract the gold of those rich mountain souls
Who lived the message that they taught,
Like Krishna, Buddha and the risen Christ.
A tunnel I will run beneath the shaft
That bears the gold of ev'ry age; and so
From each will draw the wealth to build
The temple spires that upward point to God!

I shall absorb from ev'ry source all that
I can of systems known to man; let them
Assume a single body with a Voice
That speaks to me as though it were
The Primal Voice, which first proclaimed,
"Let there be light."

The Voice Celestial
Page 9

The Science of Spirit

Journal 1
The Call to Truth

If you go a few miles south of Boulder, Colorado, on Highway 93, you will come to a large reddish-brown sign, a typical national park sign with deeply grooved white lettering. The sign reads, "El Dorado Springs National Park 5 Miles." When the signal light turns green, you turn your car right onto El Dorado Springs Road— where it immediately makes a sharp turn to the left, as if to tell you what the rest of the road will be like. The road very quickly turns back to the right and goes downhill. At the bottom of the hill, you find yourself in paradise, surrounded by multi-shaded green grass and trees. Farther up the road, the black, brown, and rusty-red peaks of the magnificent Flatiron Mountains can be seen towering above the trees.

After traveling about eight minutes, you see a new brown sign: "Mesa Trailhead." Turning your car to the right and driving down a steep, curving gravel road, you find yourself in a parking lot twenty feet below the paved road. Once parked up against one of the log fence railings, you no longer just see all the surrounding magnificence. You can feel it, taste it, and smell it. You become a part of it.

After a brief walk down a neatly groomed, gray-clay gravel path, you hear the sound of water cascading over rocks. Soon, you find yourself standing on a log bridge just large enough to allow a very small car to pass over it. Beyond this bridge lies the Mesa Trail, with other trails branching off it.

As I stand at the foot of this bridge, the thought comes to me that this is a lot like life and how it begins. We all cross a bridge from our mother's womb and begin a new adventure. We don't know what lies ahead. There are choices along the way that determine where we are going. But we are eager to move down the trail.

The Call to Truth

    I crossed my bridge on Father's Day 1943. The United States had been involved in World War II for two and a half years. The combined English and American forces had just pushed the Nazis out of North Africa and were preparing it as a staging area for an attack on Central Europe. My father, who had joined the Army just six months earlier, was stationed in Missouri. He had asked for a pass to go see his first child's birth, but his pass was denied. He was crushed and could not believe that they would deny him the opportunity to be present at his child's birth. After all, they weren't in North Africa.

    My mother, Nola Pearl, had traveled by bus all the way from Hayden, a small mountain town in northwest Colorado, just so my father could be at my birth. He knew from a phone call, after she arrived, that it had been a miserable trip. She was close to delivery, and her ankles were so swollen she could hardly walk. How could he not go?

    But the risk of leaving one's post in wartime would surely mean brig time or worse. He did not see any other option. He had promised my mother that he would be there, so he left the base. After all, nothing was more important than his new son.

    Once off base, he went around a corner, and there was his commanding officer— walking straight toward him. What should he do? What could he do, but salute him. Surprisingly, his commanding officer returned the salute and walked on past, never saying a word. This incident exemplified my dad's inner moral compass and need to put others above his own needs. This was also a foreshadowing of a strong father-son relationship to come.

    After my birth, Mother could not afford a motel, so she rented an old, converted chicken coop from a local farmer. It had a dirt floor and was large enough to have a bed and a small table with chairs. There was also a small chest of drawers, and Mother

The Science of Spirit

fixed up the bottom drawer as my crib. So I began life in a chicken coup in a chest of drawers!

As I grew up, being a minister's son, a deep belief in God was not questioned and was just a part of my Reality Box*. After the war, when I was in my preschool years in the late 1940s, we moved to Denver, Colorado. There my father used his GI Bill to attend the University of Denver.

Up until this new beginning for all of us, my father had been a minister and "soap- box" preacher. (For the younger generation, that is a person who stands around on street corners and preaches to people walking past.) He passionately cared for other people and believed it was his duty to save them. He would tell people that if they didn't change their ways and believe in God, they would surely go to hell. He used to tell me stories of these radical days— about how he would look out over a crowd at a football game and then, in his imagination, see all of the people in the crowd burning in hell. He was horrified at this and believed it was his duty to try and save them. This was the Reality Box that he was raised with in an ultra-conservative church. He was convinced that the Judeo-Christian Bible contained the whole and complete Truth about how the universe worked. There was no Truth outside the Bible.

My father worked from an assumption that he was raised with, which is, that a giant being, a super human if you will, made the physical world and lived in the sky above the earth. Then this being, called God, demanded obedience to a set of laws that he had laid down in a book called the Bible. As I hope you can see, it is all about assumptions. If his assumptions were true about God, that precluded new assumptions about the Bible. These assumptions were that God wrote the Bible and that every word was therefore a fact. If all of this was true, then my father had no choice but to carry out what he believed to be his mission. But then again, if his assumptions turned out to be wrong, the Bible was just a bunch of words on a page, and my father was just some uninformed person standing on a soapbox.

Regardless of your belief or disbelief in God, I hope that you can see the dilemma here. Everything has to begin with an assumption, and once the assumption is accepted, everything from then on is built on that assumption. Religion defines the assumption as faith; however, I will call this a Reality Box because once the assumptions are made, they create a set of beliefs that seem to fit together. It is as if they were all together in a box. This makes life more comfortable because beliefs that are outside the box can be ignored as untrue, and there is no need to be bothered with them. The tighter a person holds to a set of beliefs, or Reality Box, the harder it is for that person to change and grow.

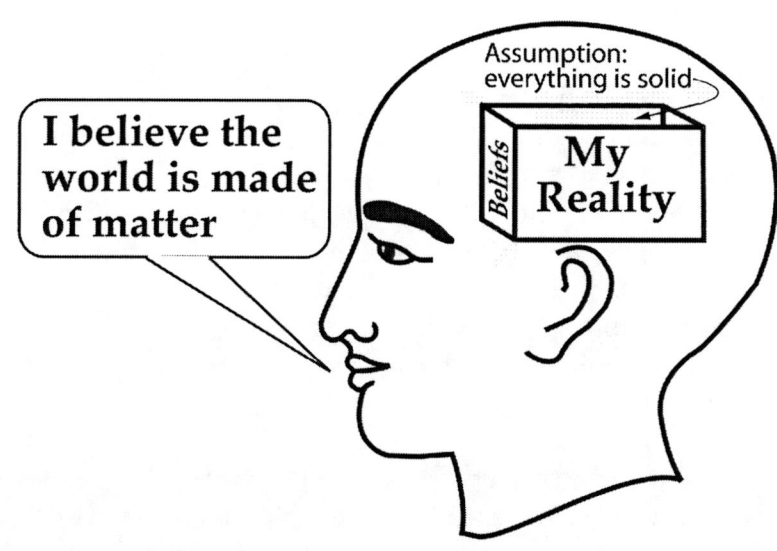

I believe the world is made of matter

Assumption: everything is solid

My Reality / Beliefs

Ben Zen believes that the world is made of matter because of everyday experience. He, as well as you, may change your minds !

The Science of Spirit

Since my father assumed that God was a perfect super human living in the heavens above earth, a whole set of beliefs went with it. God had to be the one that made the earth; and if this was true, he had to have written the Bible; and if God wrote the Bible, to say any single word in the Bible was untrue just didn't fit in the box. For science to say that man was created through a process of evolution was ridiculous because it went against everything that was in the box. My father didn't have to know anything about science or what it was doing. If it didn't fit his box, it was a waste of time looking at it.

In general, we have only one Reality Box. This is because it is our brain that creates it based on the information we grow up with. Once we think we understand the world and seem to be doing okay, it is then a lot of work to look at the world in a different way. People who don't understand Reality Boxes become very upset at information that does not fit in their Reality Box. They perceive it as an attack on them and their very essence.

The original purpose of science was to sort out conflicts between Reality Boxes. Most people understand that religious beliefs are based on an assumption, i.e. faith. But they are surprised to learn that science itself is also based on assumptions, that science has its own Reality Box. Obviously, then, if the assumptions that scientific experiments are based on are untrue, the experiments must be re-examined or re-interpreted.

Around 1948, my father went through a very painful Reality Box shift when he started his philosophy classes at the University of Denver. He told me that he would become extremely angry and upset at his philosophy professor. What they were teaching was complete "nonsense" (outside his Reality Box), and he could not accept it. He said that he would lie awake thinking until two or three in the morning, and then after pacing the floor, he would call his professor up at three in the morning and argue with him. (In 1980 when I moved back to Denver, my dad gave me the phone number of his old philosophy professor. I called the professor to see if he remembered my father. I hardly had his name out of my

The Call to Truth

mouth when he said, "Overton! How could I forget Overton?")

One of the things that my dad learned was what is taught in every beginning philosophy class. This is the philosophy that led to our present scientific age— the Reality Box shift away from religion and metaphysical philosophy. A metaphysical philosophy is a philosophy based on thinking and theory alone and many times then leads to religion. So all religion comes from metaphysics. Many people are unaware of this, like my dad who was raised to believe that all truth came from the Christian Bible. But the Christian Bible was written by men and therefore is based on their thinking and theory. Of course, my dad believed that these men were inspired and directed by God to write what they wrote, and this may or may not be the case. What is important here is to understand that one cannot experimentally prove that the Bible was inspired, so it is classified as metaphysics.

From the Renaissance, beginning in the 1650s, three philosophers emerged who became known as the classical British empiricists. An empiricist is a person who trusts only things that he can sense. Our present science is based on the assumption that if you can't see, hear, touch, or smell something, then it is not real. The first of the British empiricists' was John Locke, who based his philosophy on a principle from an earlier philosopher, William of Ockham. William of Ockham's principle said, "Do not multiply entities beyond necessity," which means that the simpler a thing is, the more likely it is to be true. This principle has come to be known as Occam's Razor. Given two theories, each of which adequately accounts for all the observable data, the simpler theory is the correct theory.

So Locke began by saying that when we are born our mind is a blank piece of paper. If this is true, then everything that we learn or know must come from experience. He asks what the basic or simplest things that we first learn are, and he calls them primary and secondary qualities. For example, try to explain the idea of yellow to someone; you can't. You have to point to something yellow and say this color is yellow. He made a list of primary ideas, e.g., blue, hard, cold, sticky, etc., and from these come secondary ideas, which are a combination of primary and secondary ideas. A concept of an apple comes from a combination of primary and secondary qualities: red-spherical-sweet.

From this it becomes clear that if everything in the world is made of primary and secondary things, then where does God fit into the equation? Whereas Locke assumed the existence of God, his followers did not. By the end of the 1700s and the last of the three British empiricists, there had developed a philosophy that totally excluded the existence of God. Regardless of the rightness of Occam's Razor, the empiricists' powerful arguments had left metaphysics in a shambles and my dad facing a very painful reality that he could not accept.

In case you are unaware, John Locke is the philosopher all of the forefathers of the American Constitution were reading, and just about every concept in the U.S. Constitution came from John Locke. It is even said that the United States is a Lockean experiment.

Radical shifts in one's Reality Box can be quite painful, as you can see from my father's experience. In the end, he saw that his assumption that the Bible contained the only Truth was incorrect, that indeed there could be other truths. Not only did he find that his assumption was incorrect, but he understood that his new dynamic belief system (new Reality Box) was also based on an assumption, but on better information. A belief system that understood that some truths in the Bible were meant for problems faced by ancient people and that the truth for our time may be different. So to understand the truth in the Bible one needed to try and understand the principle given to an ancient people so we could apply the same principle to today's problems.

Just by knowing that everything begins with an assumption makes a change not so painful. He still believed there was a God and that there were truths in the Bible. The difference was that if information came along to challenge these new assumptions, he would just need to evaluate and update the last assumption and go forward. My father grew from this experience, and, as you will see, this greatly influenced my life.

Because of this experience, my father began to play devil's advocate with me when I was about five years old. I remember as a teenager having every expression of a belief or thought challenged. It was somewhat painful for me because I struggled to come up with something he would agree with me on. I remember riding in a car with him one day and talking about a big controversy going on at my school. I said that everyone should just accept everyone else's side. I was trying to be as neutral as I could. He then said, "To be too neutral about everything is not healthy. In order to grow, you have to start with an assumption." Wow! Even taking all sides was out of balance.

He was right, though. We must start with an assumption. The problem only comes when we take our assumptions personally and involve our ego in them. His training had the desired effect because I became quite aware that there were two sides to every story, and it gave me an unusual tolerance for others' beliefs and the ability to change and grow. However, it also taught me to be very analytical in my approach, and that led me to science as the method for seeking Truth.

I started school in the basement of a little church in Denver, Colorado, the last year my father attended the University of Denver. I don't remember the school very well, except that I was very unhappy and didn't learn a thing. I do remember getting a dime every morning to ride the trolley car to and from school. I also remember figuring out that if I walked the route to school, I could spend the dime on an ice-cream cone on the way home.

After my father graduated from the University of Denver, we moved to the small farm community of Elmwood, Nebraska, where he was to be the minister. In the late forties the church provided us with a house, but my dad's salary was only what was in the collection plate on Sunday. With three children, my two sisters and me, my mother and father were very poor to say the least. One thing that helped with the food bill was that we always went to lunch at someone's house on Sunday after church. We had running water, but we had no bathroom and had to use an outhouse out in the back. And Nebraska has very cold and snowy winters. I could be mistaken but I seem to remember using catalogs.

The life of a minister in a small community in the Midwest was

The Science of Spirit

very difficult at best. Someone always disagreed with the minister, and since there weren't very many members to start with, it was easy to get together a quorum to fire the minister. So it was common for ministers to move yearly in a constant game of musical churches. This affected my schooling greatly. Changing schools yearly left me with no roots, no friends, and no interest in learning.

I failed the first grade in Denver and could not even spell my name. But because the school in Elmwood was concerned about my age, they put me in the second grade anyway and tried to teach me first and second grade at the same time. This just confused me even more. By the next year, we had moved to Greenwood, Nebraska, where my third sister was born. The school there put me in the third grade— even though I could not read a word or spell my name. Then my dad got a much better paying job at the First Christian Church in Omaha, Nebraska, where I repeated the third grade. But Omaha turned out to be a painful experience for us.

It started out great because my dad had a good income, and we had our first TV. Then Christmas came, and Dad invited an African American chorus to sing *The Messiah* for Christmas service. This was a disaster. A number of influential members of the church board were very racially biased and were so angry at my dad for letting "niggers" sing in their church that they called a board meeting after church. They gave my father two weeks to move out of the parsonage.

My father now had no job, so he called the store to come and pick up our new TV. He had no choice but to move to my grandparents' house in Oklahoma until he got a job. He was so discouraged with so-called Christians that he decided to quit the ministry and got a job working for the YMCA in Muskogee, Oklahoma. The school there, you guessed it, made me repeat the third grade yet again. My teacher, Miss Lemon, was horrified to learn that I couldn't even spell my name and gave me special attention. So at age nine, I learned to spell my full name and began to read.

My Dad then offered me a dollar if I got a 100% on my spelling

The Call to Truth

test. I was thrilled and began working hard to learn my spelling words. I worked very hard. I would have to write each and every word over and over one hundred times to learn it. Even then, when I took the spelling test at school, I missed one of the ten words and got 90%. My Dad would not give me anything for my effort. I was very disappointed and gave up learning any spelling words at all. It wasn't until I started college that I learned why I had so much trouble learning spelling words. My severe dyslexia would have a clear impact on my life down road.

The greatest impact on my development was our move when I was ten years old. We moved to Chinle, Arizona, on the Navajo reservation. My father had gotten a job with the U.S. Government. His job was to oversee the living quarters of a boarding school for Navajo school children. In the early fifties, the government was trying to move Navajos off the reservation. They believed that if the Navajos could read and write American English, they would no longer want to live on the reservation. Most of the Navajo parents saw no reason for sending their children to the white man's school, so the government gave them a monthly check.

In the early fifties Chinle was nothing but a government town. It consisted of two large barracks, one for the boys and one for the girls. There were also several school buildings, a power plant, and about thirty houses for the staff and their families. The nearest town was Gallup, New Mexico, 90 miles to the east. About one or two miles to the north, at the mouth of Canyon De Chelly (which has numerous famous ruins of Indian cliff dwellings), there were two trading posts where the Navajos would trade sheepskins and rugs for food. These trading posts were our only source of food and other commerce. The trading posts will give you a good picture of the Navajo culture and the primitive nature of life on

The Science of Spirit

the reservation in the early fifties.

The trading posts were similar to the general store that you always see in frontier movies, mostly old one-room buildings. Inside, all of the food and merchandise was kept on shelves that circled the room. There was a counter in front of the shelves that also went around the room. Because customers were not allowed access to any merchandise, most of the room was empty space, except for an old black potbellied wood stove standing in the middle. There were always a half dozen or more Navajos standing around this stove getting warm, talking, and drinking pop.

The men were dressed in blue jeans and colorful shirts. They

Family in front of a Navajo Hogan

always had necklaces, most made of turquoise and silver, and earrings that consisted of a string through their earlobes with a hunk of turquoise on the string. The women had even more jewelry with large turquoise bracelets and brightly colored blouses and skirts. Also, the women quite often had brightly colored wool "Indian" blankets wrapped around their shoulders.

To buy anything, you had to wait until someone waited on you. Then you told the clerk what you wanted, who would then stack it on the counter in a pile. Once you had everything, the clerk would then ring it up on an old mechanical cash register. Cash or trade only, no checks (the nearest bank 90 miles away), and the idea of a credit card had not even entered our heads. There was no paper or plastic. If there was too much to carry, and you didn't bring

The Call to Truth

your own box, you could use an old cardboard box that food had been shipped in.

Once when we were getting groceries, the clerk, I think her name was Margaret, was having trouble getting all of our groceries into the box. After she had made several frustrating tries, my dad said, "I'll bet you that watermelon on the shelf that I can get everything in the box in one try."

"I'll bet you can't," replied Margaret.

He did, and we got a free watermelon.

In Chinle they saw that I needed serious academic help. It was

Navajo Boy Scout Troop - Chinle 1954

worked out so that I would go back to the first grade for half a year and then to the second grade for the next half. By the end of the first year I was reading some. The Navajo school in Chinle went only to the third grade. This was a problem for some of the staff because they had children who had moved beyond the third grade. So the government set up a little one-room school for the fourth through seventh grades.

I was sent to this one-room schoolhouse. It had four rows of seats, with a grade in each row. The teacher would walk from row to row giving each class a lesson. Shortly after I started in the one-room school, the original teacher left. A retired professor of botany, whose real interest was studying the plants in the area, replaced her. He would give us an assignment, expecting us to do it like college students, and then go to the back of the room where he had a small botany lab set up. There he would study and dry plants on an old potbellied wood stove. While this was a great arrangement for him, I was again left in limbo.

One Room School Navajo Reservation 1954

Probably the most horrifying experience I had growing up happened in Chinle. There were lots of stray dogs running around the area. Every once in awhile these dogs would form packs. As far as I know, no one was ever hurt, but most of the white people were afraid of these packs. So a group of white men got together to do something about them.

One Sunday morning they formed a hunting party and went around the neighborhood shooting wildly at every dog they saw. This was clear stupidity and was just an excuse to go around shooting dogs. While no humans were hurt, several houses wound up with shot out windows and bullets going through walls into the living rooms. To make matters even worse, a number of pet dogs inside fences were killed, including ours.

I remember coming home from church and seeing our pet dog lying in the yard inside our fence, blown apart by a shotgun. The entire front of our house, which was painted white, was covered with blood and globs of fat. I clearly remember the shock and disbelief that this had really happened. For a ten-year-old to lose a pet was bad enough, but to see it brutally murdered was truly horrifying.

My dad was very angry and wrote letters to the government and the National Humane Society. The government then got thousands of letters from members of the Humane Society. It got so bad for the government that they sent the FBI out to Chinle to see what was going on. In the end, the supervisor of Chinle was severely reprimanded.

After that I drew a clear demarcation between whites and Navajos. I could not imagine the gentle Navajos that I knew even thinking of such a mass killing just for the fun of it. The Navajos did not think of animals as lesser beings. They believed that we were all equal partners. This impression has only been reinforced over the years.

I also learned that as an individual you can make great changes in the world. My father had done it, just by writing, in this case, to the Humane Society. The individual is not powerless, as many believe.

Despite all of this, as I look back, the period in Chinle was the happiest of all my years growing up. Here I was fully immersed in a simple culture that gave me a sense of spirituality and connectedness to nature that I have not found since. All my friends, except one, were Navajos. I was even given a Navajo name. It was pronounced ch'ééhdigháhí and meant "turtle." This name was in no sense a put down as it would be in the white culture. It was just a true description of me, a slow-moving person. My Navajo friends would come to my house, like kids everywhere, knock on the door, and say, "Can ch'ééhdigháhí come out and play?"

We spent most of our playtime involved in nature, looking for horned toads and raising tadpoles in a big wash tub in the yard. I went through puberty while on the reservation, and my first love was a pretty Navajo girl. We would meet on the school grounds after school and talk while we sat on the swings.

It is clear to me, looking back, that you do not need lots of things and nice houses to be happy. Happiness clearly comes from within. When you live in the desert, you are forced to look inward. Superficial things do not distract you. We have clearly lost this in our American culture. Things are no longer looked on as tools or life enhancements, but as necessities. We have forgotten where we came from and are paying dearly, emotionally, for this oversight.

In 1957, after three years on the reservation, we moved back to "civilization." Tishomingo, Oklahoma, was where my father resumed his ministry. This was a radical new world to me after the reservation— very noisy, busy, and uncaring. The school system

The Science of Spirit

was again concerned with my age and started me out in the seventh grade. I never did go to grades four through six. But this time I saw it as a new beginning, and, for the first time, I was excited about school. I got into the band and learned to play the drums, but science class was the most fun. The science teacher was a hands-on person, so we did lots of experiments. I remember him bringing a Bible to school one day and showing us that the creation story in the Bible did not conflict with science. He said that just like science, the Bible version started with the creation of the earth and lower animals up to man.

The Navajo culture had instilled a special sense of spirituality in me that was now missing. My belief in the existence of God was just there, part of my Reality Box and not questioned. So, within a year of coming off the reservation, I joined the church and was baptized one Sunday morning in May. The whole congregation gathered at Pennington Creek after church. Here my father petitioned my belief, placed a cloth over my mouth and nose, and in the name of the Father, Son, and Holy Spirit immersed me in the gently flowing water of the creek.

Here it would seem that my Reality Box was pretty well fixed in a Judeo-Christian belief system. There were, however, some cracks. The need for everything to yield to analysis was there, as was the gentleness and different spirituality of the Navajos.

A hateful incident took place about a week after school started. On my way home from school one day, I was challenged to a fight. As is common in our culture, someone always has to be the toughest or the king of the mountain (unlike in the Navajo culture, where there is no need for this dominance behavior). Here I was, surrounded by a gang of young teenage boys, with one of them calling me obscene names intended to insult me. I did not have the slightest idea what he was talking about. I had just spent the last three years on the Navajo reservation. Those words he was calling me sounded like some foreign language. He was calling my mother something, but whatever it was, I hadn't a clue. So I just walked away, and he won by default.

Another common experience that I had growing up involved ghost stores. My parents would tell of talking to spirits. One of the stories that they told was of "tipping tables." Two to four people would sit around a card table and hold their hands several inches above the table. They would then, in a meditative state, ask the table to rise. The table would then rise up off the floor and touch their hands. Or they would ask the table questions and it would lift a leg once for yes and twice for no. My mother said the table would accurately answer personal questions that only she knew the answer to. Once they asked the table to knock a picture off a wall. The table then slid several feet hitting the wall.

How could I not believe that there were ghosts? I knew my parents, and they were both very reasonable and rational people. But unlike my mother, who accepted spirits as normal and unfrightening, I was very frightened. I did not want this to be true. I wanted reality to be simple and solid. Even as a child I was very logical, and ghosts made no sense. So I was trapped in this dichotomy of not wanting to believe what they said was true, but knowing in my heart that they were right. If one is truly looking for the Truth of reality one cannot conveniently ignore strange events and honestly say that one has looked at all the information. I cannot say what made the table hit the wall, but I know it hit the wall— and *that* is outside of normal experience.

From as young an age as I can remember, my father would take me with him when he visited his friends, where I would sit listening to them discuss science and philosophy. One of the hottest topics that my father and his friends discussed was Albert Einstein's theory of relativity. This is how I was first introduced to Einstein.

It was called a theory because it was based on a picture painted by math. One of the assumptions that science works from is that math is an analog to the real world. This has been shown to be true constantly throughout the history of science. By first working out what the math says about something, one can then do an experiment to see if the math is right. Since the math has always been right in the past, there is little doubt that it will be right in the future about things that are difficult to test. In fact, after 90 years of experiments, science has yet to disprove any of Einstein's theory of relativity.

I was just blown away by the concepts that Einstein laid out

The Science of Spirit

in this theory. Einstein's math said that it was not possible to travel faster than the speed of light. That as a person, spaceship, or whatever begins to increase in speed, it would also begin to increase in size, and at the speed of light would convert to pure energy. Of course, at the speeds that we travel here on the earth, the changes would be so small that it would be very hard to measure. But for a space ship traveling in space, once it reached the speed of light, it would become pure energy, with all time and aging stopping.

Stop aging! What a concept! How could that be possible? It made no sense. Just look around you at the world. It's like a machine. There is a cause and effect for everything, just like one gear pushing a second one.

Machines I understood. When I was sixteen and got my driver's license, my dad got me an old '53 Chevrolet. It was obvious that he didn't want me driving his car. He was right, because within a few months, I tried to read a map while driving at the same time. The car jumped a ditch, plowed into a farmer's fence on the other side, and did a lot of damage to the right side of the car.

I was able to drive the car home, but then had no way to fix the body damage. Someone then told me about a '53 Chevrolet body that had no engine. The owner sold it to me for $50.00, and I helped him tow it to my house. I then set out to move the engine from my wrecked car to the new body. I had never worked on a car before, but I had this innate confidence that I could do it. Someone told me that it would be silly to go to all the trouble pulling an engine out of a car without replacing the rings. I wasn't even sure what rings were.

I jerry-rigged a hoist and just started unhooking everything that was preventing the engine from coming out. I got the engine out on the ground, then walked down the street from our house, and asked an old mechanic how to change the rings. He explained the basic process with tips like how to lay the head bolts out so they go back in the same hole. I then overhauled the engine and put it in the new body. After more conversations with the mechanic down the street, I got the car running. (I drove that car until I went in the U.S. Navy at age 20. I had learned my lesson about trying to drive and read a map at the same time.)

When I told people what I had done, most would not believe me, but a few were quite impressed. I was amazed at this. Maybe I had a talent for mechanics, but mostly I just didn't understand why other people thought it was so hard. To me, it was so very obvious and simple. Maybe this is why I wanted the world to be the same way, simple and elegant like a machine.

My Call to Truth

When I was seventeen, I left home for the summer to work as a staff member at a Boy Scout camp. While at camp, on my eighteenth birthday, I received a happy-birthday letter from my dad. The letter began, "I have chosen this, your eighteenth birthday, as the day to write you this special letter." Then after talking about how proud he was of me (for fathers can be a touch on the biased side, as you know) and after listing some of my accomplishments, he said:

> Now for the wisdom I would pass on to you. It is first of all that wisdom is the most worthwhile goal a man can seek in life. Seek it. And second, only thinking, observation, reading and experience can bring wisdom. No one can give it to you as a gift; you must claim wisdom through your own efforts. But the seeking is worth the struggle. Make wisdom your goal.

He then gave me an assignment "in wisdom." He asked me to write four essays, one each on the following statements or proverbs:

> Those whom the Gods would destroy, they first make mad with power.

> The mill of God grinds slowly, but it grinds exceedingly fine.

> The bee fertilizes the flower he robs.

> When it is the darkest, you can see the stars.

He then said that a philosopher, Dr. Charles R. Beard, believed that these four proverbs contain all the wisdom of the ages. My father added, "But then you are not going to take his word on it, are you?" (See Appendix B for the full text of the letter.)

I never did write the four essays for my dad, and he never asked me for them. Nevertheless, the letter affected me profoundly. It was the first "belief" that my father gave me that was not challenged by the devil's advocate. From that point on, I knew my mission in life. My mission was to seek the Truth at all costs. I knew then that the Truth would sometimes be difficult to accept, but it had to be supreme over all my needs. My Reality Box was now based on a belief in God but with Truth as my purpose in life. I understood that I didn't have the luxury to accept anything at face value.

Few people understand this commitment. They just accept the beliefs they were raised with as fact. But once you learn not to accept things at face value, there is no turning back. It is like trying to unlearn driving a car. This is probably as it should be because it is a changing, uncertain way to live. For the world to grow and change, a few must live that uncertain life, and I appear to have been chosen. At this point, however, I had misinterpreted my father's words and translated wisdom as intellectual truth. But that is as it should be also, for the search for intellectual truth often leads to wisdom.

The next chapter leads to a traumatic experience that lays the ground for my doubt in the existence of God.

New Reality Box 1

We all grow up with a set of beliefs that we get from our parents, schools, and churches. We are convinced that these beliefs are true. In our minds, these beliefs all fit together as if in a box. Then when information comes along that is outside this box, and would challenge the beliefs in the box, most people would rather fight than to change their Reality Box.

Science also has a Reality Box. All experiments and math have to be interpreted in order to be of value. What is in the scientists' Reality Box directly affects what their interpretation will be and what experiments they will do.

Over the last 75 years, experiments have shown that the basic beliefs of many scientists are wrong and therefore much research needs to be re-interpreted.

Perhaps I am my self the Sphinx, the dumb
Unblinking stone that broods but does not think.

O God, if God there be, O Soul of souls,
I cannot bear the hollowness and pain
That fells my heart with loneliness and grief;
How can I bear the emptiness of ignorance?
I WANT TO KNOW AND KNOW I KNOW.

> *The Voice Celestial*
> *Page 4*

Journal 2
The Eye That Sees the World Out There

As I walk up the Mesa Trailhead, I come to a very old building made of large stones mortared together. The building is fenced off with a wood-rail fence to keep me at bay. Just outside the fence there is a stone column with a plaque indicating that the building was the Doudy-Debacker-Dunn house, the people who homesteaded this land. Compared to a modern home, it is very small, only about twelve feet square. This makes it look very tall because it has two stories. The reconstructed wood door blends with the house and the two boarded-up window upstairs. The building has a new pyramid-shaped roof made of tin, with modern downspouts. The thought comes to me as I look at this old, long-deserted building that life is always changing and moving on.

It was now time for me to make my transition out into the world. Shortly before I graduated from high school, my school counselor called me in and tried to encourage me to go to tech school. She said, "There is no way you can ever make it in college with your academic record." I was quite crushed as I had counted on a college education to begin my quest for the Truth.

So after graduating from high school, I joined the U.S. Navy. This was partly to avoid being drafted and having to sleep in the mud in a tent in Vietnam. I knew that, on a ship, I would at least have a clean bed. I also had no interest in going on foot patrol every morning with snipers shooting at me. I was very naive and believed the hype of the Navy recruiter. He told me that if I joined the Navy, they would train me to be a Naval photographer.

But that never happened. I was sent to school to be an airplane airframe mechanic. I was devastated. I could not believe that the recruiter could have lied to me. I could not believe that I was going to have to learn such useless skills as riveting, spray painting, and working sheet metal. I was upset and wrote home of

The Eye That Sees the World Out There

my terrible plight. My father responded with a three-page, typed letter. He explained the realities of life and told me that there was no such thing as useless skill, that one never knows what life will hold and what information will be useful and what will not.

He was right. The skills that I learned as an airframe mechanic have proven invaluable in the last 40 years, from making a living for my family while going to college to painting numerous cars over the years.

I then began receiving a similar letter every month from my father giving me fatherly philosophical wisdom and advice. One letter that stands out came after I had visited Japan for the first time. I had written home to say that I had gone out and seen the "real" Japan. I meant that I had seen more than the tourist side of Japan and had not just gone to the bars like most of the sailors. My dad wrote back and said that the bars and prostitutes were also a part of the "real" Japan. He was right, again. I was feeling superior because I recognized that there was more to life than just bars and prostitutes.

Another letter may have saved me. In 1966 our ship, the USS Coral Sea, was off the coast of Vietnam doing bombing runs into the country. My co-worker friend and I were working on the joint of a wing. Planes on aircraft carriers fold their wings up over the body of the plane to make more room on the flight deck. As we were working, I noticed a strange little lever that I had not seen before. I had been working on these planes daily for several years but had never seen this before. I just touched it with my finger, and by spring action the lever flipped. Suddenly two 500-pound rocket launchers came loose from their mountings on the wing towering above us. Time literally stopped.

What obviously took only a second appears in my memory as if happening in slow motion. As I watched the launchers hurtling down on us, I started to yell, "Look out!" But before my words could leave my mouth, one of the launchers struck me a glancing blow knocking me back several feet to the deck. The other launcher landed in my friend's arms pushing him to the deck and crushing him.

Words cannot describe the fear and denial that go through one's head when tragedy strikes. My mind kept pushing the rocket pods back up onto their mounts and saying: "THIS DID NOT HAPPEN! How can I undo this? There must be a way to put them back and start over." Then, before my mind could clear, I found myself in a ready room, with tears running down my face and surrounded by sailors and officers asking over and over and over, "WHAT HAPPENED? WHAT HAPPENED?"

By the next day, the noise and commotion was over, and the ship was back to business as usual. But my stomach had not stopped churning, and I was still in a daze. I was left with the extreme realization that I had been guilty of causing my friend's death. The Navy didn't help matters much. They expected me to get on with my airframe work while the investigation into the accident got under way. I began to spiral down into a deeper and deeper depression. I tried going to the ship's chaplain, but that didn't help.

Two of the planes from my squadron leaving on a mission over Viet Nam. You can see how the wings fold with the loaded bombs.

Finally, I got a letter from my dad who helped me understand that it was an accident and that someone does not always have to be at fault. Fault involves intent, and there was no intent. Things just happen. We all do impulsive, stupid things on the spur of the moment, which we have to live with the rest of our lives. But by dwelling on them and feeling sorry for ourselves, we just create more victims. This helped me see that even if the investigation went against me, I could be assured in my heart that it was just an accident, a lesson I needed to learn, and that I should think of the pain that his family would have to live with. This was indeed a hard lesson. I couldn't bring my friend back, and I just needed to get on with my life and get my focus back on seeking the Truth.

I started feeling better, and then a few weeks later, I was exonerated from being the cause of the accident. It was determined that a warning sign should have been painted around the lever, and our airframes shop was asked to invent a cover. So I volunteered to come up with a device. I invented a device that covered the lever automatically as soon as the wings began to fold up, exposing the wing joint. Then, when the wing came down, it would move out of the way so the lever could do its job. Never again will someone be lost because of this lever.

Even though I was no longer punishing myself for the accident, I was still in pain and dwelled on it constantly when I was alone. Why did this happen? It really brought home the mechanicalness and randomness of the universe. Even though I did not consciously question the existence of God (for my religious Reality Box was still in place), this was the first seed of doubt. I was asking this question: "If there is a God, why does the world seem so cold and random, and why do I feel so alone?" My whole world was the Navy, a world based on destruction and the killing of other human beings. All I heard were cheers and congratulations every time a plane would return with reports of more killing, day after day. The pilots all had small replicas of all the planes they had shot down. Each replica represented not a toy plane in an arcade, but a real human life— a human who had once lived, cried, and had a family.

When I tried to talk to others about God and war, I was given the same simplistic answer. "God gave us free will, and it is that free will that has led to war and killing." But this answer bothered me. It sounded like an "easy way" to explain away a troubling subject, and if this was wrong, what else was being just "explained away?" It seemed to me that if God was so perfect, he ought to make humans better so that they would not enjoy killing. If we were forced into war, like everyone said, then why did everyone look at it as a fun game? Why did we not have prayers seeking to be forgiven for the horrible things we were forced to do? No! I could not believe the answer was that simple. There was more going on than free will.

I also began to think a lot about self-awareness, our sense of time perception, and where it came from. Why did I remember the event on the flight deck as taking minutes and not seconds? We all have this experience that we are really separate from our body, and yet still feel our body. We feel as if we have put our body on like a piece of clothing. But there were no books on the ship that would give me these answers, and no one that I knew of to talk to. This is when I decided that I MUST find a way to go to college even though I had academic problems. I was never going to find the Truth in the Navy.

College

It was in college that my mechanical, clockwork thinking became truly entrenched. When I first started college in 1969, my father's words vibrated through my being. I was setting out to find the Truth, but I was very quickly overwhelmed. Who was right? At the time, there were over two hundred different Christian denominations, each claiming to know the "Truth." Every person I talked to and every class I took offered different ideas and ways of thinking. So it became apparent that I would have to find a way to cut through all the "opinions" and get down to the "facts."

Science fit this bill perfectly. It was based on experimental evidence only— and not on opinion. No speculating about the number of teeth a camel had here, like the Old-World philosophers did. I was going to actually count them. If the "Truth" was ever going to be found, it would be through science. But I had no math background at all and learned this the hard way.

Here I was, a freshman just out of the Navy, and I tried to take college chemistry after only a "D" in high school algebra. What followed was five semester hours of "F." If I had been smart, and not stubborn, I would have realized that there was no way, at that time, that I could have made it in chemistry. I needed to have at least a couple of courses in algebra. If I had dropped out of chemistry at the half-way point, I could have had a "drop" and not five hours of "F," which destroyed my grade point average forever.

To make matters worse, at the beginning of my first semester, I was failing all of my classes. I was reading too poorly to keep up with the huge volume of required reading, and my professors where upset with my very poor spelling on essay tests. I knew that I had to do something fast, or I was not going to make it. I turned to one of the psychology professors who sent me to a speech pathology professor. This is how I first heard of dyslexia and found out I am severely dyslexic. The speech pathology professor and I were a great match. He was just in the process of testing a new phonics system, and I was a great candidate to test it on.

He had taken the seventeen vowel sounds in the English language and drawn seventeen boxes on a piece of paper. He then put all the letter combinations in the box for that sound. For example, box number one had OO and stood for the sound like the O's in "loop." Box two also had OO but signified the sound like the two O's in "look." Box three then had O-E, OA, -O, and OW. So this box had the long O sound as in "home" or "boat." The dash between two letters, like O-E, stood for a consonant, which mostly meant that the second letter was silent.

He tested me and said that I was reading on a third-grade level, and, because I was dyslexic, I could not hear the difference between vowel sounds. I was then given an assignment to start learning the sound boxes, along with a stack of children's books to read. It worked. By the end of the semester, I was re-tested and had jumped to a seventh- grade reading level, which was as high as this test would go.

Psychology

Psychology was great. It not only was considered a science, but it also involved philosophy, which I grew up on. And a lack of algebra was not a death sentence. Also, my dad would be truly proud to have a son who was a psychologist. Amazing, isn't it, the influence our parents have over us? So my decision was made and written in stone as they say.

The first lesson that every psychology student learns is that there is no one-to-one relationship between what our five senses take in and what is really out there in the world. We all grow up with the assumption that if we look at a red ball, there really is a thing out there that is a ball covered with a substance that is really the color red. So the assumption is made that everyone who looks at the red ball is seeing exactly the same thing, in all its details in the same way. The hard concept to master here is that everything is just made up in our brain. We've agreed that what we're seeing is a red ball, but we don't know what others are really seeing; and the red ball doesn't even need to be there for us to see it. Also, red to me could look green to you, but we both call it "red" because we have agreed that when we perceive that frequency of light, it's called "red."

Even when we understand this— that everything our senses tell us is just made up in our head— we can't really accept it because we have to get on with our day-to-day living. To go around reminding yourself that the fork in your hand or the food on your plate may not be real would make life very difficult at best. This is true with all our five senses. We can not only see a red ball that is not really there, but we can also hear the imaginary ball bounce on the sidewalk, smell the rubber, and taste the imaginary dirt on it with our tongue. We always think, "Well, I could tell the difference between an illusion and the real thing." But, sadly, that is not always the case. You only need to experience a good illusion once to know how real an illusion can be.

This is such a critical point that we need to explore it a touch longer. Let's take the eye because sight is the most convincing illusion of all. And we may just learn some fun facts about the eye in the process.

Most people think of the eye as a simple camera that takes a picture of the world. The first problem with this belief is that the eye is filled with a somewhat milky fluid. Did you ever look at an

The Eye That Sees the World Out There

object through a milky fluid? Everything at the bottom is fuzzy. The edges do not appear sharp and clean, but soft and out of focus. Well, that is just the way the image looks when it reaches the back of the eyeball, as if it's out of focus.

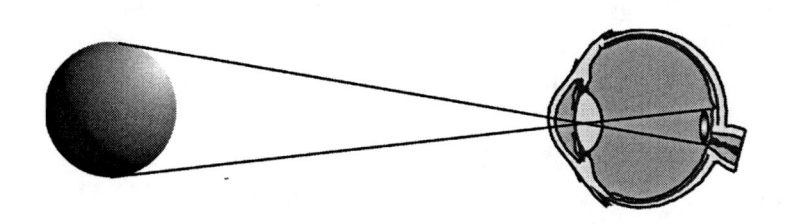

If this is so, then how come I can see nice sharp edges on everything I look at? Because of a ganglion. Let me explain. The simple picture of the eye that we learned in school is of light going through a lens and forming this sharp image on the back of the eye. This image is picked up by the rods and cones and sent on to our brain. But there is a lot missing in this explanation.

First, the light image travels through a fluid to the back of the eye and arrives in a somewhat fuzzy state. It then goes through a relatively transparent membrane where a group of nerve-like structures called ganglion cells reside. The light image goes through a second, relatively transparent membrane that contains more nerve-like structures called bipolar cells. The image then goes into a third transparent membrane where it finally meets these famous rods and cones that we all know about. To top it off, the rods and Cones are turned backwards towards the back of the eye, i.e., not facing towards the light coming in.

Some animals have a reflective coating just behind the rods and cones. The purpose of this coating is to reflect the light back to the rods and improve night vision. This is why some animals' eyes seem to glow at night. You are seeing light reflected off the reflective coating at the back of their eyes.

The Science of Spirit

Here is what seems to happen. The fuzzy image hits the back of the retina behind the rods and cones. The image is reflected back and is picked up by the cones (rods if it's dark) and converted to an electrical pulse— not a steady flow of electricity, but a set of digital pulses. The rate of the pulses tells the brain the brightness of the light. The fact that it is pulses going to the brain shows that we must make up a picture because when we look around, we see what appears to be a smooth flow of light coming into our eyes. We can not tell that what the brain is getting is just a series of digital pulses. The electrical pulses then travel from the cone to the bipolar and ganglion cells, which look like a string of Christmas tree lights. This is where the first processing of the light begins before the light signals leave the eye. (Things get very complex from here on, so I won't go into any detail.) Just understand that one thing the bipolar and ganglion cells do is to take the fuzzy image and clean it up in much the same way poor quality photographs are enhanced by a computer. When the signal then goes on to the brain, the brain gets a higher quality image. But this also means that the final image may not represent exactly what's actually out there in the world.

Even if there is a "real" box out there that you are looking at, the box you see is really just an illusion that happens to correspond, in some way, with a "real" thing out there. And, as we'll see later, even the "real" box out there in front of us can and will be called into question as being "real."

The Eye That Sees the World Out There

This idea— that what we see with our eyes is just a perception (a picture made up in our head) and may not be an accurate representation of what is really out there— is extremely hard to accept. It is something that many people just cannot accept. It is just too frightening to think that we are not looking at a real thing in all its concrete detail. Remember, though, at this point I am not saying there is no box, just that the box we see is coming from our head and is not a 100% true representation of the box out there.

Now for some fun before reading further, look at the three images above and see if you can tell why Einstein, a short man, is taller than his colleagues at the blackboard.

One day when I was in my second year at Phillips University, I walked into my Perception Class, and there was a screen made of cloth, mounted on a wooden frame, at the front of the room. The screen had a hole in it about the size of a quarter. Through the hole we could see that there was something pure white behind the screen. After we sat down, the professor, Dr. Drumright, asked the class to guess what was on the other side of the screen. Most of the students agreed that it was something white and glossy, maybe a piece of equipment that had a white plastic cover. Someone suggested that it could be a white porcelain plate.

Then Dr. Drumright flipped a switch on a cord he was holding, and whatever it was that we could see through the hole started changing color. It then started to blink. When the blinking stopped, we could see that whatever was behind the screen was really black with a single white stripe. He then removed the screen, and there was a motor with a black disk mounted on it. The black disk had a white stripe radiating from the center outward. He then turned the motor on again, and as it started to spin, the disk turned gray because the spinning mixed the white and black together creating gray. The disk was tilted so that once it began spinning, it reflected a light in the ceiling above it. This made it appear to be glossy. "But," everyone protested in unison, "that's not what we saw through the hole in the screen. It was glossy white!"

Dr. Drumright then put the screen back over the disk, and what could be seen through the hole was again glossy white. Then

The Science of Spirit

someone made the observation that the screen was not as white as we had first thought. "That is it," said Dr. Drumright. "The screen is a darker gray than the spinning disk. So your brain interprets the disk to be white. This is because your brain is making a judgment by comparing the two grays. We make this kind of perceptual mistake on a daily basis. We see a piece of paper and see it as white. But most paper is really some shade of gray."

A few days later when we got to class, Dr. Drumright asked, "Who knows what creates our depth perception?"

Someone then answered, "It's because we have two eyes. Each eye picks up the image from a slightly different angle. As objects get farther away, the difference gets smaller. The brain then does simple trigonometry calculations, like we learned in high-school geometry, and uses this information to make a judgement of how far away something is. It then uses this information to make a picture in our head that is three dimensional."

"That's exactly right," said Dr. Drumright.

Dr. Drumright then said, "Everyone close one eye and look around the room. Now, let's see a show of hands of everyone that can't see a three-dimensional image of the room. . . . What, no hands? Then if everyone still sees a three-dimensional image, maybe the eye theory is wrong."

"But," said a student, "if what we are looking at is really just a 'made-up' image in our head, then wouldn't it still make up a three-dimensional image? After all, we still know from experience that everything we see is three dimensions."

"That's right," said Dr. Drumright. "So people that have lost an eye still see everything as three dimensional, but because their brain does not have the information from two eyes, they make a lot more mistakes as to how far away things are. Now I want everyone to get up and go down to the large room at the end of the hall."

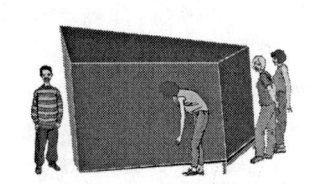

Girl looking through eye hole in this cardboard room

When we got to the other room, there in the middle of the room was a

The Eye That Sees the World Out There

huge cardboard box six feet in all dimensions sitting at an angle on a plywood ramp. One side of the ramp was on the floor, and the other side was held a couple of feet off the floor by some wooden legs so the box tipped to one side. (See drawing previous page.) If you walked around the box, three of the sides met with ninety-degree angles at the two corners, as you would expect. The forth side, however, met its two corners at angles that were more then ninety degrees on one end and less than ninety-degrees on the other. If you were to look at the box from above it would look like half a trapezoid. Then, to top it off, the top of the box slanted like a shed roof on a house, slanting down to the side off the floor. The box was high enough to stand in and was about five and a half feet on the low side and seven feet on the high side.

Inside a similar box at the Exploratorium in San Francisco

If you walked around to the back, you could see there were a couple of distorted trapezoidal-shaped holes cut in the side. "Who's the tallest person here?" asked Dr Drumright. "I want the tallest and the shortest persons to get in the box. I want the tall person at the high end and the short person at the low end." Once they got in the box by pulling one of the sides open, he had us all look through a single hole in the box that was opposite to the slanted side. This hole forced us to use one eye at a time to look into the box. When we looked into the box through the hole, the shortest student was now taller that the tallest student in the class. Trying as hard as I could, I just could not see it any other way while looking through the hole. The shortest was now taller than the tallest!

He then had two students stick their heads through the two diamond-shaped openings, and we again looked through the peephole. Through the peephole the diamond-shaped holes were no longer diamond shaped, but perfectly rectangular, just like windows. The students' heads sticking through the openings were different sizes. One was twice as big as the other was. He then had the two students switch sides, and the size of their heads also switched.

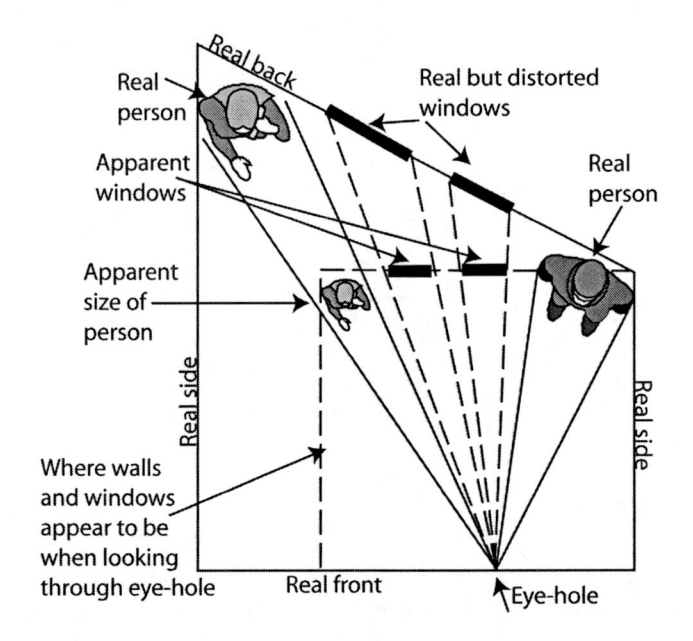

This is called the Ames Distorted Room. If you are ever in San Francisco, go visit the Cavernous Exploratorium, where they have a real room made into an Ames Distorted Room. It's not made of cardboard like the one I saw at Phillips University. On page 35 is a photo of the Ames Distorted Room at the Cavernous Exploratorium in San Francisco. The two children are really about the same height.

The peephole, of course, forces you to lose your binocular cue. The drawing to the left shows why the two children look so different in size. Remember, as you look at the photo, that you are looking through a peephole with only one eye. When you look at anything with just one eye, your brain cannot tell how far away it is, so it assumes that it is all the same distance. But perspective make things get smaller the farther away they are. If you look at the drawing of Einstein at the blackboard, you will see a similar illusion. Note that the lines get smaller as the distance perspective goes away from the eye but the people stay the same

The Eye That Sees the World Out There

size. This fools the brain into thinking it's a normal perspective when it is not.

I missed the real message of that exercise. I was just looking at it as a fun illusion. What I failed to see, down deep in my soul, was that every time we look at something in the world, we are seeing only an approximation of what is really there. We are seeing just what we need to see to get around and do things in the world. The real illusion is in our head.

If you look back again at Einstein at the black board and measure each figure with a ruler, you will see that all three are the same height. Although this illusion is not as dramatic as seeing it in the distorted house, they both work the same way. Everything in our day-to-day world has a "square" relationship to everything else. In the Einstein picture, the perspective is drawn backwards. What we see is miscalculated in our head.

We misperceive things in our day-to-day world, but we don't recognize this because we assume that what our eyes see is accurate. A good example of this is the harvest-moon illusion, in which the moon looks much larger on the horizon than it does at the zenith. As I grew up, I was told that this phenomenon occurred because the atmosphere was magnifying the moon on the horizon. So, when I learned that if you take a picture of the moon on the horizon, and again at its zenith, the moon at the zenith is slight larger. I was stunned.

How can this be? Well, no one knows for sure, but the best experiments say that when we look at the horizon moon, our brain perceives the background against which the moon appears as about twice as far away as the zenith moon's background. This is because when you look up at the zenith, there nothing close by, except stars, to judge the size of the moon by. But when you look at the horizon, there are lots of trees, cars, and roads to compare it to. Go outside and look at the sky. If you look up, it looks flat; but as your eye moves closer to the horizon, it seems to curve sharply. Now, the image of the moon that falls on the back of the eye is essentially the same size at both the zenith and the horizon. But if it is perceived as sitting against a horizon background that is farther away, then the moon is going to appear larger.

The Science of Spirit

Later that semester, we were studying our skin's sensation of hot and cold. The theory was that we have a set of receptors that respond to cold and a set of receptors that respond to heat. To prove this, we had a bunch of needles in cold water and a second bunch in warm water. We then drew a one-centimeter sized square on our forearms with a black ink pen. Someone then randomly touched our skin with one of the needles until we felt something. Let's say we took the cold needle and touched the skin. In some spots we would feel nothing, and in others we would feel cold.

It was assumed that because we could not feel anything in some spots, we were not touching a cold receptor. We marked the spot where we felt the cold with a blue ink pen. Then we would repeat this using the warm needles. In this way we were able to plot on our skin where the cold and heat receptors were. This seems very simple, right? Well then, when we were all through, Dr. Drumright said, "A few years back, a researcher mapped his hot and cold receptors and then physically cut out the centimeter of skin and looked at it under a microscope. No receptors were found! He could not find anything." So what is going on? "No one knows," said Dr. Drumright.

As far as I can ascertain, it is still believed by most scientists that we have little hair-like receptors in the skin that sense cold and hot. This is a good example of how humans refuse to see something that makes no sense in their Reality Box. The assumption is always made that the researcher must have made some error in judgment. And then the research is shelved as unimportant. In recent years, I have come across an explanation of why there were no matching receptors to the ink dots when the skin was cut out. It appeared in a book by Robert O. Becker, M.D., titled *Cross Currents*.[2] In the process of his research, Becker discovered a primitive DC electrical system in humans. This system works similar to a modern solid-state transistor system, with the skin cells acting as the transistors, passing the current from cell to cell.

I was struck by the idea that if the individual cells acted like transistors, then the cells themselves were the receptors. This would also make sense because the DC system is one of life's

The Eye That Sees the World Out There

earliest systems. One of the first and most important evolutionary systems to develop would logically be temperature sensing. This DC system has been confirmed in Europe, but U.S. biologists are afraid of being called "Vitalists." So it will be another twenty years before a DC system is accepted in the U.S.[2]

One of the more bizarre experiences that I had in Perception Class occurred one time when I was helping a classmate on a project. He was doing a paper on the Phi-phenomenon, as it was called then. The new term is autokinetic movement or AK. In autokinetic movement a small spot of light in a dark room appears to move even though it is stationary. If you have not seen this before, it is easy to duplicate. Place a small hole in a small piece of paperboard and tape it over the end of a flashlight. Turn on the flashlight and place it on a table so that it creates a small light spot on the wall. Then turn the overhead light out. Sit still watching the spot. It will begin to move. If you watch it long enough, you can see it make letters. Experiments have shown that slight movements of the eye cause AK.

This student wanted to see if the power of suggestion could make the spot move in predictable ways. After all, if it was the eye movement that created the phenomenon, one may be able to cause a person to move his eyes in a predictable pattern and therefore make the spot move in patterns. His plan was not to tell his subjects that the spot was stationary, but that he was controlling it. He would then tell the subject watching the spot that he was going to make the spot make an O and then see if indeed they saw an O.

One day a female student, who was the experimental subject for that period, was watching the spot. In the middle of the experiment she suddenly stood up and said in an angry voice, "How did you know that about me? That's not very nice." She then left the room. The experimenter ran after her, but she refused to talk to him. To this day, no one knows what she "wrote" on the wall with her eye, but it points out the power of personal influence on what is seen.

Then, of course, as a psychology student, I was immersed in Sigmund Freud's personality theory. Freud believed that the personality was divided into three parts, the Id, the Ego, and the

The Science of Spirit

Super Ego. Freud did not intend for them to become three different parts of the brain, but that is what happened. The Id involves basic or animal instincts and is the seat of motivations. If the Id were left unattended, it would have no morals and would be "out of control" to use today's terminology. The Ego is what keeps the Id "in check" and gives us a sense of self. Then the Superego is consciousness and contains the idle self. Thus the Ego and the Superego are both in the conscious part of the brain.

Over the past forty years it has been a preoccupation of psychology to locate where in the brain the Ego and the Superego are, i.e., where consciousness is. No one to date has found definitive proof of a location in the brain for consciousness. A number of researchers are now saying that consciousness must comprise only a small percentage of the brain. This is because nearly all of the brain is needed to account for other functions.

This makes me wonder, then, if consciousness is even in the brain. And this is why many researchers believe that consciousness is just a by-product of the brain's functioning. This by-product is called an epiphenomenon.

In the early seventies a new science thrust began, known as consciousness studies. These questions were asked: "Why do we have this experience of seeing the world out there? Where do we get our sense of Intentionality, of Self-awareness, an awareness of being aware, and the experience of 'I'?" It is as if we were a little man or woman inside our head controlling and using the body. But this makes no sense because there would need to be a little man or woman inside of the little man's or woman's

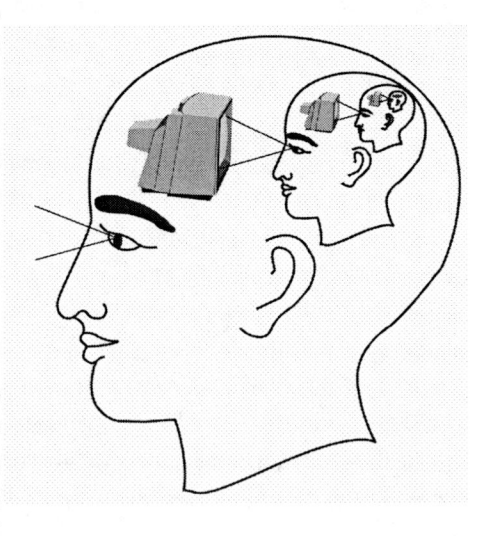

The Eye That Sees the World Out There

head inside our head. Where would it all end?

Physicist Amit Goswami has put together a list of nine common experiences that we all have and which he calls The Salient Experiences of the "I"[3]:

> 1. Intentionality (purposeful, directional focusing toward an object, including desire, judgment, and speculation)
> 2. Self-awareness (sense of self)
> 3. Reflectivity (awareness of being aware)
> 4. Ego-experience (feeling that the self is a unique entity with a certain character, personality, contingent personal history)
> 5. Attention (experience of the ability of the self to direct its focus toward one object or another)
> 6. Transpersonal-self experiences (moments of revelation or insight, as in the creative "Ah-ha" experience)
> 7. Implicit experience of the self (experiences in which there is division of the world into subject and object but not explicit experience of "I")
> 8. Choice and free will Experiences related to the unconscious

This sense of "I" or of seeing the world out there is indeed a very powerful and personal experience. But if the universe is just a machine, as I believed, then the only way to explain it away was to say that it was just an epiphenomenon—just a byproduct of the brain's working.

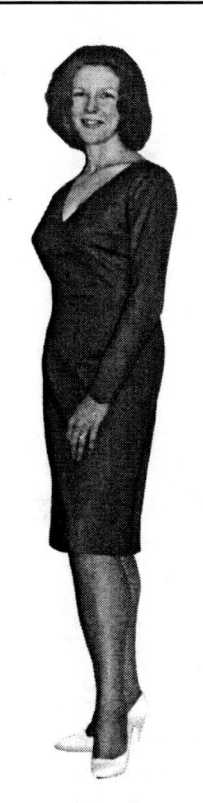

Between the Navy and college I had gotten married to an incredible lady. Her name was Joyce, and we had a daughter whom we had named Terina. On top of my working full time at night and struggling academically, the old car we had was always breaking down. Every time it did so, I could just feel my stress increasing almost overwhelmingly. I also noted that every time this would happen, I would get a boil somewhere on my body. Convinced that there was a correlation between my boils and stress, I mentioned it to our family physician. He started to laugh and said that he had never heard of anything so ridiculous. Boils were caused by staph infection, not stress.

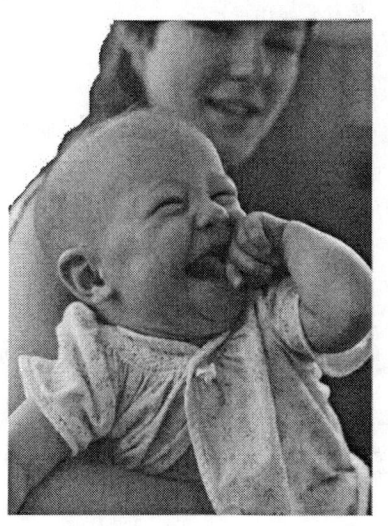

I was still not convinced, so I started going through medical journals and came across the *Journal of Psychosomatic Research*. In the early 1970s, psychosomatic illness was confined to conditions like ulcers and asthma. It was not believed that stress could cause illness in general. Because of the assumption that the universe is made of matter, modern medical practitioners believed that our body was just a machine, so it was not possible for the mind to make the machine/body ill. Looking through the journals, I came across a newly developed stress scale designed for research. It was called the Social Readjustment Rating Scale.[4] I decided to use it and just see for myself if stress could cause boils or make one physically ill.

I then made up a questionnaire to hand out to people. The questionnaire began with ten questions about a person's background, e.g., age, sex, occupation, etc. I then listed 29 common illnesses, including things like cuts, broken bones, and of course boils. Then on a second page I printed out the Holmes and Masuda stress-rating scale. I could then compare the respondents' stress rating to physical illness. I went door to door asking people if they would fill out a questionnaire for me. I wanted to make sure that I got some sick people, so I also went to doctors' waiting rooms and had people who were waiting to see the doctor fill one out. I even went to the local hospital and found some people lying in bed who would fill out a questionnaire for me.

My results were amazing. In all categories for which I had enough data, there was a dose-related response. This means that as the dose or conditions got higher numbers, the stress increased; and as the stress increased, the number of illnesses increased. This was true for injures as well. The boil question had quite interesting results. In the first range of stress, there was one boil reported. In the second range, there were none reported. But in the third range, there were ten reported, and this was significant to the .005 percent level (a very good rating). It is not likely, though, that this would have impressed the doctor who had laughed at me. Most doctors don't like research that uses correlational data.

By the end of the first year of college, I already had very grave doubts about the existence of God. Before college my Reality Box had not let me question where God would reside. My concept of God was of a separate being, the super human, the concept we learned at Sunday school. It was now obvious that he could not live in the heavens because man had been to the heavens in a space ship, and there was nothing there except empty space. So if there was a God, he had to be in a spirit form. But why bother? It was clear that if there was this super-spirit-human, he would have to be very complex to have "made" the universe. Anyway, this begs the question. Who made this complex being, an even more complex being? Science could show that from nothing more than a soup of hydrogen atoms the whole universe could evolve. It was a lot easier to believe that hydrogen atoms just happened to exist than that a complex being did.

This may sound like a

Reality Box shift, but really it was not much of a change. The concept of a God had already been in conflict with my mechanical, analytical way of looking at the world. I understood machines, and all I could see was the mechanical aspect of everyday life. I think that this is why it is more common for men to reject God than women. Men in our European/American culture grow up with left-brain, machine thinking, engaged in activities like working on cars. It makes no sense for God to be mechanical; a machine cannot create other machines.

New Reality Box 2

We are told in school that our eye works like a camera. But in reality, the image on the back of the eyeball is very fuzzy and is then broken up into hundreds of pieces that are sent all over the brain. There is no picture in your head. The brain uses the information to make up a picture.

If there be God, why, it is well, but I
Seek Truth and whether there be Mind or no
Within the Cosmic Scheme: and should it be,
Then shall I further quest a way to speak,
Perhaps to hear; and should It speak to me,
Then gladly to obey.
But Truth Itself can never lay commands;
For dogma is the mummy of the past,
Long since embalmed but not interred,
Wrapped round with gravecloths of intolerance.

The God of such belief is not the God I seek,
Nor can be real to me. I search for God,
Unfettered, free from cloying garb
Of priests whose bony hands and tonsured pates
Bespeak a niggard faith.

> *The Voice Celestial*
> *Page 8*

Journal 3
The Five Assumptions of Science

Just past the Doudy-Debacker-Dunn house, there is a dirt path that branches off the main Mesa Trailhead's wide, neatly groomed trail. This trail is called Homestead Trail. As I stand here, I have to make a decision.

Life is full of decisions, and to leave the main trail is often a bad one. But I believed that I had a mission to explore Truth. I couldn't do that staying with the rest of the group.

In 1973 I graduated from Phillips University with a Bachelor of Arts degree in psychology. This had been extremely tough for me because of my severe spelling problem. Most professors were quite understanding of this problem and said they could read my essays well enough to know what I was saying. I would write term papers by hand and then dictate them to Joyce, who typed them on an old Sears typewriter. The real problem, though, was that I was required to have four semesters of foreign language. For a person who couldn't spell his full name until he was nine, this was an impossible- sounding task. It was hard enough just keeping up with the English language, much less a second one.

First, I tried French. This made me incredibly miserable, but I managed to get through it with a "D." I knew I could not continue this way, so I went to my language professor, and he agreed that I would not make it the way I was going. He said that one of the problems was that French was a hard language and that I needed to switch to Spanish. He then set me up with a programmed self-

The Five Assumptions of Science

learning machine that would teach me Spanish. He gave me a semester hour of credit for completing a set number of pages in the machine. It worked. Even though I wouldn't win prizes for my Spanish, I got the credits I needed.

The next problem was that my GPA (grade point average) was too poor for me to get into graduate school. This was because of the low grades I had gotten in my first year, including that five hours of "F" in Chemistry. There's not much you can do with only a BA in psychology, but graduate school looked out of the question. Graduate admittance boards wouldn't even consider a candidate unless he had at least a 3.0 or better GPA. Although I did have a 3.0 in my psychology major, my overall average was 2.5. At graduation, one of my psychology professors shook my hand and said that he thought I had great potential. He said that there was a way to get into graduate school with my low GPA. He told me just to move to a graduate school, start taking individual classes, and show the professors there that I could do the work. He then told me about a great little school called Fort Hays State University in Hays, Kansas.

We moved to Hays, Kansas, to see if it would work. It did, and I settled into graduate school. We no longer had any G.I. Bill money, and now we had to come up with school tuition ourselves. The only jobs around were at a medical supply plant outside of town, and they would only hire women for their assembly line. Joyce jumped at a chance to get out of the house.

Our family now consisted of two little girls, Terina Louise and Alta LaVina. Terina was always sick. She was very skinny, had a distended stomach, indicative of malnutrition, always had a cold or something, and was constantly at the doctor's office. No one could come up with a clue as to what was going on. Then about halfway through graduate school, we took her to a new pediatrician in town. He took one look at her and asked what her stools were like. I told him, and he immediately said, "I want you to take her to the hospital for some tests right now. I'll call ahead and set it up." The tests confirmed what he had thought: she had Cystic Fibrosis (CF). In the early 70's, this was like a death sentence. Joyce cried for days, and I was working hard to remain calm and see what needed to be done.

Cystic Fibrosis results when the body makes improper mucus. Mucus is very critical to our survival because it is the first line of defense for the body. The mucus of CF kids is too thick to do its job. This causes the lungs and stomach to become clogged. So not only do the lungs do a poor job of taking in air, but there is no mucus to stop microbes that are breathed in. Then the thick mucus in the stomach clogs the ducts so that only small amounts of digestive enzymes get through to digest food. The only consolation, if there was one, was that now we knew what was wrong.

Very little is more painful than not knowing, but now we knew and we wished we didn't. Terina started taking digestive enzymes with her food, which helped improve her nutrition and made her stomach look more normal. We were also trained to do respiratory therapy and began cleaning the mucus from her lungs twice a day.

By 1976, Joyce had moved from the assembly line in the medical supply plant to being a supervisor. She also had become interested in chemistry and was accepted in the undergraduate program at FHSU. This made things really tight.

We now had to come up with tuition for two and handle Terina's illness. Our grocery budget was $14 a week for four people. Adjusting for inflation, that would be about $30 a week today. If it had not been for the CF foundation and the county health department, we could not have made it.

But Terina's illness was still quite expensive because the closest CF care center was in Kansas City, 260 miles to the east. So every time we had to go, it meant over 500 miles worth of gas and a night in a motel. Plus, the old 1960 Falcon station wagon that I had gotten in the Navy was our only source of transportation. It always had something wrong with it, and quite often would break on the way to Kansas City. I spent many trips lying under that old car out on the road, sometimes in the snow.

Graduate school further entrenched my mechanical thinking. The early seventies were the heyday for behavioral science. A psychologist, B.F. Skinner, was making Behaviorism popular.

The Five Assumptions of Science

Behaviorists believed that our complex behavior was the sum total of thousands of classical and operant conditionings. Each was building on top of the other. In other words, humans were just machines responding to a complex environment.

Classical conditioning, sometimes called a conditioned reflex, was discovered in 1890 by a Russian physiologist named Ivan Pavlov. He invented a way to accurately measure the amount of saliva produced when a dog saw food. He then accidentally discovered that if he rang a bell at the same time he showed food to the dogs, the dogs would become "conditioned" and salivate at the sound of the bell only. B.F. Skinner introduced operant conditioning. It is a more complex form of classical conditioning, which involves a set of conditioned reflexes. Skinner believed that everything we learn, like driving a car, occurred by learning a "chain" of conditioned reflexes that "shaped" our behavior. The "chain" of conditioned reflexes was called "operant conditioning."

Skinner said that there was no way to know what was going on inside someone's brain, which he called a "black box." He said that what we needed to do was to control what went into the black box and then see what came out. In other words, we needed to learn what motivated people to act in certain ways. By learning ways to modify or manipulate the environment to make people behave in predictable ways, we could then make an environment that would make people conform to society's needs. He believed that concepts like freedom and dignity were outdated ideas that just got humans in trouble and that all people really wanted was to be happy. Therefore, by developing behavior technology, we would give everyone what he needed and really wanted. If everyone was happy, there would be no need for wars or crime.

Operant conditioning proved to be great for training animals. One could start at the bottom of the chain and build or "shape" the animal into performing very complex tasks. Skinner was most famous for teaching pigeons to play ping-pong. He began by giving the pigeons a treat or reinforcement every time they just turned their heads toward the ping-pong ball. Once the pigeons learned to look at the ball in hopes of getting food, Skinner would stop reinforcing "looking at the ball" and reinforce only when the pigeons actually touched the ball. Once the pigeons knew that to get food they would have to touch the ball, he would up the ante again and not reinforce them until they pecked the ball to make it move. He then continued this chain of reinforcing until they were playing ping-pong with other pigeons.

This was so impressive that large numbers of psychologists joined his school of thought. Psychologists were excited about psychology becoming more accepted as a science. Physics had a base unit, the atom, from which everything was made, and biology had the cell. Now psychology had its base unit, a conditioned response. This was very exciting at the time, because it made psychology a "real" science. Psychology was kind of snubbed by physics and biology because it relied on correlational data. "Real" science was thought to rely on cause and effect experiments which "proved" that something was true.

Psychologists could now do experiments and show a causal relationship between a set of states and behaviors. Besides, it was a lot of fun. The Psychology Department at Fort Hays State had a well-equipped behavior lab with all kinds of cages and mazes to run mice and pigeons through. Someone even put one of the cages in a tree outside the lab to experiment with a wild squirrel living in the tree. The cage door was left open so the squirrel could come and go as he pleased while the computer in the lab kept track of everything he did in the cage.

One of the unexpected things we learned was that animals were smarter than we had thought. The operant chains were developing weak links. One of the students in the lab trained some pigeons to peck on a button 3 times for food when they saw a small circle on the cage wall and then to peck 9 times for a large circle. Once the pigeons were trained, the student then put an intermediate-sized circle on the cage wall. Amazingly, the pigeons "knew" to peck 6 times to get their food. What was believed to be a simple animal with a pea-sized brain, which operated by conditioned responses, was capable of understanding the mathematical relationship of relative circle size.

It was experiments like this that convinced many psychologists that behavior was more complex that operant conditioning could account for and that you did have to try to understand what was going on inside the "black box." By the time I graduated, the school of thought called Cognitive Psychology was already being favored over behaviorism. Cognitive psychologists believed that we learn by concepts, that we develop a picture in our brain that is a complete thing. If the pigeons were learning by a series of conditioned responses, they would have to learn the intermediate circle by conditioning also. But the pigeons didn't. They developed a concept of what was going on and followed through when presented with the new situation, i.e., an intermediate-sized circle.

About halfway through my graduate training, I was stunned by a series of amazing experiments done in France and continued in the United States. The researchers set up a cage in a remote room. They then built a small enclosure around the cage so no one could see what was going on in the cage or influence what happened in it. Photo sensors were set to tell a computer where the subjects (gerbils and hamsters) were in the cage at all times. The floor of the cage was divided into two separate electrified grids, i.e., the subject had to be on one or the other grid at all times. The computer would then randomly turn the electricity on to one of the two grids. If the subject happened to be on that grid, it would be shocked and have to jump to the other grid to avoid the electric shock. If the subject just happened to be on the grid that was not turned on, it would not get shocked.

If the universe was mechanical and the subject was just learning by conditioning, then the subject would stand a fifty-fifty chance of getting shocked. The computer would report this. But this is not what happened. The subject quickly learned to "read the computer's mind" and was away on the grid that was off and never got shocked.[5]

This experiment touched something inside me, but I couldn't place it at the time. I knew then that something extraordinary must have been going on. But to be a good scientist, I could not take it at face value. Still, I did not try to "wash it away" like some of the students and faculty had done. I knew that something was going on that we didn't understand, but, surprisingly, it didn't change my Reality Box. My purpose for knowing the Truth and the analytical method had now taken over my Reality Box. I could not see any way to bring a purposeful creation, therefore God, back into the picture. This experiment, though, did put a crack in my Reality Box. Where the whole concept of God seemed silly, it was still based on the Sunday-school concept of God, the super

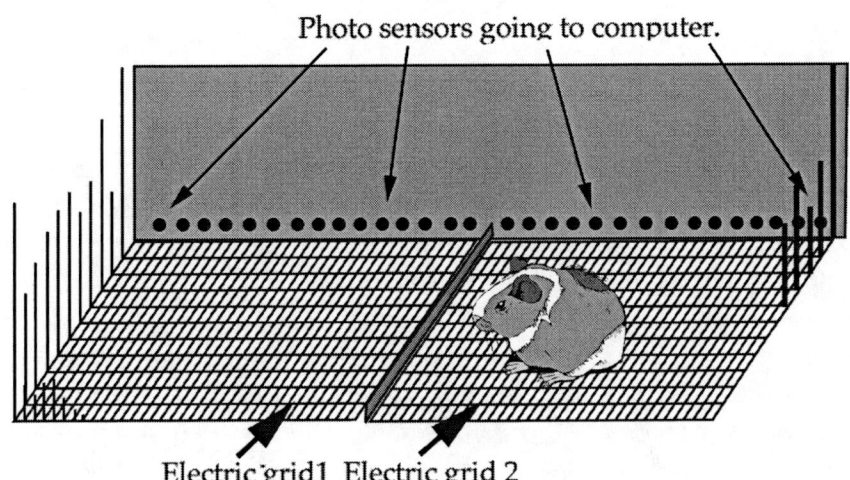

Photo sensors going to computer.

Electric grid 1 Electric grid 2
Computer turns electric grid 1 or 2 on randomly

The Five Assumptions of Science

human in the sky.

There had to be some other explanation. I decided that if you thought about it, it was not that incredible. It just meant that there was some undiscovered radio frequency that brains could read, and that would explain it. You see, there had to be an explanation. There is always an explanation for everything. So I chose the only explanation that was possible, something that would fit in my Reality Box, something that seemed mechanical: a radio frequency. I was unaware of the assumptions that set the boundaries for my Reality Box. It was just obvious that the world was solid and made of matter, and so I didn't even question it.

I was aware, however, that science was based on a set of assumptions. We had studied these assumptions in a class I took called Scientific Methodology. To my mind, the fact that science was based on assumptions was trivial. After all, once an experiment proved something was true, it didn't seem to matter what assumptive base was being used. Besides, the assumptions had to be true, which makes them not really assumptions. But little did I know that the basic assumptions of science were critically important, as you will see in later chapters.

According to physicist Amit Goswami[3], there are five assumptions that make up the foundation of classical physics and most people's Reality Boxes. They are:

1. Our mind is separate from the world. Therefore, we can influence the world only through control of our body. He calls

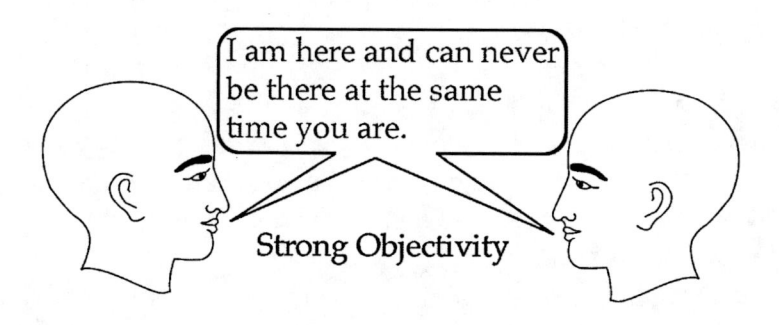

I am here and can never be there at the same time you are.

Strong Objectivity

this assumption "strong objectivity."

2. The universe is a machine like a clock. If you had enough information about an object, you could predict future outcomes or behaviors of that object. This includes the mind, which is also just a machine made of circuits instead of gears. Therefore, if you had a computer powerful enough and could program it with someone's thought patterns, you could predict what that person would think. This assumption is called "causal determinism."

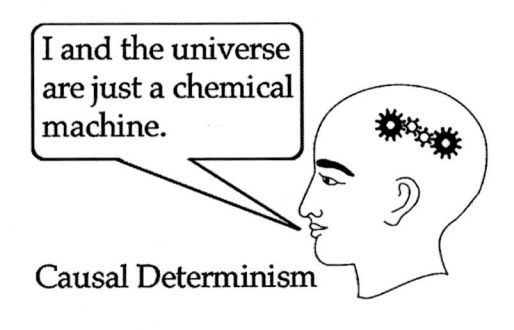

> I and the universe are just a chemical machine.

Causal Determinism

3. Everything is bound by time. For example, let's say it takes me ten minutes me to go to the store. I will first have to walk to the table. I will pick up the car keys, walk out to the car, and so on. In other words, everything takes place in a step-by-step sequence. If I try to skip a step, then I cannot go to the store. If I go from the house to the car without my keys, I can't start my car. So I would have to go back and complete the step of getting my keys. For light to get from the sun to the earth, traveling at the ultimate speed limit, step-by-step, it would take about 8 minutes. In other words, everything happens one bit at a time, and you cannot disappear from one spot and reappear in another without traveling step by step from the first spot to the second. This

> I am bound by time. I can never go to the ball without traveling through the space between me and the ball

Locality

The Five Assumptions of Science

assumption is called "locality."

4. Everything is made of matter, including our minds. You learn in school that matter can never be created or destroyed. Therefore, nothing can exist that is not made of matter. This is called "material monism."

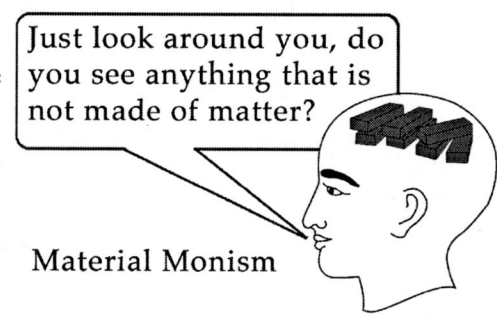

> Just look around you, do you see anything that is not made of matter?

Material Monism

5. The final assumption then comes from material monism and is the idea that since everything is made of matter, then mind, thinking, and things like love are just secondary side effects. This side effect or secondary phenomenon is called an epiphenomenon, so we call this assumption "epiphenomenalism."

> If everthing is made of matter, then thoughts cannot be real things, and are just a by-product of the brain. This is called a epi-phenomen.

Epiphenomenonism

How can these be assumptions? Aren't they facts? You couldn't get any more solid than this. Everyone knows that I'm separate from you and that it takes time to go to the store, sometimes all day. Can you find anything that is not made of matter? Of course, if everything is made of matter, love can't be a real thing. It's just a feeling. Right? It is hard to accept that these are assumptions. And therein lies the problem. Even physicists have trouble accepting these as assumptions.

By this time, I was quite anti-religious and was clearly an atheist. I did, however, consider myself a Christian in a totally non-traditional sense. I grew up with the teachings of Jesus and believed that he was correct in the way we should conduct ourselves in the world. Most Christians did not appear to have a feeling for or did not care for what Jesus was trying to tell us. I

The Science of Spirit

even thought about writing a book on Jesus for atheists.

At the same time, I was quite critical of religious organizations, mostly because they appeared so irrational to me. Especially far right-wing groups that spent most of their time worrying about gays instead of trying to help the sick and homeless like Christ did. Also, if you look at most of the world's wars, you see some religious group behind it. I still firmly believed that the only way to know was through scientific experimentation and math.

So by the end of graduate school in 1978, my thinking went like this:

In a scientific "mechanical world" (based on the assumption that the universe is made from matter), any rational person should be able to see that the traditional idea of God makes no sense whatsoever. To believe that there's a God up in heaven, therefore somewhere in the sky, makes no sense. We have seen to the farthest points in space and seen no man with a long beard. This is especially true when you look at the theory of human evolution, which, contrary to popular belief, is as close to a fact as one can get. People who do not accept the fact that humans evolved from lower species have just not looked at all the evidence. They are working from an emotional perspective, not from rational thinking.

Not only is the anthropological, genealogical, and biological evidence overwhelming, but computer modeling shows that evolution is the norm. It's just the way everything in nature works. If you set up a simple model of the early Earth on a computer and then just let the program run, it evolves very quickly in the most amazing ways— even creating virtual bacteria that attack the virtual creatures that are evolving. And then these virtual creatures develop immune systems to attack the virtual virus. This is true even in creating computer programs. Many programmers today are now evolving software rather than writing it because the evolution can create software far more complex than humans can write.[6,7]

Where the amount of accumulated data in support of human

The Five Assumptions of Science

evolution is overwhelming, no scientific evidence is needed. Just common sense tells you it makes the best sense. Look around you. Everything in the world works by growing and developing from a simple form to a more complex form. Humans start as an egg and sperm, then grow more complex. Humans once lived in caves, and now we live in warm homes with running water. And it is still evolving. We can now go into space and talk on cell phones.

The only assumption here is that evolution is random, and therefore we are created in what is referred to as a bottom up manner. In other words, a simple creature randomly mutates, evolving into a more and more complex creature, ending up with us. Of the majority of evolutionary biologists who still believe in the bottom-up creation, all agree that it is a far more complex affair than random mutation can explain. But because the bottom-up manner is an assumption, religious groups can rightly argue that evolution was guided. They just can't argue with the physical facts that human evolution occurred. The philosophical question here is: Why invoke guidance when the evolutionary system seems to work just fine without it? Then, if you add to that the obvious fact that there could not be some giant super human living in the skies above us, it makes even more sense that God could not be real. Therefore, science can explain the entire creation of the universe, from the first atom all the way to man. So why drag God into a system that works without it?

A common-sense argument for the existence of God says that evolution makes no sense because a pocket watch could never create itself—it has to have a watchmaker, i.e., God. From a rational point of view, this is a very poor argument. First of all, it has nothing to do with the way evolution works. Of course, a watch would need a maker. But we are not made of metal like a watch. Evolution is organic and very dynamic; it is in a state of constant flux and change. The watchmaker argument is a poor argument because, if it takes a watchmaker to make a watch, it begs the question:

Who created the more complex being that made the watchmaker? This starts a never-ending cycle of who made whom. Some try to end the paradox by saying that God just always

The Science of Spirit

I made the Universe and a lesser God.

existed. But why not just say that the watch just always existed, especially since science has shown a way for the human to come into being? Then there is the problem of thermodynamics. (See drawing on next page.) Thermodynamics is a fundamental law of physics that says in a closed system there is a set amount of energy that can neither be created nor destroyed. The universe is considered a closed system by science, like a balloon that has a set amount of air in it. Once the balloon is blown up and tied off, there is a fixed amount of air. New air is not created or destroyed in the balloon, it just moves around. Up until the 1970s scientists were sure they could account for all of the energy in the universe.

If God or Spirit exists, then God or Spirit must use energy to

The Five Assumptions of Science

In a mechanical world, the laws of Thermodynamics forbid the existence of spirit.

What is Ther-mo-dy-nam-ics?
   Thermo = Heat or energy.
   Dynamic = In a state of change.

The first law of thermodynamics says that energy (heat) is neither destroyed nor created, just moved around.

This is demonstrated in the drawing below.
1) Wood is really just stored energy.
2) When it is burned the fire converts the stored energy.
3) The heat makes the water in the pot boil and turn to steam.
4) The steam, another form of energy, pushes the piston and changes the steam energy into mechanical energy, wheel turns.

If spirit existed then it would need energy to move and science should be able to measure the energy change to work, but no one has ever seen spiritual energy.

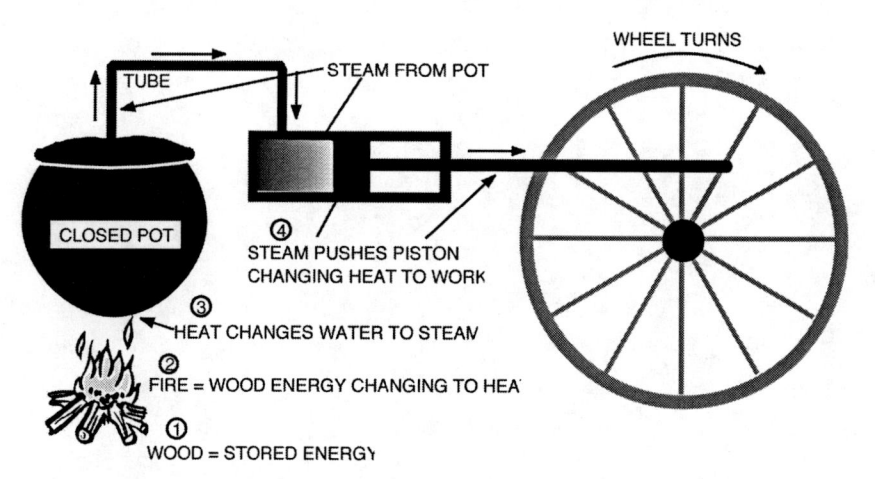

WHEEL TURNS
TUBE
STEAM FROM POT
CLOSED POT
④ STEAM PUSHES PISTON CHANGING HEAT TO WORK
③ HEAT CHANGES WATER TO STEAM
② FIRE = WOOD ENERGY CHANGING TO HEAT
① WOOD = STORED ENERGY

interact with the universe. Since the universe is a closed system, we should be able to see that exchange of energy, which we do not see. So the laws of thermodynamics forbid the existence of God.

Therefore, in a mechanical world, God or Spirit makes no sense. (This is an old argument that has lost its cogency. In recent years, science routinely sees what appears to be new energy being created.)

Most Christians don't realize that they are trapped in a dichotomy, trying to ride the fence, having both God and science. They don't understand that they cannot have it both ways. They are afraid to question science because it can prove its side with experiments and proofs. Besides, just look at the technical marvels science has unleashed. If you accept present science, you have to accept the scientific assumption of a matter-based universe. Most Christians try to get around this by saying that there are two worlds: the spiritual world and the material one. But if you accept western science with its matter assumption as true, then the laws of thermodynamics are laws that cannot be broken. The laws of thermodynamics forbid a spirit.

End

Please understand my point here. I am not saying that there is no God or Spirit. I am saying that if your Reality Box holds only the assumption that the world or universe is made of matter and is a machine, then God cannot exist because then God has to be made of matter and be a machine. So you may be trying to mix two different belief systems that do not mix.

The Five Assumptions of Science

Graduate School Ends

My last year of graduate school started with a class on a psychotherapy approach, one of many I'd had. This time, the psychotherapy approach was a newcomer called Rational Emotive Therapy (RET). A former Freudian psychoanalyst named Albert Ellis had developed it. You know the stereotypical approach that you see in all the movies and cartoons, like Woody Allen movies. The patient lies on a couch and spends years talking about his past, while the psychoanalyst points out where the patient went wrong. Ellis claimed that he had gotten tired of his clients never getting better, and while reading some works by some old philosophers, he came across the cause of most of his clients' problems. He believed that his clients were acting on a set of irrational beliefs (assumptions) that were getting them in emotional trouble. As soon as he started pointing out that they were setting themselves up from assumptions they were making and taught them to be more rational, they got better very quickly.

Rational Emotive Therapy has become extremely popular and today is one of the favorites of pop psychology. One of the basic principles of RET is that we alone are solely responsible for our emotions. People or environmental events outside of us do not cause us to get upset. It is what we tell ourselves that gets us upset. What we tell ourselves comes directly from our belief system that sometimes stems from our upbringing and innate human irrationality.

A common example is the one about money. Imagine that when you leave the house in the morning, you say to yourself: "I'd like to have $5 with me today. It doesn't have to be any more than $5, and it's not that I must have $5 dollars, but I'd prefer to have that much money in my pocket." Then later that day, you checked in your pocket and found that you had lost one of the dollars. How do you think you would feel? Well, you'd feel disappointed, but it's not like the world is over because one dollar is missing.

But now let's change what you had said in the morning from "I would like to have $5" to "I must have $5." "If I don't have $5, I won't have enough money to do anything. I'd be trapped." Now if you lost the dollar, how would you feel? You see the difference in the feeling of the two? In the second case, you would be more upset because you had "set yourself up" to be more upset. You turn a not-so-important $1 from a nicety to a necessity. Therefore, if it is a necessity or imperative that you have that $1, then you have no choice but to be upset if it is lost.

We do this all the time. We meet a new friend and say, "I'll just die if this person doesn't like me." Or, "There is something wrong with me if this person does not like me." Or, "This is my last chance to ever be happy." Now, we have put so much pressure on ourselves that we can't be at our best and wind up making a fool out of ourselves or even worse, making the person not like us. Just look at the number of hostage takers and shoot outs with police that occur. When these events are over, we find out that the shooter was upset because his girlfriend had just left him. Or look at the number of people who end up in the hospital because their team lost the Super Bowl.

Have you ever seen a very upset, crying person— and then the phone rings? Within seconds of answering the phone, the crying stops. You can't cry unless you are thinking about the subject that's making you cry.

Did you see what I just said? I just did it. I said, "the subject that is 'making' you cry." See how pervasive it is in our language? The "subject" did not make her cry! She was crying "about the subject." This psychotherapy approach just resonated with me instantly. And from then on, I would call myself a RET therapist.

The next semester I had to do my "practicum," which is like an internship for a physician. I got accepted at a psychiatric hospital across the state, so I had to live at the hospital during the week. It was a large hospital with a number of buildings. There was a building for women, another one for men, one for children, one for criminals, and one for dementia patients. There was also a cafeteria, an office building, and a building which had staff apartments.

It was very old and dirty and was built on the old "snake pit" concept. This meant that the nurses' station was built very high, overlooking the day room. This way, the staff could see what was going on in the day room without making contact with the patients below. This arrangement made the day room appear as if you were looking down into a big pit with dozens of ill people milling around below.

A psychiatrist ran it, and all he did was prescribe drugs. So all patients were on some kind of drug, and a large number were on as many as 20 drugs. Some of these drugs had very bad side effects, and many patients were suffering more from the side effects than they would have from their illness. But all that mattered was that the patient was passive and didn't give the staff any trouble. It just happened that the psychologist in charge of the men's ward had just quit, and they had not found a replacement for him. So I was put in charge of the men's ward and my supervisor, Dr. Phillips, was the psychologist in charge of the women's ward. This was a very scary situation.

I was a total rookie and knew nothing about running a men's psychiatric ward. I had never even seen or talked to a psychiatric patient. We had worked with clients in school, but they were all college students who had minor problems like homesickness. It was not as bad as it appeared to me, though. This was because Dr. Phillips was really heading both wards, and I was more like his assistant. But they said that I was in charge, and that forced me to get my feet wet, so to speak. Within a week I had my feet on the ground, and it was not as bad as I thought. There was very little real therapy going on. This hospital was more a warehouse than a place that was interested in doing everything it could to help the patients.

But Dr. Phillips was great. He was truly interested in finding ways to help his patients. He had been studying a new system developed in a hospital on the East Coast. This system made all staff, including the psychiatrist, equal members of the team. The therapeutic approach was a combination of behavior modification and cognitive therapy. The basic program was what is called a "token economy." All the patients had to "earn a living" within the hospital, but instead of being paid money, they were paid tokens. It was set up to be as fair as possible. Patients were given tokens based on what the team thought they could do or what they needed to learn.

This experiment was done on the worst ward in the hospital because if it worked there, it would work on other wards as well. For example, this ward had a number of patients who were completely dependent. The nurses brushed their teeth and dressed them every day. So these patients would get tokens for brushing their teeth and dressing themselves. If a patient did not brush his teeth himself, he would not have enough tokens to buy a meal, and his meal would be dumped into a blender and blended to a liquid. This way they were not being deprived of their food; it just did not taste good because they had to drink it. So to get hot mashed potatoes, they would have to earn enough tokens to buy it.

The first task was to take all patients off of all drugs. Then, for those patients who could not function without medication, drugs would be gradually reintroduced. But the team worked hard to find the one, or two at most, drugs that would help the patients function as normally as possible.

It worked. Within two weeks, patients who had been completely dependent were getting up every day, getting dressed, and brushing their teeth. Once a patient was taking care of his own hygiene, he would have to start going to a job every day just as in the real world. The hospital had set up a workroom and started a small business making doormats to sell to the public. If a patient had a handicap, then a special tool would be made so that patient could work. Within a few months, they were sending patients home who had been in the hospital for many years. Even a lot of patients who were too crippled ever to go home were happier because they had a sense of dignity and purpose that had just not been there before. The point here was that by truly caring, it was possible to make patients' lives better and even send patients home who normally would not go home. Dr. Phillips worked hard to get the hospital to use the new program, but, in the end, the psychiatrist won. When I left the hospital, it was still a human warehouse.

Towards the end of my practicum, they hired a new psychologist for the men's ward, and I was sent to the children's

The Five Assumptions of Science

ward to do testing on children. Here I had a new supervisor. One of the tests that he had me do was a subjective test in which you had the child draw a picture of a man, a woman, and a house. One day we had a child come in from another hospital, and I was asked to give him this test. This boy, who was about ten, drew me a picture. When he left, I looked at his picture. On the figure of a woman he had drawn a strange plaid skirt. The plaid was drawn with a heavy hand, i.e., when he drew the horizontal and vertical stripes that made up the plaid on the skirt, he had pushed down much harder on the pencil. My supervisor looked at it and said, " See this plaid skirt? That means that he is a homosexual. He makes these heavy lines to try and hide or deny female sexuality."

I objected strongly. I wanted to know where his scientific proof was that drawing plaid skirts was a sign of homosexuality. He then said, "I don't need scientific proof. I see it all the time, and when you check it out, it is always true." I said that I could not buy that and went on about my business. The next day the young boy's file arrived from the hospital he had come from, and I started going through his records. There it was: he had a long record of sexual encounters with other boys. I was very amazed but decided in the end that this had to have just been a lucky guess. How can you really "know" without some experiment to prove it? What I was missing was that experience could be a valid form of research.

Summary

In the beginning I was not going to include my poor grades and dyslexia. But then I thought that it might inspire someone. It is clearly a story that shows "where there is a will, there is a way." I can assure you that I am just as lazy and procrastinate as much as anyone. But I had a goal that was of the utmost importance to me. Discipline is a myth. A disciplined person is really just a motivated person. If it is truly important to you, then you will do it. The only thing I had that many people seem to lack is the belief that I could do it. The point here is that if you have a dream, the only thing that is standing in your way is the will to make it happen.

I also went through, very briefly, a simple understanding of psychology. My intent here was to show how I was led deeper into mechanical thinking. I could not see how it was possible to know something without experimental proof. If everything is just made up in our head, then any experience that we have could be an illusion. So, really, we can never know anything. Math and experiments give us the best information we can get—i.e., you can never trust feelings or subjective experience. At least that's how I felt then.

But the most important point to understand here is that if the universe is a machine, then God has to be a machine; and we would see God sitting out there in space somewhere, but we don't. So if there is a God, then the universe cannot be ultimately made of matter.

New Reality Box 3

If matter is real as everyday experience tells us, then the world is just a machine, and God would have to be a machine also, because thermodynamics forbids an interaction between matter and spirit. Therefore, God is not possible. But if we can show that matter is not real, and just an illusion, then God is possible.

The Science of Spirit

*Then suddenly the air was stirred as by
A fanning wing, and in it flamed the light
So luminous it veiled the Presence from
The Farer's eyes; although, bedazed, he knew
Those lips had framed an answer to his need.
Yet as he spoke, self-pity welled so high
It choked his words and he was still.
At which the Vision too began to fade
Into the darkness of the room.*

                        Alarmed,
*The Farer shook through all his limbs, yet half
Relieved, for still his reason could not bear
True witness to his sight, nor could he tell
The nature of the apparition who
Had come from Nowhere into Now, or man
Or God, or what? Distraught, he wondered if
Some evil visitant had come to claim
His soul.*

*And then he laughed in pure delight
At his own fancy. "Who can claim my soul
Until it first be proved I have a soul?*

                        The Voice Celestial
                        Page 29

Journal 4

Cracks in the Machine

On up the Homestead Trail, just as it starts to curve, I find another path branching off. It has no sign and must not have a name. Curious, I decide that I will go only a short way and then come back, so I take it. I have gone only about 30 feet when it curves to the left. Going around the curve, I come out into a clearing with a beautiful, gently flowing stream about ten feet below. The sound of the water trickling over stones as it sparkles in the morning sun makes me take a deep breath. There the path ends, at a large wooden bench inviting me to sit and bathe in the sounds and smells that surround me. As I sit, I reflect on where I have been and what might lie ahead on my path. I remember seeing a very steep hill ahead of me back on Homestead Trail.

At Christmas break 1976, we drove to Denver for Christmas. Älta and Terina were very excited about getting to spend Christmas with their grandparents, and Joyce had not seen her parents in a number of years. Within a day of arriving in Denver, Terina began to cough constantly, and by the next day she was having trouble breathing. We decided that it was the high altitude causing the problem, so we got an oxygen tank. We hoped that it would help her make it through Christmas. The oxygen did help. But she couldn't stop coughing, and we couldn't get her lungs to clear with therapy.

Everyone was becoming increasingly worried. So we decided that I would take Terina back to Hays in the car, and Joyce would bring Älta back on the bus just after Christmas. We decided to do it this way because we did not want to disappoint Älta as well. Once back in Hays, Terina did a little better, but I still could not get anything out of her lungs. Terina was very disappointed that she had to come home early, so I took her to see a movie that she had wanted to see. This was a rare treat on our budget.

As we were coming out of the movie, a strange feeling came over me, and I began to cry. I worked hard not to let Terina see me crying, but the crying was uncontrollable. It was as if I had jumped into the future and could see and feel her death. Up until this point, the idea of losing Terina had been merely theoretical. When she got sick, I would get a sick feeling in my stomach and would feel worried, upset and sometimes very afraid. But this was clearly different. It was as if I could accurately see and feel the future. Something was telling me that Terina was not going to get better.

Once home, the feeling was gone, and I was back to normal. I explained the odd experience away as just a fear reaction. But Terina never did get better and within a week went into the hospital. Then, on January 20, 1977, less than a month after her Christmas, she was gone. There is no way to describe this pain. I have experienced a lot of deaths over my 60 years, including that of my father, who was my mentor, but the pain of Terina's death has never left. I can return to it in a heartbeat.

Within two weeks, Joyce and I began to have problems in our marriage. Every time Joyce was near me, she would start crying and did not want to be around me. About a month later, Joyce said she wanted a divorce. This was the bottom of the barrel.

I reacted first with rage, screaming and begging her not to do this. I slammed my fist so hard on the kitchen stove that I broke a burner, cutting up my hand. I then became extremely depressed. I just could not deal with anything anymore. I was emotionally drained. Eight years of constant worry about school, Terina's illness, and trying to keep food on the table had drained me. Then if Terina's death was not the last straw, Joyce's depression was more than I could take. A few days later, I began to feel suicidal and knew I needed help. So on a Sunday afternoon, I called one of my psychology professors, and he met with me at the school. After a long talk, I went home with an appointment to come back in a few days. After a few sessions, I accepted that I needed to separate for a time from Joyce and give her some space.

But I did not see how this was possible. I didn't have a job or any place to go. My masters' thesis was about three quarters done, and it was all that I needed to finish school. By the time I got back home, after deciding to start with a separation if that was what Joyce wanted, an amazing thing happened.

Some people we knew, who lived two trailers down, had gotten a new job out of state. They needed to leave right away. They asked me to watch their trailer for them until they could rent or sell it and agreed to let me stay in the trailer. So I moved down to their trailer and kept myself busy finishing my thesis.

Thesis

The title of my thesis was "Ethical Attitudes Among and Within Divisions of Psychology." I was quite interested in ethics because of my philosophical upbringing, and I had noted that different divisions within psychology seemed to have different attitudes about ethics. For example, experimental psychologists believed that ink blots were unscientific and therefore unethical to use when working with a client. Clinical psychologists, on the other hand, who got information they believed was useful from ink blots, considered their use ethical.

To find out what the differences were, I sent out 400 questionnaires, 100 each to people within four divisions of psychology. What is interesting here is that the questions on the questionnaire were set up so that the answers could be analyzed with a new statistic that had been developed for market research, "nonmetric multidimensional scaling." One of the criticisms of statistical research is that people lose their identity. It is argued that the statistician forces everyone into a generalized pigeonhole of percentiles and probabilities. With multidimensional scaling, though, each individual is represented as a point in a geometric space. This way the individual is not lost because his opinion can be seen relative to those of other individuals. This geometric space can be in two, three, four, and more dimensions.

In the mid-seventies there were no PCs, and data was fed to the computer via punch cards. So I had to get the use of a punch card machine, punch all my data into a stack of punch cards, and then hand my stack of cards through a window in the computer room. The computer operator then ran the program on a computer that filled the room. It took a few days to get my results. (Boy, am I dating myself here!)

When the results came back, my data came out as points or dots sitting in a four-dimensional space. Because there is no such thing as four-dimensional paper—paper being considered as two dimensional, with width and length only—the computer printed out the four dimensions two dimensions at a time. So the computer printed one graph with dimensions one and two, another with dimensions one and three, then one and four, two and three, two and four, and dimensions three and four, i.e., all combinations. Thus the computer printed six graphs just to represent one four-dimensional space.

Imagine a small ball hanging in mid air over the book you are reading, representing one of the points sitting in space. Only this ball would be sitting in a three-dimensional space. We cannot picture the ball hanging in a four-dimensional space. If we were to do the same computer graphing with our ball in a three-dimensional space, we would need only

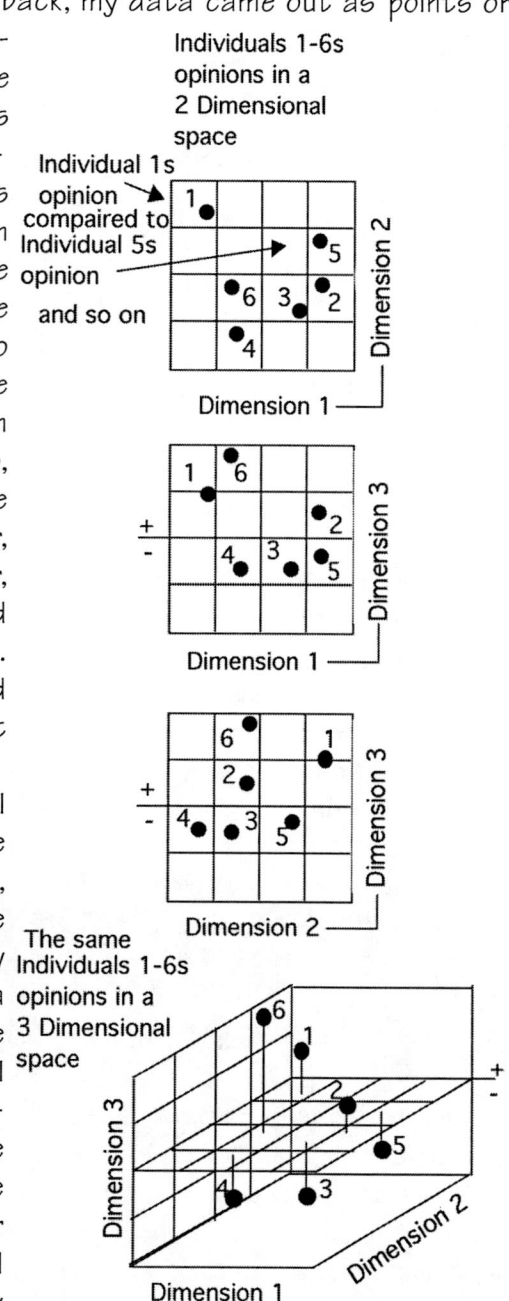

Individuals 1-6s opinions in a 2 Dimensional space

Individual 1s opinion compaired to Individual 5s opinion and so on

The same Individuals 1-6s opinions in a 3 Dimensional space

three graphs or pictures. A picture of the ball would show only dimensions one and two. If we then took a second picture looking down on the ball from above it, the picture would show dimensions one and three. If we then took a third picture from the side it would show dimensions two and three.

Since I had four groups, there were a total of twenty-four graphs, six for each group. As I started to work with these graphs, I kept trying to imagine a point sitting in a four-dimensional space. It was totally beyond my comprehension. And then, to think that sometimes results came back in more than four dimensions! I also knew that some physicists have math results showing that the universe may exist in as many as ten or eleven dimensions. They believed that since our brain could only see three dimensions, there might be other dimensions we could not see. Working with these graphs really made me realize the possible existence of other dimensions of which we are entirely unaware.

This reminded me of an old book written in 1874 by Edwin A. Abbott, called *Flatland: A Romance of Many Dimensions*[21]. In this book Abbott pretends that he is a two-dimensional square living in a two-dimensional world called Flatland. As a square in Flatland, Abbott is writing this book from Flatland prison. To explain why he is in prison, a little background is in order.

Flatland is a class-conscious society made up of lines, triangles, squares, pentagons, hexagons, and other figures. They all move around and live out their lives on a two-dimensional plain like a huge piece of paper. Women make up the lowest class and are lines. The next class is composed of extremely acute triangles, and as the base of the triangle lengthens, the class status rises. Then there are squares, to which Abbott belongs, and they are the professional class. As the number of angles increases, the class status goes up. The circles, the priests, make up the highest class.

But everyone in Flatland looks like a line to everyone else. The main way that they tell one another apart is by voice or touch. In order to understand why everyone looks like a line, imagine a quarter lying on a flat table. If you look down from up above (three dimensions), the quarter would look like a Flatlander priest or circle. Then if you moved your eye down so as to view only across the surface of the table, all that you could see of the quarter would be a line. Keep in mind that Flatlanders cannot rise up out of or go below the flat two-dimensional surface they live on.

The story begins one night when Abbott is helping his grandson, who is a very smart pentagon, do his math lesson. As they work on the math, Abbott shows his grandson that by squaring a number one can represent the two-dimensional reality they live in, with math. This is because any single number, such as 11 inches, represents a straight line that is one-dimensional. Then the square of any number, such as 11 inches times 11 inches, represents two lines, and so it is two-dimensional. As they work, Abbott then shows his grandson that it is possible to cube a number, e.g., 11 inches times 11 inches times 11 inches. The grandson is fascinated with this and says, "If a single number represents one dimension, and a squared number represents our two dimensions, then can a cubed number mean that there is a third dimension?" At this Abbott scolds his grandson for talking nonsense and tells him to go to bed and get such silly ideas out of his head.

This may sound strange to us because we live in a three-dimensional world; however, if someone were to say to us that raising a number to the forth power (11 inches times 11 inches times 11 inches times 11 inches) means there is a fourth dimension, we would think it is silly. The same is true for two-dimensional Flatlanders, for they cannot imagine three dimensions.

Then that night Abbott has a dream in which he comes across a strange land that is only one-dimensional, called Lineland. He then tries unsuccessfully to convince the people of Lineland what two dimensions look like. After all, if your world has only one dimension, there is no way you can imagine two dimensions. Just as we in a three-dimensional land cannot conceptualize four dimensions.

The next night he suddenly sees a very short line appear in his house that grows longer. The stranger then speaks to him and tells him that he is from Spaceland, which is a three-dimensional world, and that he was a sphere. Abbott cannot conceptualize such a thing as three dimensions or a sphere, so the sphere

The Science of Spirit

Hi! My name is Edwin. I am a square, and I live in Flatland. Squares are the professional class in my society.	My world is flat and two-dimensional. I cannot see or conceptualize you three dimensional beings.	My grandson, Charles, is a most promising young hexagon.
One night, when I was helping him with his homework, I showed him that we could represent our 2-dimensional world by taking any length and squaring it. So any number X squared, X^2 stood for a 2-dimensional world.	Then I showed him that it was possible to cube a number, so any number X could be taken to a third power, X^3. He then said the most absurd thing.	If X^2 represents our world, maybe X^3 represents some other type of world that has 3 dimensions.
Well, I told him that was ridiculous. Anyone can see that only 2-dimensions are possible.	The next day I met this strange person who claimed that he was in fact 3 dimensional, what silliness.	My silly friend's name is Henry. He claims to be a sphere, which is 3 dimensional
Henry looks like an ordinary person to me. He claims that what I am seeing is where he pokes through my world. Henry as seen by Edwin	Henry can do a magic trick where he disappears. He claims that he has moved above my world, whatever that means. what a kidder. Henry as seen by Edwin	Henry claims that when he is above me, he can see my insides. I don't believe him however.

spends most of the night trying to convince him that there is a place called Spaceland that exists in three dimensions. Finally, in the midst of a fight, the sphere lifts Abbot up out of his flat world into three dimensions. At first he cannot believe what he sees, but then he understands and can conceptualize three dimensions. Once back in Flatland, he tries to convince his countrymen of the existence of Spaceland, but eventually ends up in prison for teaching lies.

The point of the book was to make us aware that we may be doing the same thing as the Flatlanders. Because we cannot see more than three dimensions does not mean that more dimensions do not exist. In fact, there is little doubt today that there are more than three dimensions.

Here again, the information is indicating that the universe could be, and probably is, very different than we know it to be in our day-to-day mechanical experience. Why is it that I've so disliked this picture of the universe? Is it because I would lose control of the comfortable three-dimensional world that I grew up with? Why do we dislike change so much?

Did you ever notice that even if you like taking showers, there is always the discomfort transitioning into the shower? Some of us may repress this and not remember it. Once you get adjusted to the water, it is great, and then you don't want to leave. But then you know that the water will soon turn cold or you have to get someplace, so you muster up the courage and turn the water off. Then you have to go through a distasteful transition again. Once dried and dressed, though, you feel good again. If you haven't noticed this, think about it next time you take a shower.

There is a psychological theory based on this principle, called "cognitive dissonance," that was developed when I was in school. The word "cognitive" simply means the act or process of perceiving or knowing, and "dissonance" means conflict. Cognitive dissonance theory simply says we will not change until we are in a state of conflict with our knowingness or the way we perceive the world to be. In other words, we will not change our Reality Box or the way we perceive the world. More precisely, it says that unless we are in a state of mental unbalance or dissonance, i.e., cognitive dissonance, we will not change, no matter what anyone says or what information we are receiving.

Cognitive dissonance seems to come in two forms. First people enjoy seeking knowledge because they just want to know the truth (a form of self-induced cognitive dissonance). The second form occurs when people are forced by an event or circumstance into a state of cognitive dissonance. Have you ever known something and tried to explain it to someone else who would just not listen?

Someone who would just push you away by saying things like, "I just don't believe that," or "That's crazy," or they just walk away? I am talking about Reality Boxes in case you hadn't noticed.

According to cognitive dissonance theory, we develop a set of beliefs that are comfortable, like when you are in the shower. We know what is true, what we like, what's not true, and what we don't like. This makes life easier and makes it feel in balance. When something comes along that does not fit within what you have accepted as true, you reject it out of hand. From what you know, it can't be true, and it would require work on your part to change. So it is easier to reject it and go on about your business. A good example of cognitive dissonance in play involves the Wright brothers' flight at Kitty Hawk.

Five months *after* the Wright brothers flew their airplane at Kitty Hawk, the prestigious journal *Scientific American* printed an article stating that flight was impossible. After that first flight, the Wright brothers set up their plane in a field where they could fly back and forth to test and improve their plane. This field was bordered on one side by railroad tracks and by a busy road on the other. So, as they flew back and forth across the field, everyone on the road and everyone on the train saw them flying. Word spread quickly that flight was possible. But no one would believe the witnesses, and newspapers refused to print the stories. Science said it was impossible, so it had to be a hoax. *Scientific American* then printed an article to try and dispel this nonsense going around that human flight was possible.

The story is told that one of the local newspapers did send a reporter to check it out. When the reporter came back and wrote a story about the airplane he saw fly, the paper refused to print it. His editors had expected the reporter to come back with a story of a hoax.

Flatlanders are the two-dimensional people I talked about earlier, and they don't believe in spheres because they can't see them. But does that mean that spheres do not exist? Are we doing the same thing as the newspaper editors and the flatlanders? Are we missing a lot of wonderful things because we don't want to step outside our Reality Boxes? There is a psychologist, Wallace Johnston, who did a little study on cancer cures. He believes that we may already have a cancer cure, but because we are afraid of new ideas, we won't check it out. Another example of cognitive dissonance and refusal to change a Reality Box can be seen in the story of Louis Pasteur.

In the 1800s, Louis Pasteur proved that bacteria could make people sick. He showed that just by washing our hands we could prevent some illness. But it was 20 years later before doctors were *ordered* to wash their hands between patients, and that was only because they had been embarrassed by the midwives who had a lower birth mortality rate as a result of washing their hands.

We have this idea that science is on a steady march forward and that every experiment takes science one step closer to the Truth. But according to Thomas Kuhn, in his little book *The Structure of Scientific Revolutions*, science is especially bad about changing.[20] Mr. Kuhn calls science's Reality Box a "paradigm." Paradigms are especially hard to change because science works so hard to set up laws to fit their data. Once something is a law, then the generation that set up the law is resistant to change, even when there is evidence to the contrary. Thomas Kuhn says that quite often these scientists never change, even in the face of overwhelming evidence. The paradigm changes only when a new generation takes over, a generation reared with the new information.

The book from nowhere

Just as I got my thesis completed, a job as a counselor became available at a counseling center just 60 miles to the south of Hayes. I got the job and moved there while Joyce stayed in Hays. I then worked at the counseling center for four months before I graduated with my master's degree. Then Joyce and I sat down and had a long talk. We figured out that the real problem was that I reminded her of Terina, so it was hard for her to be around me. We decided to move to Denver together and see if we could make our marriage work. So I quit the job and made plans to move. The plan was to move our trailer to Denver, but since we could not find a trailer park to move it to, we decided to sell it. We moved everything in the trailer to Joyce's parents' house in Denver. Joyce and Älta then stayed with Joyce's parents, while I drove back to stay in the trailer until it was sold.

I had been in the trailer for about a week, when one day I walked back to the kids' room. I don't remember why I did that because it was empty except for a bed we were leaving with the trailer. As I stepped into the room, there on the floor was one of Terina's books. I was shocked and felt a hollow feeling sweep over my body. Where in the world did that book come from? We had carefully cleaned the trailer so it would be ready for a prospective buyer, and I had walked through the trailer earlier to make sure it was ready when I got back from Denver. All of the kids' books had been moved to Denver. This was indeed a profound mystery. However, I just could not accept that there was not a simple explanation.

I decided that I had somehow overlooked it, that it had just accidentally been left behind. My Reality Box would not accept that there was more here than just finding a book. But why had I not noticed it before? It was unavoidable. It was lying almost in the doorway. Of all my strange experiences, this is the most painful, because, as I will show, I might have missed an incredible opportunity to experience something profound. I might have been able to communicate with Terina. But I was afraid and grounded in everyday reality. Spirits were not real; the world was just a machine.

Once the trailer was sold, I went back to Denver to live with Joyce at her parents' house. I learned very quickly that it was going to be an impossible task for me to get a job as a counselor. In Kansas I had been considered a master's level psychologist, but in Colorado one had to have a Ph.D. to be called a psychologist. Statistically, Colorado had more psychologists and counselors per capita than any place in the country. So I was competing with Ph.D.s with many years of experience. I could have gotten a job if I had been willing to move out of state, but Terina's death was still too painful, and she was buried in Denver. Denver was also Joyce's home, and Joyce and I were beginning to flow together again. That meant, in the short run, that I would need to get some other kind of job. So I got a job as an industrial spray-painter, and we were able to rent a house. Looking back now, I can see that this was a good thing because I was not emotionally up to counseling other people.

Within a year we had bought a house, and I took a correspondence course in electronics. For the next six years I worked as an electronics technician. I then got a job at a psychiatric center for children and teens. I had worked at the psychiatric center for about three years when Älta graduated from high school, which meant money for college. I was not making much at the psychiatric center, and I really was not very happy there anyhow, so I went back to electronics.

Throughout these years, I continued to read as much as I could, and my dad and I continued to correspond. Our hottest debate was over artificial intelligence or more precisely whether or not computers would ever have consciousness. I, of course, argued that computers would someday be conscious. My then Reality Box said that the five assumptions of science were true. This meant that consciousness was nothing more than an epiphenomenon or a by-product of the right amount of computing power. So it was just a matter of time before computers would have the required power.

Dad argued that consciousness was not an epiphenomenon, but something more. He could not give me any scientific proof, so there was nothing he could say that would convince me. He once had a profound experience during which he experienced a loss of his individuality and experienced oneness with the universe. I did not doubt this experience, but I was skeptical that it was anything more than some unusual psychological experience. After all, I once

The Science of Spirit

had some strange experiences around Terina's death and had concluded that they were nothing but strange experiences.

In the mid-eighties my dad sent me a book written by a scientist named John Gribbin. It was called *In Search Of Schrodinger's Cat*. This title may sound like a mystery novel, but it turned out to be anything but. It was about a new branch of science called quantum physics.

> Epiphemomenon: A by-product of the brain working that results in our consciousness, i.e. consciousness is not a real thing.

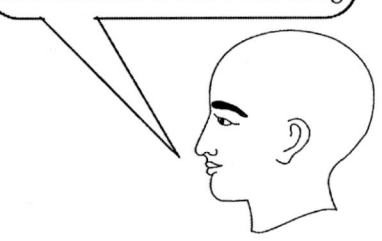

This branch of physics was developed around 1925, but the findings were so strange and unbelievable that most scientists' Reality Boxes would just not accept it. As a result, it has only been since the mid-seventies that the discovery of quantum physics has started to come out into the general population.

Quantum theory created a crack in my Reality Box, but I was able to explain it away. However, there was one experience my dad had that was very hard to explain away, and it was another crack in my Reality Box— one that I realized was a crack. It seems that he had a dream one night in which he was back at his old junior high school. When he arrived at the junior high, he found they had built a new gymnasium onto the old building he had gone to class in. He then, in his dream, flew through one of the high open windows and looked around inside. The dream was so vivid that the next day he told my mother about it and wrote down a detailed description of the building he had seen.

He wanted to write the school and see if his dream was true, but was embarrassed to contact the school about a dream. So a number of years passed before he finally got up the courage to write a letter to the principal of the school. Amazingly, the principal wrote back and told him that he was right: they had built a gymnasium just as he had described. The principal also sent a picture of the new gymnasium and a number of essays that students of the school had written about how amazing this event was.

I really wanted to know how this could have happened, and I worked hard to come up with a good explanation. It's harder to call something like this simply a coincidence when it happened to someone you know. The best I could do was to say that it must have something to do with quantum theory— but what? The truth is that I just didn't understand quantum theory in spite of the number of books I had read on the subject. I was trying to understand it with intellectual eyes that saw the world as a machine.

This is exactly what many scientists do now. They look at the world with mechanical eyes and then come away totally bewildered, explaining away inexplicable events by saying things like, "That only happens on the quantum level and not here in the real world."

In November of 1991, I got a job with a large electronics firm. As I was working there, I met another employee who was a design engineer. Soon after I met him, he left to work for a new start-up company called Environmental Services and Products, Inc., ESPI for short. They were going to make a shield for computer monitors. This shield was installed inside the monitor and blocked EMF (electromagnetic) radiation believed to cause health problems.

I thought that since this was a start-up company, it might be a great opportunity to get in on the ground floor and grow with a company, so I sent them a resume and got a job. It seems that the design engineer had not worked out, and they gave me his job! I wasn't a trained design engineer, but the owners thought that with my electronics background I could do the job. This, however, meant that I needed to learn all I could about EMF radiation, so I started reading some books. One of the books I read was called *Cross Currents* by Robert O. Becker, M.D.[2] The blurb on the cover said that the book was about the health effects of EMF, so I was totally unprepared for some of the other concepts in the book. Becker began with a history of medicine.

I was very surprised to learn that medicine, at the core, was not a noble science dedicated to the betterment of man. Although most physicians are very honest and want to do their best for their patients, some are not, and the core, the American Medical Association (AMA), is run by arrogant, politically motivated bureaucrats. The AMA is the organization that decides what the doctors learn.

Becker said that at the beginning of the 1900s there were two major schools of thought. Both were just as scientific and had good research to back up their statements. The two groups were called the vitalists and the mechanists. The vitalists had done a great deal of research on the DC (direct current) system in the body. This research showed that living things were living because of a field or force, which they called the life force. As a result, the vitalists believed that medicine should try to work with nature and find ways to prevent illness. The mechanists, on the other hand, believed that life was just a chemical machine and that by researching the chemical cause of disease, they would rid man of all disease. Then in the 1920s two things happened.

First, the vitalists bet everything that the nerve impulses in the brain were electrical, while the mechanists said they were chemical. The mechanists were then able to show that brain nerve impulses were chemical. At just about the same time, the mechanists developed antibiotics. This gave them enough clout to go to the government and say, "See! We practice the only truly scientific medicine, and therefore people who do not do things the way we do are quacks and should not be able to practice. They may harm people." It was all a matter of politics and had nothing to do with who provided the best care. The vitalists didn't completely die, however; they were just pushed underground. Today they are on their way back and are called holistic or alternative medicine practitioners.

Before reading Dr. Becker's book, I had always thought of Chinese medicine as inferior to our "scientific" medicine, which I felt was clearly superior. I was shocked to realize that this was not necessarily the case. Chinese medicine, like that practiced by the vitalists, was just a different approach and was superior within that approach. We really need both approaches, but the AMA has not allowed that.

The main difference between Chinese and Western medicine is

Cracks in the Machine

that Chinese medicine tries to prevent disease, but western medicine, or the mechanists, tries to cure the disease after it has manifested. It became clear to me that preventing makes more sense. There is no comparison between the rate of degenerative disease in the United States and in China. Per capita, the West has almost double the degenerative diseases of the East. The number one tool that the East uses is diet. So while we may marvel at the incredible technology utilized in western heart surgery, we need to remember that in the Chinese systems, there would be little need for the heart surgery in the first place.

The Placebo Effect

Dr. Becker said something that surprised me. One of the main problems with the mechanists'/modern medical thinking is the belief about the placebo effect. (The placebo effect occurs when someone is given a sugar pill that has no medicine in it, and yet that person gets well.) This makes no sense to the mechanists' way of thinking and is therefore looked upon as a nuisance. All drugs are tested to weed out this pesky phenomenon, the placebo effect. This is because it is said to mask what the "real" drug is doing.

It works like this. Let's say that you want to test a new drug that cures a certain liver problem. The researcher would then find a group of people with this type of liver problem. The researcher would then divide this group into three sub-groups. One group (called the control group) would not get any of the drugs. The second group (called the placebo group) would get a placebo, or sugar pill, that looked just like the test drug. And then the third group (called the experimental group) would get the drug.

At the end of the experiment, the results are tallied up. If all three groups have the same number of people who get better, then the drug is said to have no benefit because the group that got the drug did no better than the control group. On the other hand, if no one in the control group gets better, but one third of the placebo group gets better, as well as those in the experimental group, then the drug is still said to be no good. This seems to make good sense because, after all, the drug did no better than a sugar pill.

But wait. We just walked past something very important. Why are one third of the people getting better just by taking a sugar pill? Here we have a third of the people getting better just on the belief that they will get better. This is powerful and would seem to be clear evidence that the body is not a chemical machine, as the mechanists believe. Dr. Becker says that sometimes as many as 60% of patients get well just by taking a placebo.

To make this even more obvious, recent experiments have shown that this phenomenon occurs even with surgery. In these experiments, the doctors used the same procedure we just described above, but instead of a drug, they used surgery. The group with the problem was divided into three groups: an experimental group, a control group, and a placebo group. The control group got no surgery, the experimental group got the surgery, but with the placebo group the doctors would merely make an incision and then sew it closed without doing anything else, i.e., making the subject think that he really had surgery. Believe it or not, one third to one half of the people in the placebo group improved as much as those in the experimental group![8,9]

Modern western doctors have always used the word "fake" to define placebo. But for being "fake" it sure is powerful. They also put down alternative health, saying, "It is just the placebo effect." This is always said in a manner to imply that alternative healers are fake and just treating patients for the money. But it sounds to me like the pot calling the kettle black. This put down has no effect on alternative healers because most are more interested in making the patient better and knowing that they are helping. When you consider that prescription drugs are the fourth leading cause of death, it would seem to me that it would make better sense to try a placebo solution first.

The second thing that happened was that I was introduced to the idea that diet was critical for good health. It not only could affect how well you felt and thought, but also was probably responsible for most of the degenerative disease in this country. For example, osteoporosis is rampant in the West, but in the East it is rare. And the people in the East do not take calcium supplements. The difference is believed to be due to diet. The main difference is that in the East they do not consume cow's milk, and meat consumption is very low. It would be unheard of for a Chinese person to eat meat without eating lots of green veggies with it. Many studies have shown that cow's milk and meat are very acid forming in our blood. This acid is what causes you to lose calcium. Eating large amounts of green veggies balances the acid.

The owner of the little business I was working for had been trained in Chinese medicine, and he introduced me to blue-green algae. Within two weeks of taking blue-green algae, I began to feel better and had a strange feeling that I can only describe as a sense of well being. Then, after taking the blue-green algae for several months, I suddenly had an experience as if a fog was lifting off of me. I immediately felt I could think more clearly and wasn't as depressed as I had been since Terina's death. It was as if I could see colors better: they seemed brighter. I have no way of proving that this change was brought about by the blue-green algae. But if not, it surely was an interesting coincidence. Also, digestive problems that were getting worse as I got older suddenly improved dramatically.

I then heard about a survey, which I have not been able to confirm, that asked physicians going into medical school if diet had any effect on health. Some 80% believed that diet was very important for good health. They then asked the same number of medical students who were graduating from medical school the same questions. Fewer than 5% said diet had anything to do with health.

So now not only could I see that the physicists and physicians all had blinders on. But I did too. They had been my mentors; they represented wisdom and Truth to me. I felt cheated. I felt as if I had been lied to. I knew on an intellectual level there was not any purposeful intent on their part because they were stuck in their Reality Box. But I felt quite angry, almost anti-science. This, however, was just my Reality Box beginning to give way. Little did I know that it was about to explode in a million pieces.

Summary

Learning about flatlanders, I saw more evidence that the universe might not be what it seems on the surface. I have tried to show how hard it is to change and why we do not like change. In spite of the fact that I was at a dead end in my career, I never lost sight of my goal and continued to read and correspond with my dad in my quest for Truth.

In Chapter 5, my job at ESPI begins an amazing chain of events.

We will always hold Terina in our hearts.

New Reality Box 4

> Everyday reality says that the three dimensions we see around us, i.e. length, width, and height, are all that is possible. But lots of scientific evidence says that as many as eleven dimensions may be possible.

Part II

> O. Frank claims that matter is an illusion but I don't buy it. Last time I checked bricks were as hard as ever, and it still hurts to kick a bed post.

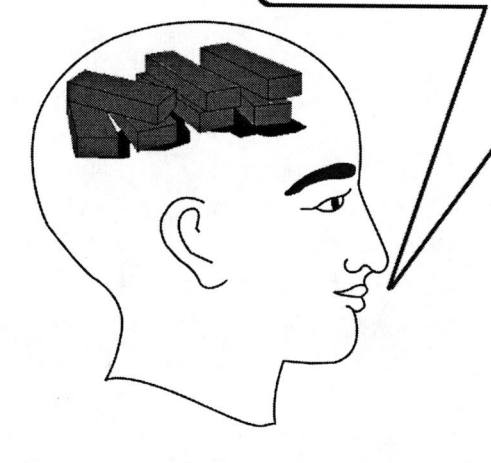

The Science of Spirit

When I was a child, we lived in a small town where the downtown streets were paved with red bricks. Once, as my dad and I came into town, he said, "If we were in heaven, those bricks would be made of gold." I was surprised and puzzled at this picture of heaven as a physical place like earth. Not that it wouldn't be possible for God to have a place that had streets lined with gold bricks, but my innate feeling of heaven was not of a physical place at all. I could not describe my feeling or explain it. I just knew that heaven was something more than this physical world.

Now, fifty years later, I have come full circle and again believe that heaven is not a physical place. This time, however, thanks to science and mathematics, I can describe it to some degree. But in order for you to understand my picture, I will need to take you on a quick tour of science history. In order to believe this picture, you must understand where it came from.

In case you haven't noticed, I have already been laying a foundation of information that will make the next three chapters easier to follow. First, we learned that there is no one-to-one relationship between what we see, hear, smell, taste, or touch, and what is really out there in the world. The only way we can experience the world is through our five senses. Our brain then just "makes up" a picture from this information. We do not even need the information to make up a picture. We make up pictures of, or "see," what is not really there all the time— and don't even know it.

Second, we saw that our self-awareness, our consciousness, was really quite mysterious, that it can't be explained in mechanical, scientific terms. If we stop and try to analyze it, our consciousness seems to be something separate from our body. It not only gives us self-awareness, but we are also aware that we are aware. Mainstream science tries to explain it away by saying that it is just a "by product" of the working brain. But there is a consensus among researchers who study consciousness that it is more.

We then learned the five basic assumptions that science and which most people have in their Reality Boxes. These assumptions seem so obvious that we can see no way they could be wrong. They can't be assumptions: they must be facts! The most important of the five assumptions is called "locality." Locality says that everything is "bound by time," meaning that everything must be done in a stepwise manner and that you can never skip a step. You can never disappear from one spot and reappear in a different spot without moving between the two spots.

We learned that if the five assumptions are true, then God makes no sense. This is because if the world is solid and is a machine, as the five assumptions say, then God must be a machine also. The laws of science forbid an exchange of energy between a spirit world and our mechanical world.

Finally, we learned that if there were more than four dimensions, there would be no way for us to know. The only way we can experience the world is through our five senses, and thus everything is just made up in our heads. Our brain has only the ability to make up three-dimensional pictures. So if we were to get information through our senses of four or more dimensions, our brain would still make up just a three-dimensional picture.

Many people are afraid of reading books with science in them. Science seems arbitrary and can't make up its mind. It has a stilted, technical, and boring way of talking, full of terms that are hard to understand. Human nature is such that when we don't understand something, we distrust it. This distrust then leads people into believing many strange things and in turn creates bitter debates, which can hurt people and even destroy lives. The Scopes trial* is a good example.

But these people are missing an important piece of the puzzle by avoiding science. I didn't say the only piece, just an important piece. It is not necessary to learn science language and math to have a basic understanding of what science is trying to say. I have gone to great lengths to make the next three chapters understandable to anyone and have included lots of illustrations. But no matter how clear or how many pictures I use, you must have a basic understanding of what science is about. So I will try to explain that too.

---

*The famous trial where a high school teacher was put on trial for teaching evolution.

The Science of Spirit

There are many people, regardless of the religious group, who believe that their scriptures are the only word of God and that it will give them a complete picture of reality, if they just interpret it right. But even within Christianity, there are several thousand different groups all claiming that their interpretation is the right one. Most likely they all have some piece of the "real" reality, but how do you sort through all of the differences and get closer to the complete reality? All of these people see their truth clearly and cannot understand why other people do not agree with them. What they don't understand is that their Reality Box determines what makes sense and what does not. So people with different basic assumptions, different Reality Boxes, are going to see things in different ways. As we discussed earlier, we can never escape the dilemma of the Reality Box coloring what we believe. But by testing and experimenting, we can improve the information in our basic assumptions. This experimenting is called science. This should not be confused with technology, which comes from science. Technology is about making a better machine or cell phone, whereas science is the study of the basic laws of nature (i.e., God).

Although testing and experimenting sounds simple, it turns out to be complex and very hard to do. The first problem that one runs into is that everything touches everything around it. So it was necessary to break systems down to the smallest possible unit and then study that unit. Thus where science is now starting to look at things as a whole, in the beginning that was not possible. Science is severely criticized today for not being holistic. But if you try to understand all of the problems and complexities in studying nature, you will understand that in the beginning a holistic approach was not possible. The way science is and has been is a necessary stage. The danger, however, in looking at a piece at a time is the temptation to say that the piece represents the whole.

This is what is happening when science appears to be arbitrary. Science has assumed the whole from just one or a few studies. But science as a whole recognizes this problem and from one generation to the next pulls itself back to its basic principles.

Part II

Where one generation may become dogmatic the next generation will change to a new dogma, which is growth. But in the beginning, because of human nature, this was the only way it could work.

The first thing that was discovered when science began was the power of mathematics. Nothing is more solid and absolute than math. The only problem lies in interpreting what the math is telling us, bringing us back to the Reality-Box problem. Math can tell us things we cannot know any other way. A good example of the power of math is the story of Eratosthenes.

Eratosthenes was an early scientist/philosopher. In or around 230 BCE he was able to calculate the diameter of the earth with only a simple experiment. First, he determined the distance between two cities with some accuracy. Then he placed two sticks of the same length in the ground, one in each city. Eratosthenes and a friend measured the angle of the shadow from the sticks at noon on the same day. He then used the two different angles to calculate the diameter of the earth. So seventeen hundred years before Columbus, the Greeks not only knew that the earth was round, but they knew how big it was, all by using math. Of course, it was not until modern air travel that we could actually measure it and know he was close to right.

This is how the history of science works. By using math, science can figure out how something works without seeing or touching it and then later perform experiments to test and see if the math is right. The math has always been right; it has only been our interpretation of what it says that has been wrong. Why math is such a good analog of reality I don't know. (Maybe God is playing a game with us, and math is the clue to the game). But after twenty-five hundred years of testing what the math says and the math always being right, it becomes hard to doubt it even when it says something that makes no sense to us. And, as you will see in the next few chapters, the math has told us some of the most amazing things. Hidden beneath our everyday reality is an unbelievable world no one ever imagined.

*At last you see! The heart can understand
And lead the mind into the Holy Land.
This truth doth hold in life and death the same,
That he who seeks with an unfailing aim
Shall reach the goal of wisdom for today,
And at the hour when he shall put away
This mortal world, his new-built soul shall be
So filled with memories of the self that he
Shall wake Beyond still conscious of the Me.*

**The Voice Celestial
Page 342**

The Ghost in the Machine

Journal 5
The Ghost in the Machine

Back on Homestead Trail I have finally reached the summit of the hill. It has been a very hard climb. I am hot and my muscles ache, but there is a sense of accomplishment. I have finally made good headway up the trail.

This is the way I felt having finally found a fun job. But I was not aware of the dramatic shift that my life would take.

Working at ESPI, I met Richard France, a holistic healer who did nutritional counseling. He had a degree in world religions and was involved in everything New Age. He believed in crystal energy, auras, and all types of metaphysical concepts. He knew that I was very "straight laced" scientifically, and so he would try to start discussions with me. I had no knowledge of metaphysics because it was generally considered pseudo-science. That meant it was not "real" science and could not be trusted in my Reality Box. I had bought into that belief from my training, but I was trying to be very open minded because I was truly interested in the Truth. Some of his concepts were really strange to me.

One day, as I was trying to present some scientific argument, he stopped me and said, "You don't know that because everything is based on an assumption, including science." Somehow this statement hit me just right and really took me back. I immediately started thinking about quantum physics and knew that I had not been facing up to all the facts. Quantum theory did violate every basic assumption that science had been built on. I went into a state of cognitive dissonance, and the walls of my Reality Box went into meltdown. Richard's statement wasn't much, but it was the proverbial straw.

In an instant I knew why my parents' card table hit the wall, why the hamster in the split cage did not get shocked, and why my dad could travel in his dreams. It all made perfect sense, and I

The Science of Spirit

knew why our mind perceives the world as out there and why there is not a little person in our head. I suddenly understood that it was not possible for the universe to be a machine. I now possessed the key that would unlock the door to a truth I had looked for my whole life. That key is simple. You just have to flip your assumption that the universe is made of matter. It is not: it is made of conscious energy! The five assumptions of science are wrong.

I can hear you crying foul. "What? That makes no sense. What does conscious energy have to do with it? How does this answer all of the above paradoxes? How can the five assumptions of science be wrong? Everyone knows that I'm separate from you, and that it takes time to go to the store. Can you find anything that is not made of matter?" Of course, if everything is made of matter then love cannot be a real thing: it's just a feeling, Right?

It is hard to accept in our day-to-day life that these are assumptions, they seem so real and right. So it will take some pretty darn good proof to prove that these assumptions are wrong. If the five assumptions are wrong; then two things can be in the same place at the same time; I would be able to disappear from my house and reappear at the store without traveling through the space in between; the chair that is holding me up is just energy; and love may be something real, like matter. This makes no sense! How can this be?

The answer lies in understanding quantum physics. Did I hear you say again that this isn't fair, that you don't even know what quantum physics is, much less understand it? "Besides," you say "I'm right brained and can't understand this science stuff."

Well, I hear you, but it's not as bad as it sounds. Let me give you a little secret. When most people say they don't understand science, what they are really saying is they can't conceptualize science, and don't understand all the big words and math, and it doesn't always have to be that way. I have worked hard to remove most of the big words and math, and when I need math to explain something I use everyday addition and subtraction type of math only. As far as conceptualizing science, no one can. For example, science says that it takes light, traveling at 186,000 miles every second, 4 years to reach Alpha Centauri, the nearest star to earth. Anybody can learn this simple science fact, but not even the most brilliant scientist can conceptualize the vastness involved in traveling at 186,000 miles a second for four years. So if you give me a chance and look at it as fun, you may learn something wondrous.

Ether

From the time of Galileo, light has been the enigma in physics. I say this because of all the phenomena in our physical world, nothing refuses to yield to mechanical theory like light. Mechanical theory says that the universe is a giant machine like a clock, and some scientists still believe that this is the case. Around the year 1670, light was shown to have a set velocity or speed. Since light had now been shown to be a real "something" and not some magical thing with instantaneous velocity, it was assumed that it must be in the form of a wave, like sound waves or ocean waves.

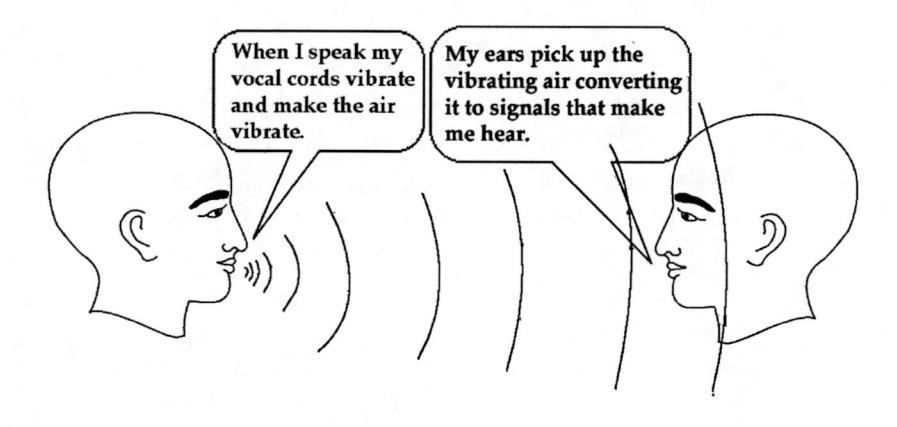

Sound, as we all know, has to have a medium such as air to travel through. If you remember from science class, sound is not really a thing, but just the movement of air. When we talk, our vocal cords make the air vibrate. When this vibrating air goes into our ear, it makes our eardrum vibrate, and we hear a sound. But then, with light, there was a problem. There is no medium like air in the vacuum of space. So what is one to do? It was proposed that there had to be something, so it was assumed that this something was outside of our awareness, and so it was given a name. The first scientist, Aristotle, lived around 300 BCE and called the substance that makes up the heavens ether, the medium was then called ether.

Once something has a name, it takes on a life of its own. So scientists started to use ether to explain other things that were not explainable in mechanical terms. They now had a way to explain gravity, i.e., waves of gravity. But what if the ether that carries light is different from the ether that carries gravity? Then new names were invented, and they called the one carrying light "luminiferous ether." It's easy just to give something a name, but now how could one prove that ether existed? Calculations were done using the same math used to describe sound.

If sound is traveling though air, the air molecules vibrate causing them to snap back and forth at the speed of the sound wave. By calculating the speed of the snap back, one could calculate the density or thickness of the medium the sound was traveling through. So if sound were traveling through, say, steel, the steel molecules would snap back much faster than air molecules. When the calculations were done, it was found that luminiferous ether would have to be denser than steel. But at the same time, it had to be an extremely tenuous gas to exist everywhere in the universe without our being able to see it.

Where is the Ground

This may seem crazy to us today, but if it were believed that the universe was a giant clock or machine, then some weird things would need to be accepted in order to put the theory together. Besides, it was inconceivable in the early scientists' mechanical Reality Box for there not to be "something" for light waves to travel in. They were working from the base assumption that the universe was made of matter. This is what everyday experience tells us. It was believed that our solar system was floating in space. So something had to be there for it to float in; there had

The Ghost in the Machine

to be a "ground" or reference point from which everything came. This is a clear dilemma in the matter assumption/mechanical theory. If you think about it, this was really just a new version of the old world story, of the world resting on the back of a turtle. It could be seen that there was no turtle, so something invisible, ether, was substituted.

There is an old story, which I have heard in more than one version, about a teacher trying to explain to a young student about the earth floating in space. The student said that the teacher couldn't be right because he was told that the earth rested on the back of a turtle. To this the teacher replied, "But what does the turtle rest on?" The student then came back with, "Oh no, you can't fool me; it's turtle all the way down."

What ground or sea is the turtle walking on or swimming in? This is a never-ending cycle. Because with mechanical thinking, which is the way the brain works, one cannot conceive of infinity. Our brains just will not accept the reality of something going on forever. We can say intellectually that we believe the universe goes on forever, but by the very nature of time and space, this makes no sense. Matter must begin and end at some point.

By claiming the existence of ether, the scientists were trying to ignore the philosophical paradox of turtles on top of turtles. The ether was the one and only ground or reference point because it filled all of space. The ether was the ground of the universe and was called "absolute motion." Absolute motion means there is no motion whatsoever. So everything moved relative to the ether, and the ether had no motion.

Think of it this way: imagine a swimming pool as all of space. This would then make the water in the pool the ether. Then imagine someone swimming in the pool with the water flowing over and past his body. The water, or ether, is completely still, but if you were a germ on the swimmer's head, you would feel the water, or ether, moving past you just like a wind. You, the germ, would then feel like as if you were standing still, with the water, or ether, moving. This apparent motion is called the ether wind. The ether just appears to be moving, but it is really the earth that is moving.

At the beginning of the 1880s, Albert Michelson came up with

The Science of Spirit

In a scientific, mechanical universe, there has to be a ground or reference point on which everything stands. Matter is solid and cannot exist without a foundaton or ground to stand on.

This is called absolute motion by science. A place where nothing moves, the ground or foundation of the universe. This is a serious challenge to a matter universe. What is it standing on???

To try and solve this, physicists invented a substance called Ether. Ether filled the universe and was the foundation which held all the bodies in space. But this is really just an updated version of the ancient belief that the would was on the back of a turtle. The problem is still there. Where do the turtles end??? What is holding all of the Ether???

a way, he believed, to measure the ether wind. He said that since the earth was moving though the ether and since light was just vibrating ether, there was a way to see the direction the earth was moving though the ether. To do this, all he had to do was measure

The Ghost in the Machine

the light coming from space in all four directions. His idea was simple. Light coming from space and traveling in the same direction as earth would measure slower because it was having to "catch up" with the earth while light that was meeting the earth would measure faster. It's the same thing as meeting a car on the road or having one come up from behind you. Relative to your car, the car you meet is going faster, and the one passing is moving slower.

This was really a straightforward experiment. Measure the speed of light coming from space in all four directions, and the direction in which light is moving the fastest would indicate the direction the earth was moving through the ether. But after repeated measurements and instrument refinements, light always moved at exactly the same velocity in all directions. Physics was at an impasse and didn't know what to do. Physicists just could not understand why light always moved at exactly the same speed.

Then in 1893, George FitzGerald proposed a new approach. He assumed that all objects grew shorter in the direction of their motion. In other words, if you throw a ball, the ball will flatten out, because the air pushing on it pushes it flatter in the direction of the motion. What if the ether wind did the same thing to the earth and light traveling by it? This would account for light measuring the same speed in all directions.

FitzGerald put together a ratio equation that matched the

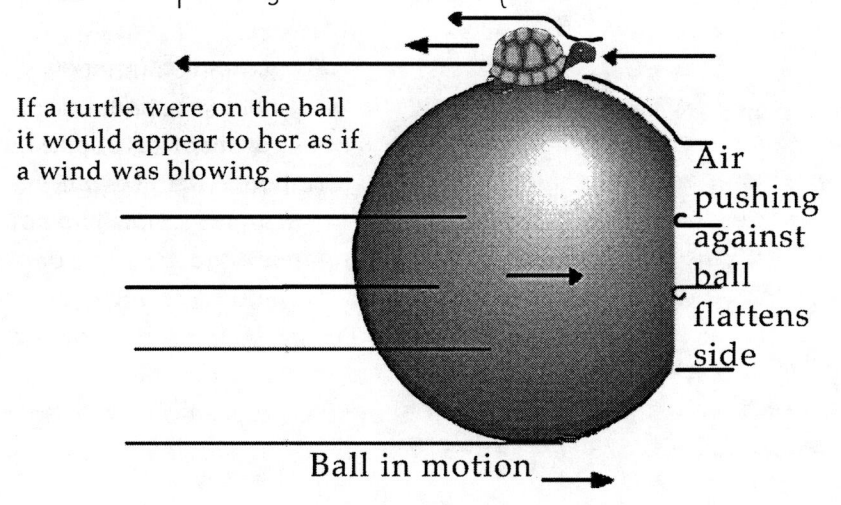

If a turtle were on the ball it would appear to her as if a wind was blowing

Air pushing against ball flattens side

Ball in motion

119

The Science of Spirit

facts exactly. It showed that because the measuring instrument was moving right along with the earth, it would mis-measure the light's speed and always come up with the same measurement for the speed of light. This meant that as long as we were on the earth, there was no way to know whether there was ether because any instrument used would shorten with the direction of the ether wind.

The equation also showed some very strange anomalies at very high velocities. For example: if an object, say a space ship, were to reach the speed of light, it would foreshorten completely and become a pancake of ultimate thinness. So it was FitzGerald who first showed that the speed of light was the ultimate speed. He showed that it was impossible even to approach the speed of light using a force/thrust rocket because the faster a ship goes, the more fuel it will need to push against an increasingly larger and flatter ship. This is why science fiction writers always invent new ways to move through space.

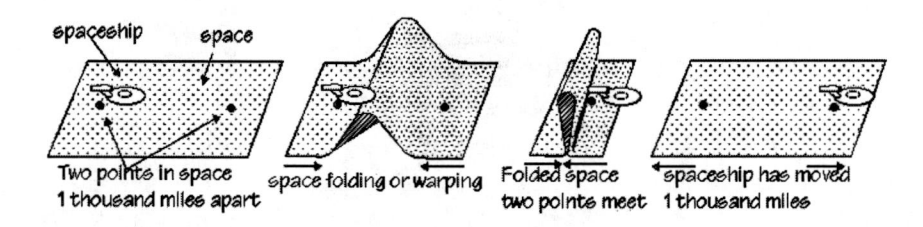

spaceship   space

Two points in space   space folding or warping   Folded space   spaceship has moved
1 thousand miles apart   two points meet   1 thousand miles

In *Star Trek*, as you may know, the warp engine bends, folds, or warps space/time. Imagine that space is like a sheet of paper. Lay a sheet of paper on a table and draw a dot an inch in from each end. (see picture above) Then put your fingers just below the dots and start pushing your fingers and the paper together. The paper will start to buckle, bend, or warp up. As your fingers move closer together the dots will move closer together until they touch. If you think of the dots as the locations of a space ship, then you can see how, if a ship could warp space in the same way, it could move very fast indeed. Thus the ship would move not by

The Ghost in the Machine

force/thrust, but in jumps between folded sections of space.

In 1905, Albert Einstein published a paper called *The Special Theory of Relativity*. The special theory dealt only with motion. First off, Einstein said, it was impossible and useless to keep searching for methods of detecting the ether wind. So we should just assume that the motion of all objects is relative to all other objects. You see, Einstein was not so much about new math discoveries as he was about changing our assumptions.

Einstein said that the velocity of light in a vacuum, *as measured*, would always come out to be the same speed, relative to some other object. He did not say that it is always the same speed: we simply cannot know. The constant speed for light may be an illusion. In other words, Einstein was the first one to have the guts to say, "Look, we have got to quit looking for a turtle/ether that may not even be there."

> If you were a 2 dimensional Flatlander you could not understand a 3 dimensional sun. We are 3 dimensional humans, and just like the Flatlanders we cannot understand a 4 dimensional object.

Einstein then went on to show mathematically that matter and time were not the simple solid things we experience in everyday reality. We think of time as one event happening after another, but this is an illusion. He said that our material world has four dimensions not three, with time being the fourth dimension. Since we experience time as one event happening after another, we don't think of time as a "real thing." It is just a name we give to this perceived succession of events. But Einstein said this was wrong, that time was a true dimension just like height, width, and length. Our perception of it is motion.

> That is what Einstein's math says. Time is the 4th dimension and not just one event happening after another. That is why relativity seems so strange, but it's not, it is just the way it really is.

The analogy always used is that of two people standing on a flat-bed truck playing baseball. If the truck is moving at 50 miles per

121

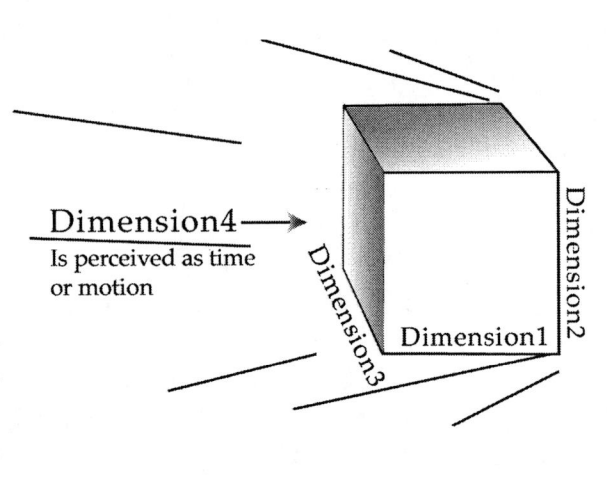

The Science of Spirit

hour (mph), and the ball is batted at 50 mph in the direction the truck is moving, the ball will be going 50 mph relative to the truck. But it will be going 100 mph relative to the ground. In other words, 50 mph on the truck plus 50 mph for the motion of the truck would total 100 mph, for someone standing on the ground with a radar gun trained on the ball.

Dimension4 — Is perceived as time or motion

Dimension1, Dimension2, Dimension3

This is what everyday experience tells us, but if the speed of light is the maximum speed, then this is not always correct. As Einstein's math revealed, the total would be some minute fraction smaller than 100 mph, but the fraction would be much too small to measure. This fraction, however, gets larger and larger as the speed increases. Let's say now that someone invents a new type of fuel that makes a ship go close to the speed of light, and we speed our ship up to 100,000 miles per second (mps), which is just 47% shy of the 186,000 mps needed to reach the speed of light. Further, let's say that instead of throwing a ball, we have a

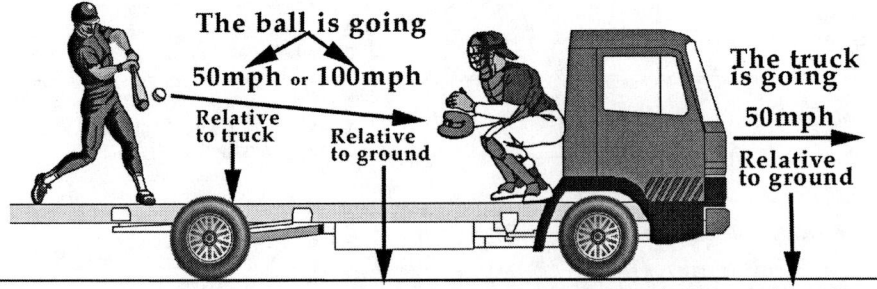

The ball is going 50mph or 100mph
Relative to truck / Relative to ground
The truck is going 50mph
Relative to ground

If the ball, relative to the truck, is going 50mph as the truck is going 50mph relative to the ground - then the ball would be going 100mph relative to the ground. This is common sense, but Einstein's math showed that common sense is wrong. The ball is really going an undetectable amount slower.

The Ghost in the Machine

rocket launcher that can shoot a rocket at 100,000 mps. What will our person who is standing on the earth with the radar gun measure? If everyday experience were true, it would be 100,000 mps plus 100,000 mps, just as above, for a total of 200,000 mps. But you cannot exceed the speed limit of light, so the radar gun would measure 176,700 mps, and that's not even the

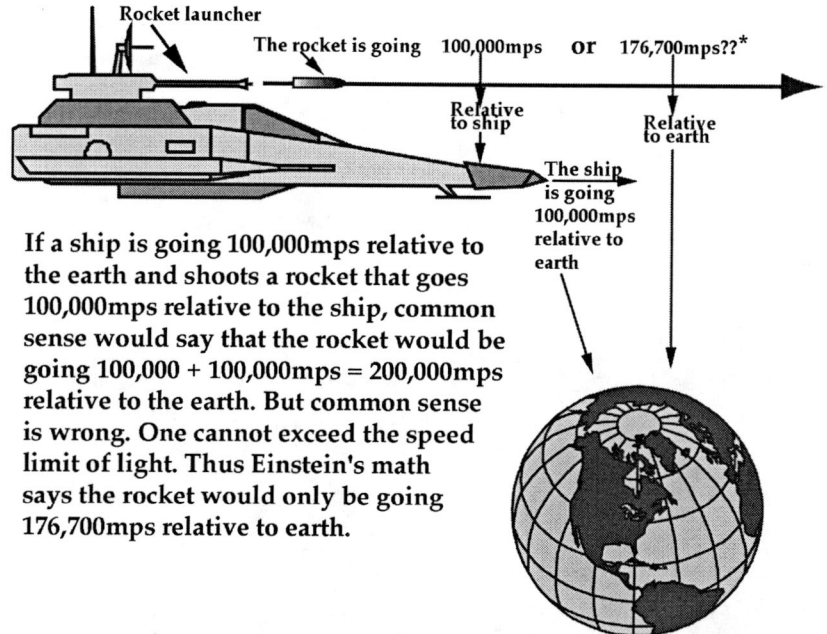

If a ship is going 100,000mps relative to the earth and shoots a rocket that goes 100,000mps relative to the ship, common sense would say that the rocket would be going 100,000 + 100,000mps = 200,000mps relative to the earth. But common sense is wrong. One cannot exceed the speed limit of light. Thus Einstein's math says the rocket would only be going 176,700mps relative to earth.

*Not 200,000 as you would expect - That would exceed the speed of light

maximum speed of light. This number may seem strange, but that is what Einstein's math says. In order to explain it better we would need to look at more detailed math. (You can see some simple math in appendix A.) But don't let this confuse you; just accept that this is the way things are.

We do not know what is really going on. All we can know is what our instruments and five senses tell us. Or maybe that is our problem. Maybe our problem stems from our assumption that the only way we can know something is by measuring it with instruments or by using our five senses. We will return to this thought later. But for now I will show why some believe that the

The Science of Spirit

above is really an illusion and, therefore, that time and matter are an illusion.

Imagine, if you will, the starship *Voyager* trying to find its way out of the Delta Quadrant. Unfortunately, the ship is trapped in a starless void, the warp drive is down for repairs, and the ship is stalled in space. Then along comes an approaching alien ship. It's important to know how big this approaching ship is in order to assess whether it is a threat, so Captain Janeway asks ensign Kim, the engineer, to measure the ship's length and mass. Kim pushes some buttons on his console and takes the measurements. The computer then says that the ship is traveling at 100,000 mps, and at that speed its length was measured to be 84% that of its resting length and its mass twice that of its resting mass.

You are mistaken, we are the ones stalled in space and you are going 100,000 mps

I assure you captain Gorn our warp engines are off-line so we are the ones stalled in space and you are the one going 100,000 mps

The starship Voyager is trapped in a starless void with another starship. With no stars they have nothing to be relative to, and therefore cannot tell whom is moving.

Janeway then asks Kim to make contact and put it on screen. The alien captain comes on screen and says, "This is Gorn. I am the captain of the starship 697. Can you help us?"

Janeway then says, "This is Captain Janeway of the starship *Voyager*, how can we help you?"

Captain Gorn then replies, "Our engines are down, and we need parts to get us moving again."

To which Janeway replies, "Are you trying to trick us? We are the ones stalled in space, and you are moving at 100,000 mps."

"No! No!" protests Captain Gorn. "I assure you that we are the ones standing still, and you are the ones traveling at 100,000

The Ghost in the Machine

mps. We have measured your length, and it is 84% that of its resting length, and your mass is twice that of your resting mass. So you are the one moving."

Who is right? If you are a *Star Trek* fan, you are going to assume that captain Gorn is the one lying. But that is clearly just a bias. There is no way to "know" who is right because both captains can know only what their instruments tell them. Relativity theory says that if the ships were approaching each other at 100,000 mps, the instruments on each ship would show the other ship to be moving and itself standing still. But how is this possible? Can we not say that relativity theory is wrong? No, not likely, this is because accurate experiments show that the mass does indeed increase with increased speed. The only reasonable explanation is that mass is really just an illusion made from something we do not understand— not a mechanical thing, as we understand mechanical things in our everyday life. Mechanical things would not act in such a strange manner.

You may be shocked to learn that we cannot prove, by any means, whether the earth is rotating on its axis or whether the earth is standing still and the universe is moving around us. We assume, like the *Star Trek* fans, that it is the earth that is turning because it would seem very arrogant to assume that the vast universe is moving around us. But one of the problems of relativity is that there is no way to measure it and know for sure. You may say it would be ridiculous to think that a star hundreds of thousands of light years away would move around us in 24 hours. But according to relativity math, the outcome would be the same. You may even try to be clever and say, "Well, the earth has a bulge at the equator caused by the centrifugal force of spinning." But you would be wrong because the mass of the universe flying around us would create the exact same bulge.[19]

You may now ask, "What about time? After all, it is just the movement of one event after another." One of the more bizarre aspects of relativity is that time and matter are all one thing, with everyday matter having three dimensions and time being the fourth. So as the speed goes up and the mass increases, time slows down accordingly. This also is a measurement illusion like

The Science of Spirit

mass. Experiments have shown that if one of two twin brothers were sent to space and traveled close to the speed of light, the one in space would age more slowly. For example, if the brother who is traveling close to the speed of light was gone for 50 years of earth time, when he returned, he would have aged only 5 years. But the brother on earth would be 50 years older.

In the seventies the first test was done to see if time would really slow down as speed increased. Scientists placed two atomic clocks aboard an airplane, which then flew, at the same speed, several times with the rotation of the earth and several times against the rotation. By flying against the rotation, the airplane increased its speed, and by then going with the earth, it flew very slowly relative to the ground. By then comparing how fast or slowly the clocks ran in each direction, the scientists could determine whether the clock slowed when the airplane was traveling against the earth's rotation. Indeed, when it flew against the rotation, the faster speed, the clock ran slower by as much as Einstein's math predicted.

Jerry! What has happened to you? You look 85 years old! What happened in the five years I was gone?

I am 85 years old! You were gone for 50 years not 5.

Here we have 2 twin brothers. Tom has been on a trip traveling close to the speed of light. To Tom only five years have passed and he is five years older. But Jerry, who was on earth, saw 50 years go by and is now 85.

If people really do age more slowly as the speed they travel increases, it must be an illusion also? To answer this we need to listen in on the dispute between Captain Janeway and Captain Gorn. Remember that Captain Gorn had just assured Captain Janeway that they were indeed the ones standing still. Captain Janeway then says, "You must be lying because we have a special sensor that can read the rate that time is moving on your ship, and at 100,000 mps time on your ship is moving 84% as fast as it is on our ship."

"But Captain Janeway, we also have a time sensor, and it is you aging at 84% the normal rate relative to our ship."

This is not just math or conjecture. Researchers have been doing experiments for over 90 years trying to disprove Einstein's theories. They have even made atomic clocks slow down by putting them in airplanes and moving at high speeds.[10]

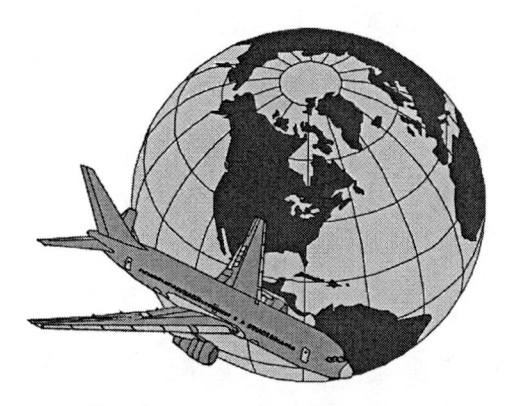

In the seventies the twin paradox was tested to see if it was real or just math. It turned out to be real. The clocks on the airplane ran slower than the clocks on the ground.

New Reality Box 5

Our everyday experience tells us that time is just the occurrence of one event after another, but after 90 years of testing relativity theory we've learned that time is a measurement illusion. Time changes as your speed changes. If two space ships, traveling close to the speed of light, were to meet; space ship 1 would see the clock in ship 2 as moving faster than their own clock but ship 2 would see the clock in ship 1 also moving faster than their own clock.

The Ghost in the Machine

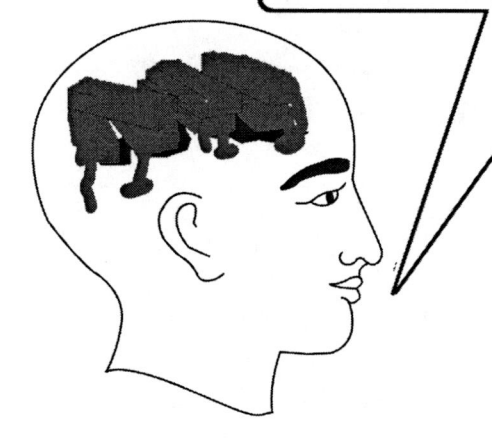

*So free yourself from the
Illusions of your senses. Sanity
Requires adjustment of the mind between
The thing as it appears and what it is
In fact and in reality.*

> **The Voice Celestial**
> **Page 123**

The Machine: She Came Undone

Journal 6
The Machine: She Came Undone

As I stand at the top of my climb, I must stop for a moment and try to understand and accept this new world up here. I must prepare myself for change. Life after all is a moving changing river, and those that try to hold on to the bank will not experience the wonders of life and the universe.

My first book on quantum physics, which my father had sent me in the late eighties was called *In Search of Schrodinger's Cat* by John Gribbin. It was an introduction to quantum physics for the layman. I was just blown away by the concepts in the book, but just the same as some physicists, I could not accept that what happens in the micro world could affect everyday reality. I could not believe that this was really mainstream science. I had thought of physicists as engineers with calculators, working out the force of a jet engine. This is called classical or Newtonian physics. But Gribbin's book said that the new physics was about things being in two places at the same time. You know, like being a little bit pregnant. This is not at all the reality of our everyday life! As a matter of fact, the truism that you can't be a little bit pregnant means that either you're pregnant or not. It is meant to show that something cannot be in two states at the same time. But on the microscopic level, from which we are made, things do this all the time. It is the natural state.

> The science that we all learned about in school is called "Classical." It matches everyday experience.

> There is a new science. It is called "Quantum" It has found that matter is not real, and everything is just energy packets called quanta.

Did I hear you say that was impossible? If you are new to the new physics, i.e., quantum physics, then hold on to your hat, because we are about to go for a ride. It is important that you begin to understand that the everyday world you grew up in is not at all the same as the microscopic world. Remember the newspaper editor who refused to print the story about the Wright brothers' airplane flying? Well, it's your turn. Flying was just as impossible to him as something being "a little bit pregnant" seems to you now. But if you are willing to grow and listen to the scientific facts, I will show you how this is possible. To make this fun, we need to go back to where we left off when we were talking about relativity.

We are now transported to the end of the nineteenth century. Physicists were worried because they believed that physics was complete— that they knew all that they could know and that they would be out of jobs soon. Students were advised not to go into physics because there were not going to be jobs for them. They believed that there were only two small problems that would be worked out shortly. This was the height of what is called classical physics, which is based on the assumption that the universe is a machine made of matter. All the mechanical laws that govern our everyday reality had been discovered and worked out. The laws that govern the entire universe were believed to be known.

One of the two problems with classical math was that it could not correctly predict the color of metal as it was heated. From common experience, we all know that when metal is heated, it first becomes red, then white, and eventually blue. But classical physics knew very little about radiation. It was believed that radiation was just waves like sound or water waves, and, working from this idea, physicists used the same math to picture heat radiation. As a result, their best math predicted that metal should be blue, not red, when it was first heated. As a matter of fact, according to the math, it would be dangerous for you to sit in front of a fire because the radiation would burn you up. So I would say they had a small problem.

No one was concerned about this problem because they were confident these little kinks would be worked out shortly. Then a

The Machine: She Came Undone

physics student by the name of Maxwell Planck decided to work on the radiation problem. He discovered that if he added a constant to the math, he could make the math agree with the real colors of heated metal. But by using the constant he created a new problem. If the constant was an accurate picture of radiation, it meant that radiation traveled in little packets of energy, not in waves as it was believed to travel. This made no more sense than the color of heated metal being blue. But in the end, Planck decided to write it up for publication. After all, he had nothing better to offer, and maybe someone else would be able to make the energy packets go away. So in 1901 his paper was published, and the first seed of quantum physics was planted. The constant is now called Planck's constant, and it turns out that it is the smallest size that anything can be divided to.

> A constant is a number that never changes like pi or the speed of light.

I would like to point out here that this is the point at which science came full circle. Plato, a philosopher in the fourth century BCE, had already dealt with this problem and concluded that the universe could not be made of matter, "matter" meaning something that had weight and dimensions like height and width. It had to be made from energy, i.e., something that was infinite and had no dimensions. This was because matter can always be divided, with the divided piece being divided again, and on and on, continuing in a never-ending cycle. Since you cannot keep dividing matter forever, there must be a point where it ends and becomes energy. Energy is clearly different from matter. It has no height and width or time that we know of.

The second problem involved the photoelectric effect. Experiments had shown that when you shine light on a metal foil and look at it with a special microscope, you can see electrons being kicked off the surface. The experiments showed that the number of electrons kicked off were not proportionate to the brightness of light, i.e., the amount of energy. This made no sense to classical physicists. They believed that the brighter the light, the more energy and the more electrons should be kicked off the surface. The analogy always used is that of ocean waves hitting a beach. The more powerful the waves, the more sand and rocks that would be kicked loose.

Then in 1905, Einstein used Planck's constant to show that the experiments were right and that classical math was wrong. He showed that if light traveled in small energy packets, called quanta, the math would match the experiments. So Planck's constant could explain both problems. Maybe classical radiation theory was wrong, and, somehow, light was made up of packets of energy. Today, light energy packets are called photons. Thus, we have the name "quantum physics" from the fact that everything is based on quanta, "pieces" of energy. The size of a quanta is very small indeed. Planck's constant, which is the size of a quanta, is represented by the letter h, and h=0.000,000,000,000,000,000,000,000,006,626 ergseconds. An ergsecond is energy times time, so if 0.1 is one tenth of an ergsecond and 0.01 is one one-hundredth of an ergsecond, then one quanta is one million, million, million, millionth of an ergsecond. Planck's constant is the smallest that anything can be. It other words it is impossible for anything to be smaller than Planck's constant according to math. This is a strange number for classical physics because it is a four-dimensional number. "Erg" stands for energy, which is a three-dimensional number times time. If you will notice, this is the same concept as Einstein's 1905 space-time, which is also a four-dimensional entity.

> Plank's Constant is the smallest anything can be, and the size of a quanta.

At the time, no one knew anything about atoms or if they really existed. Classical physics' picture of the atom was sometimes called "Christmas pudding." Classical physicists believed that the atom was a tiny sphere (matter/a hard thing), which had a positive charge. This sphere then contained small nuggets of negative charges, like raisins in a pudding. The big problem with this picture was that it could not explain how radiation worked.

Einstein, also in 1905, was the first one to show that atoms existed, using a phenomenon called Brownian motion, which can be seen under a microscope. If you put flower pollen in a solution like water and look at it under a microscope, the tiny specks of pollen will jump around as if they were alive. Einstein showed that the force needed to push the pollen around was the same force that the physicists would have expected to see exhibited by a vibrating atom. So the movement of the atom was bumping the pollen and making it move.

Then around 1907, a man by the name of Ernest Rutherford discovered that the atom was mostly empty space with a hard core. He discovered this by having his students shoot alpha particles (a type of radiation like light) at a thin gold foil. Most of the time, when the alpha particles hit the foil, they would go on through, knocking out some electrons. But occasionally, an alpha particle would bounce back. This meant that occasionally the alpha particle would hit the atom's core, which would bounce it back. By calculating the rate of bounce-back, Rutherford figured out that the atom contained a positive core with electrons in orbit around the core. This made no sense to classical physics or to Rutherford. What would keep the electron in orbit? According to classical physics, the electron would lose energy and spiral into the center within seconds.

Bohr's Quantum Jump

Around 1912, Niels Bohr began working on the structure of the atom. He used Planck's constant and Einstein's work on the photoelectric effect to make the first working model of the atom. Bohr's math showed that the atom had to be made up of different layers of energy like an onion. His math showed that as long as an electron was in one of these orbits— or shells, as they were called— it would be stable and not fall into the center. But then Bohr found a strange thing. In order for radiation to be released from the atom, as had been seen, the electron would need to jump

The Science of Spirit

to the next orbit to release the energy, in the form of a photon.

The weird thing here is that when the electron switched shells, it did so without traveling through the space between the two shells. If nothing can be smaller than Planck's constant, then the electron had to jump in increments no smaller than Planck's constant. But it didn't: it didn't "jump" at all. The electron would disappear from one orbit and reappear in the second orbit— without traveling through the space between the two orbits.

This, of course, seems impossible from everyday experience.

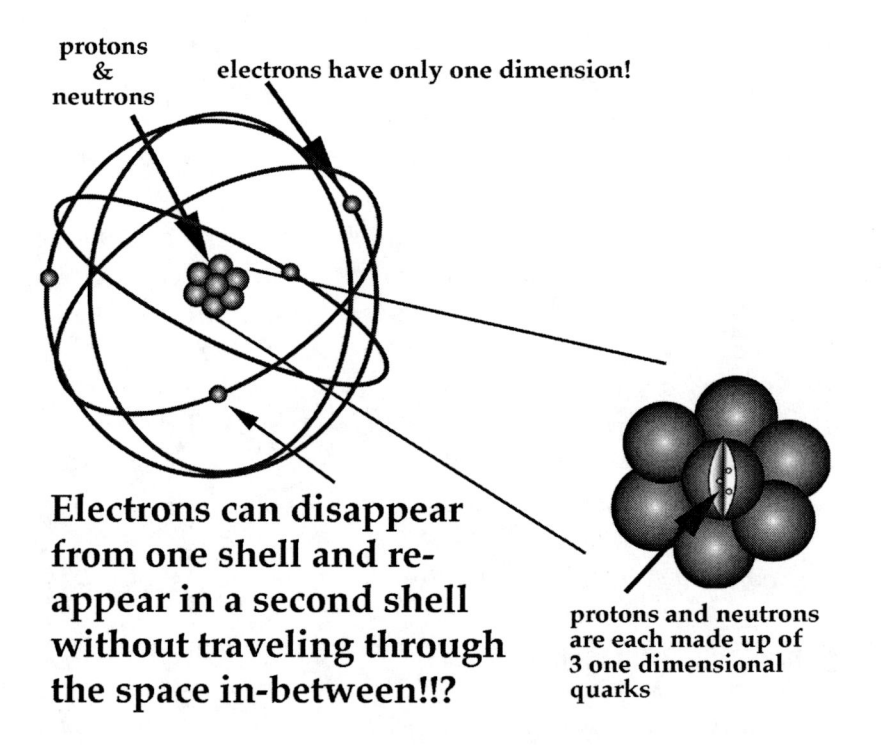

protons & neutrons

electrons have only one dimension!

Electrons can disappear from one shell and re-appear in a second shell without traveling through the space in-between!!?

protons and neutrons are each made up of 3 one dimensional quarks

There is no doubt today, however, that this phenomenon occurs. This is where the term "quantum jump" or "quantum leap" comes from. A quantum leap is a leap from one point to another without traveling through the space inbetween.

(continued on page 140)

The Matter Myth

This is what a hydrogen atom would look like if you could make it big enough to see. It, like all matter, is nothing but a ball of energy.

Scientists have run into a serious problem with their theory of the atom. Where is the mass or weight in the atom??? Atoms are nothing more than a set of balanced charges. There is nothing there that can give it mass. The electron is only a one dimensional speck of energy. The protons and neutrons in the center are nothing more than sets of three specks of one dimensional energy. There is nothing else that they can find! Nothing but one dimensional specks of energy called quarks.

There is a 90% probability that the electron is somewhere in the cloud.

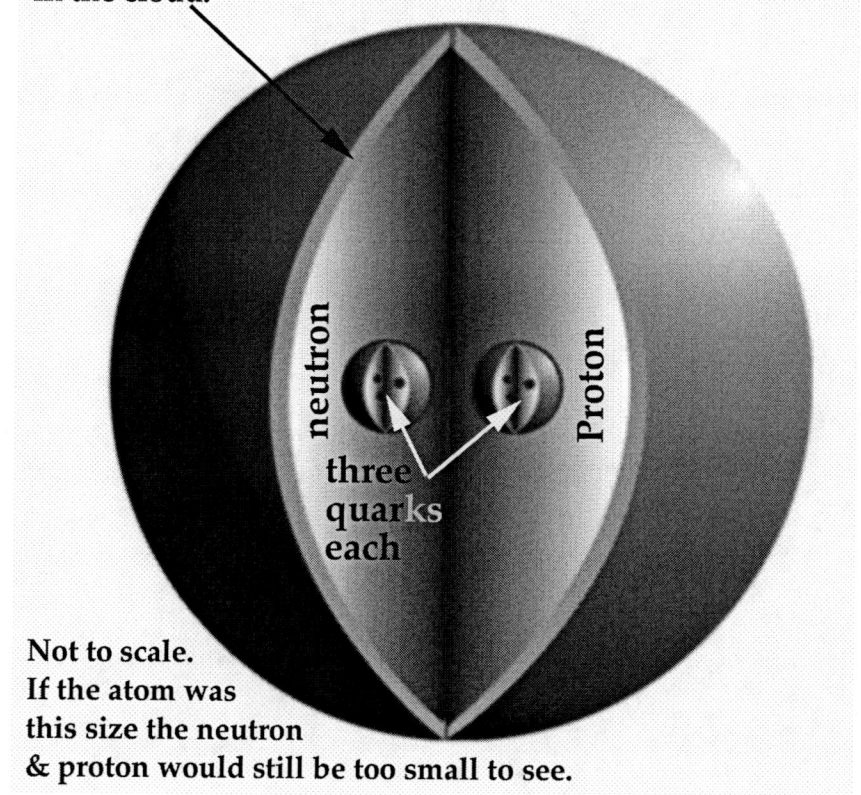

neutron

Proton

three quarks each

Not to scale. If the atom was this size the neutron & proton would still be too small to see.

The Science of Spirit

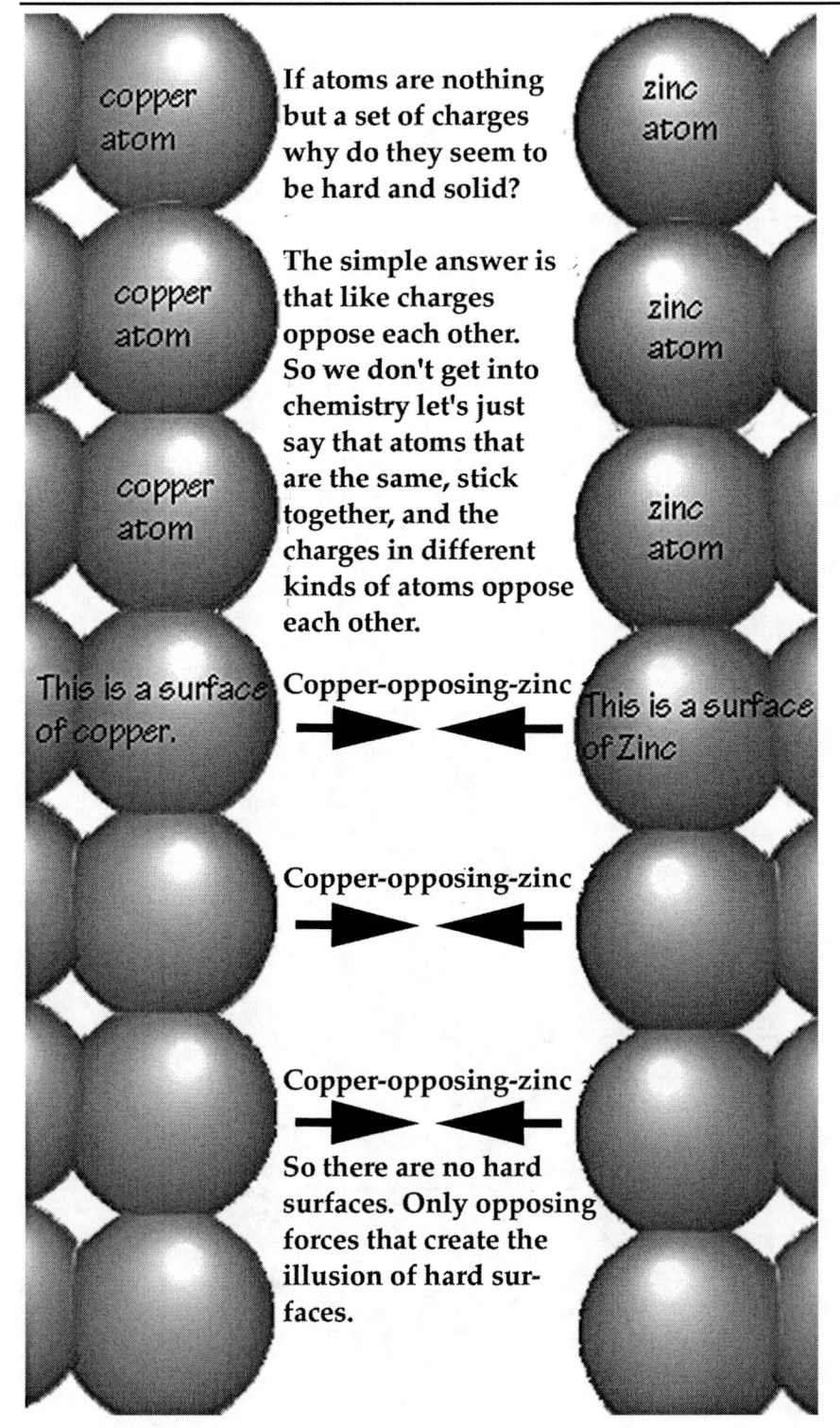

copper atom

copper atom

copper atom

This is a surface of copper.

zinc atom

zinc atom

zinc atom

This is a surface of Zinc

If atoms are nothing but a set of charges why do they seem to be hard and solid?

The simple answer is that like charges oppose each other. So we don't get into chemistry let's just say that atoms that are the same, stick together, and the charges in different kinds of atoms oppose each other.

Copper-opposing-zinc ▶◀

Copper-opposing-zinc ▶◀

Copper-opposing-zinc ▶◀

So there are no hard surfaces. Only opposing forces that create the illusion of hard surfaces.

The Machine: She Came Undone

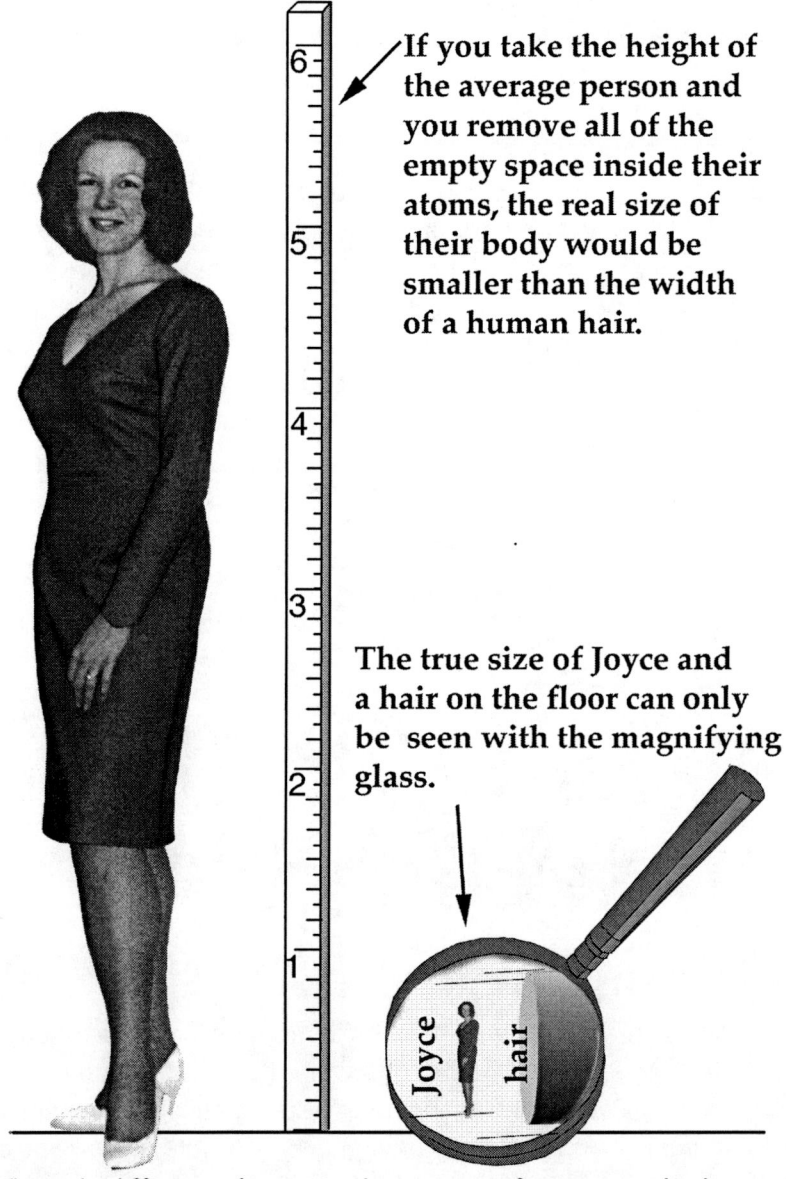

If you take the height of the average person and you remove all of the empty space inside their atoms, the real size of their body would be smaller than the width of a human hair.

The true size of Joyce and a hair on the floor can only be seen with the magnifying glass.

The only difference between the picture of a persons body on a TV screen and their "real" body is the number and complexity of charges and vibration.

How and where the weight comes from no one knows. The present theory says that there must be a "particle" that "endows" matter with weight somehow.

?????   And this is only the half of it---Read On.

Possibly the best experiment to demonstrate the strangeness of quantum physics is the "double slot" experiment. Imagine a cardboard box with a small hole in one side. Opposite the hole on the inside of the box, you tape a sheet of carbon typing paper. If you then take a peashooter and shoot a pea through the hole, the pea will hit the carbon paper and make a little mark where it knocked off some of the carbon. If you then shoot a hundred peas through the hole, most of the peas will hit the carbon paper in about the same spot and create a large spot on the carbon paper opposite the hole.

If you now cut a second hole next to the first, just to one side, and repeat the above experiment, you will then have two spots on

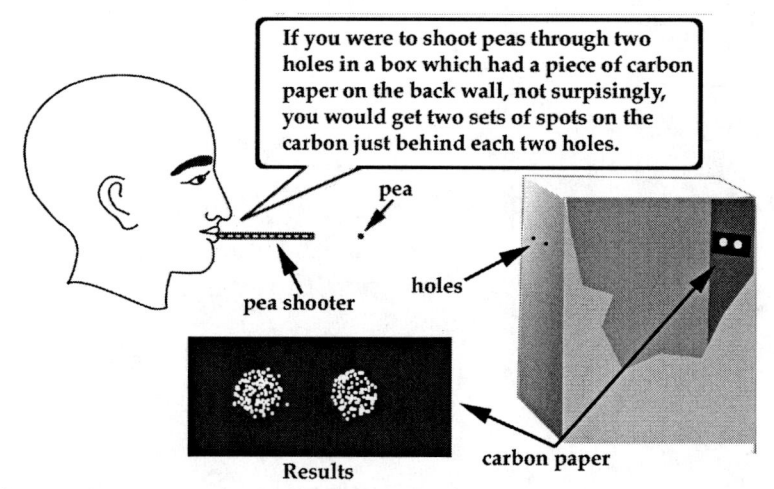

> If you were to shoot peas through two holes in a box which had a piece of carbon paper on the back wall, not surpisingly, you would get two sets of spots on the carbon just behind each two holes.

pea shooter · pea · holes · carbon paper · Results

the carbon paper just beyond the two holes— one spot for each hole. This is only common sense.

Now what if you replace the carbon paper with a sheet of camera film and replace the peashooter with an electronic device that could send just one photon, or particle of light, through the hole in the box? If you start by having only one hole and shoot one hundred photons of light through the hole and then develop the film, you will see a large spot just like the one on the carbon paper with the peashooter.

But if you then repeat the experiment with two holes, you will not see two spots as with the peashooter, but one large spot with bands of dark stripes running though it. Why? The answer is that

The Machine: She Came Undone

If instead of shooting a pea we shoot a photon at a box which only has one hole we would get the same results as we did with the peas.

photon gun

photon

Results the same as pea

camera film

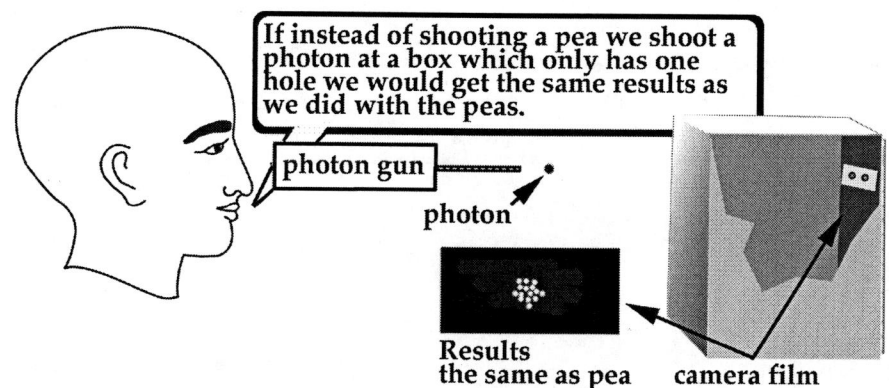

even though you are shooting only one photon through one hole, it is going through both holes at the same time. The stripes come from what is called an interference pattern. You can see an interference pattern by dropping two stones into a pond side by side. The two rings that come out from the two stones will mix and create interference patterns in the water.

So light must be a wave like the waves in a pond, right? But if photons are little particles of light like peas, how can they be going through both holes at the same time? Well, why not just put a light detector on one of the holes and see which hole the light is really going through?

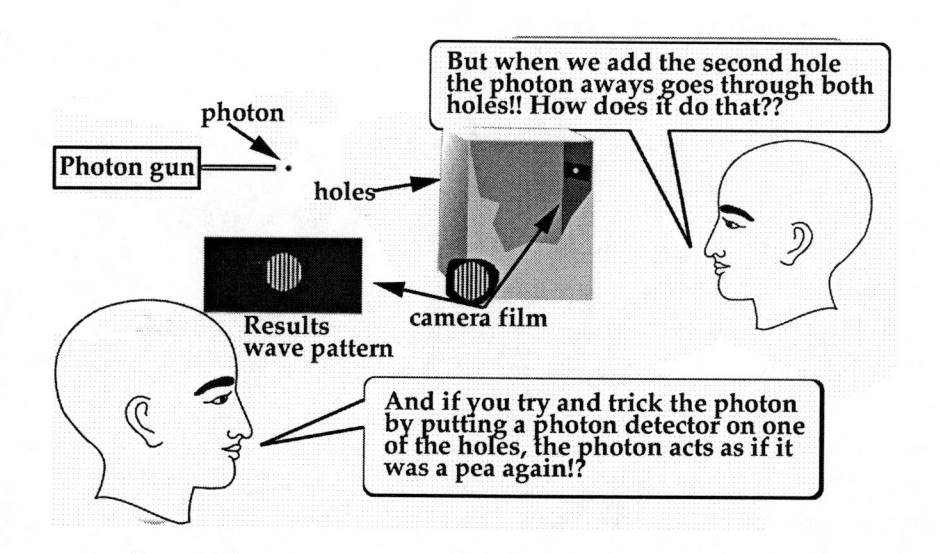

photon

Photon gun

holes

But when we add the second hole the photon aways goes through both holes!! How does it do that??

Results wave pattern

camera film

And if you try and trick the photon by putting a photon detector on one of the holes, the photon acts as if it was a pea again!?

The Science of Spirit

Light detectors were placed on one of the holes, then on the other, and then on both at the same time. No matter what was done, as soon as the scientists tried to look (using a light detector), the light would turn back into a pea and create a single spot just behind one of the holes. In other words, as long as we don't look at the photons, they act like waves in a pond; but as soon as we try to observe them, they act like peas from a peashooter.

This experiment has been done thousands of times over the years, using every conceivable apparatus. No one to date has found a way to trick the light. There is no other conclusion: light is a wave when we are not looking, but a photon when we are. This means that light is both a wave and a particle all at the same time, and just looking at it, causes light to revert to its particle state. It is as if our brain cannot accept or understand something that occurs in two states at the same time, so it picks one of the two states and says the light is now a photon or now a wave. Today, this phenomenon of things being in two states at the same time is called "super position."

The famous picture to the right is a good example of super position. This famous picture of an old/young woman exists in two "states" at once. One state is a picture of an old woman, and the other is a picture of a young woman. Note that the eye of the old woman is the young woman's ear, and the old woman's mouth is a necklace on the young woman.

By 1926 the basic quantum math was complete, and no fewer than three different types of math had been used. The first type of math is called Matrix Mechanics, and was done by Werner Heisenberg. He put numbers into a table or matrix, and then each matrix was used as if it were a single number. As you can see, this could get quite complex when multiplying or dividing whole matrixes by each other. Then an established physicist, Erwin Schrodinger, developed the second type. He did not like Matrix Mechanics or Heisenberg's new quantum theory. To begin with he did not like the concept of particles and believed that waves did a better job of representing the way the world worked. He then set out to show that Heisenberg was wrong. But to his surprise his

The Machine: She Came Undone

wave math came to the same conclusion as Heisenberg's Matrix Mechanics. Finally, the third math approach came from a young math student by the name of Paul Dirac. At a meeting he was handed a copy of Heisenberg's unpublished quantum theory. He was very impressed and set out to rewrite it using algebra, the same algebra most of us learned in high school. He then developed a new type of algebra called Quantum Algebra. The Quantum Algebra came to the same conclusion as Heisenberg's Matrix Mechanics and Schrodinger's wave math.

But, you may ask, if all this math is saying that the world is mostly quantum, then how come what I see is mostly classical? Shouldn't the classical math also work with the quantum math? You're right, and it does. All three of the above mathematical descriptions of the world also say that a small part of reality will be the classical reality that we see every day. So not only do three different math descriptions say the universe is mostly quantum, but they also describe our everyday reality, as a part of the whole picture. In other words, the picture the math paints is one of a quantum universe with a small classical world embedded in it, i.e., our everyday reality.

Many physicists, including Einstein, didn't like the new physics. It was too far outside their Reality Box. So Einstein began an open debate with Niels Bohr. Einstein argued that the quantum weirdness could not be right, that something was missing and when we found this something, the weirdness would go away and the universe would be classical again. So he argued that quantum theory must be incomplete. Bohr argued that quantum theory was complete, and we just needed to accept the weirdness. One of the things that Einstein objected to was the uncertainty principle.

The uncertainty principle says that, on the quantum level, the more accurately we know the position of a particle (where the particle is) the less accurately we know its velocity (how fast it's going) and vice versa. Position and velocity are attributes of an electron. This is like a baseball being at a precise place in space, which is called position, and moving at a specific speed, which is called velocity. But unlike with baseballs, if we know with accuracy the position of a particle, the velocity does not exist. Einstein was one of the physicists who believed that this was a measurement problem. In other words, even if we could not measure or know the velocity, that did not mean the position did not exist.

If you are new to this quantum concept, you will probably agree with Einstein. You will not be able to accept that if you know the

The Machine: She Came Undone

velocity of an electron, then that electron has no position in space. But this is because you grew up with baseballs, and ultimately believe that the world is really classical. I know: I have been there and done that. That is all right for now. Just don't be afraid of going further, because once the whole concept blossoms in your thinking, it is truly a beautiful thing. I would not have it any other way. The secret is to "accept it without conceptualizing it." Wow! Does that statement have an eastern-philosophy flavor or what?

This is all well and good, you may say, and very hard to believe, but what does it mean? One answer came in a little book called *Quantum Reality* by Nick Herbert, a physicist/scientist/philosopher.[12] Herbert looked at the underlying reality of the universe that the quantum data painted. He says that there are four main interpretations of the quantum data, and then within each of these schools there are splinter groups.

> Old classical science and everday reality says that there really is a 3 dimensional bird out there in the real world.

bird

The first and most widely accepted interpretation of quantum theory states that there is no deeper reality. In other words, beneath our everyday world there are no dynamic attributes. Attributes are things like position and velocity. Position is like the position of a baseball at some point in space, and velocity is how fast the ball is going. In other words, attributes are a measurement illusion. This interpretation was developed by two of the founders of quantum theory, namely Niels Bohr and Werner Heisenberg. It has come to be known as the Copenhagen Interpretation, as it was developed in Denmark at the Copenhagen Institute. The Copenhagen Interpretation does not say that electrons are not real, just that they do not have any attributes (like position and velocity) until they are measured.

The Science of Spirit

> The new science is called quantum. This science shows that there is no "deep reality." One interpretation of this is called the "Copenhagen Interpretation". This says that things in the world do not exist in a form we can understand. Our bird is just "waves of probability."

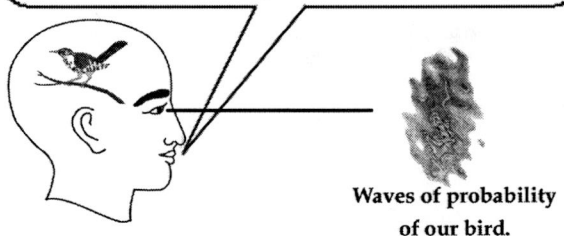

Waves of probability of our bird.

Remember the lesson that we learned in perception class? Our five senses are just measurement devices. (I'll call them M from now on.) They just take samples of information in from "out there" in the world, and we interpret the incoming data. (I will discuss who "we" are later.) This is different from being merely pragmatists. Many physicists refuse to put any interpretation on the data. They believe that quantum math is just a useful tool, which they need to make whatever it is they are studying work. For example: it is not possible to understand how our sun works without using quantum math.

The Copenhagen school believes that what we see when we look at an electron is an interaction between the electron and the measurement that creates its attributes. This includes looking at an electron with our eyes because looking at something is really an act of measuring it. In other words, the Copenhagen school is saying that the electron does not exist in a way we can understand until we look at it or measure it. (Remember what I just said above, that in the quantum world, if you look at or measure an electron's velocity, its position does not exist and vice versa.)

In the early days, it was thought that the attributes were really there, but that our measurement devices were too poor to see them. It was believed that one could know indirectly, without interacting with the electron, whether or not it was really there. For example, let's say we have an apparatus that will randomly send an electron down one of two different tubes. Let's call one tube "A" and the second tube "B." We will then watch the detector on tube "B" that is waiting to tell us if an electron goes down tube

"B" or not. If we then send an electron randomly down one of the two tubes, and the detector on tube "B" does not detect an electron, we can say that "indirectly" we know that the electron went down tube "A."

You would then think that we have indirectly measured the electron without looking at it or interacting with it. But, unfortunately, this is not the case. The assumption is that the electron went down tube "A," but it is only an assumption. In order for us to know that an electron went down either tube we would need to have a detector on "A" tube also. When the electron is then detected in tube "A," we have interacted with it. Therefore, detector "A" created the dynamic attributes. After 75 years of quantum theory, no one has been able to find a way not to interact with a measurement of a quantum entity.

What Bohr and Heisenberg believed was that an interaction between a measuring device, just the act of looking at the electron, and the action is what creates the illusion that the electron has dynamic attributes. This is a similar thing in that it is a measurement illusion. It is not an illusion in the sense that there's nothing out there in the world, but what we see does not exist in the form we think we see. It is our mind that **creates** what it sees.

Think of it like this: particles that make up atoms—i.e., electrons, protons, and so on—do not have attributes like position and velocity until we look at them. Therefore, atoms do not exist in a form that we can understand until we look at the atoms and create the illusion of attributes. So this book that you are reading is made of millions of atoms, and none of these atoms exists in a form humans can understand until you start reading the book. You then create the attributes with your mind and cause the book to come into existence in the form you see! I know that this seems impossible to believe, but hang in there.

Herbert says that the main drawback to the Copenhagen view is that it gives special status to M devices, and this runs into a philosophical dilemma. It assumes that the M device is different from the quantum world. This creates the problem of what happens if a second M device then measures the first M device.

The Science of Spirit

Does the first M device then become a quantum entity and the second a special class? What if you had a third M device that measures the second? What then? We're back to the world sitting on the back of a turtle. Then what is the turtle sitting on? And so on forever.

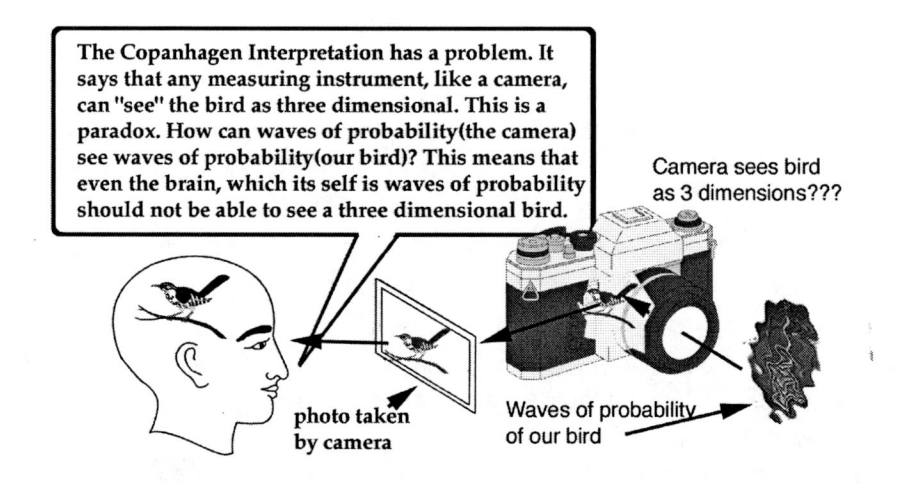

> The Copanhagen Interpretation has a problem. It says that any measuring instrument, like a camera, can "see" the bird as three dimensional. This is a paradox. How can waves of probability(the camera) see waves of probability(our bird)? This means that even the brain, which its self is waves of probability should not be able to see a three dimensional bird.

Camera sees bird as 3 dimensions???

photo taken by camera

Waves of probability of our bird

In the second interpretation of the quantum data, the Copenhagen Interpretation is carried further. This interpretation says that we actually create reality by observing it. The universe is nothing but "waves of probability," and when we look at a set of waves, they collapse to create our reality. The moon is not there until we look at it. It is nothing but waves of probabilities, and the very act of looking at the moon collapses these waves of probability into just one set of waves.

This interpretation has the same problem as the last in that it gives special status to M devices. But some physicists claim an easy solution to the M-device problem by saying that only a "conscious observer" can collapse the wave. This would mean that if you took a picture of the moon (the camera being an M device), the picture would record all of the waves of probability, and then when a conscious observer looked at the picture, he would collapse the waveform and see a picture of the moon. This makes very good sense to me, and we will look at it more later.

The Machine: She Came Undone

Many World Interpertation

The next major interpretation of quantum theory is the most bizarre of them all, in my view. This is not to say that I reject it. It does seem to explain some strange events that occur in everyday

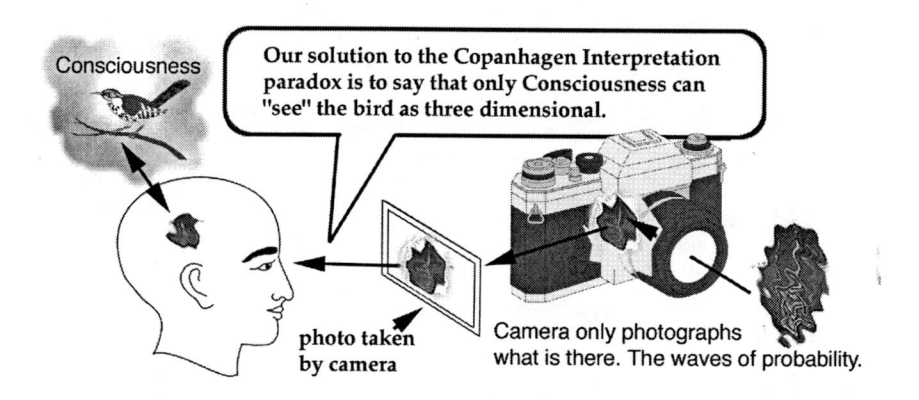

Consciousness

Our solution to the Copanhagen Interpretation paradox is to say that only Consciousness can "see" the bird as three dimensional.

photo taken by camera

Camera only photographs what is there. The waves of probability.

experience. This interpretation was formulated by Hugh Everett when he was working on his doctoral thesis. Everett was trying to get around the problem of giving special status to the M devices. He felt that M devices had to be made of the same quantum stuff as everything else. One way not to give the M device special status is not to collapse the wave. So if the M device is also made up of waves of probability, why not have each set of waves split with each M device. This way there would be only one M device with each set of waves. In other words, one M device would be looking at the old woman, and the other M device at the young woman. But let's say there were five sets of waves, not just two. They would split into five different sets of waves and M devices. This means that if a human is the M device, then the person would be split into five different humans, each one looking at his own set of waves. But since no one has ever seen anyone split into five different persons, then each of the five persons would have to reside in his own parallel universe

This is why it is called the Many World Interpretation (MWI), and it would mean that there are five of me and five of you, all

The Science of Spirit

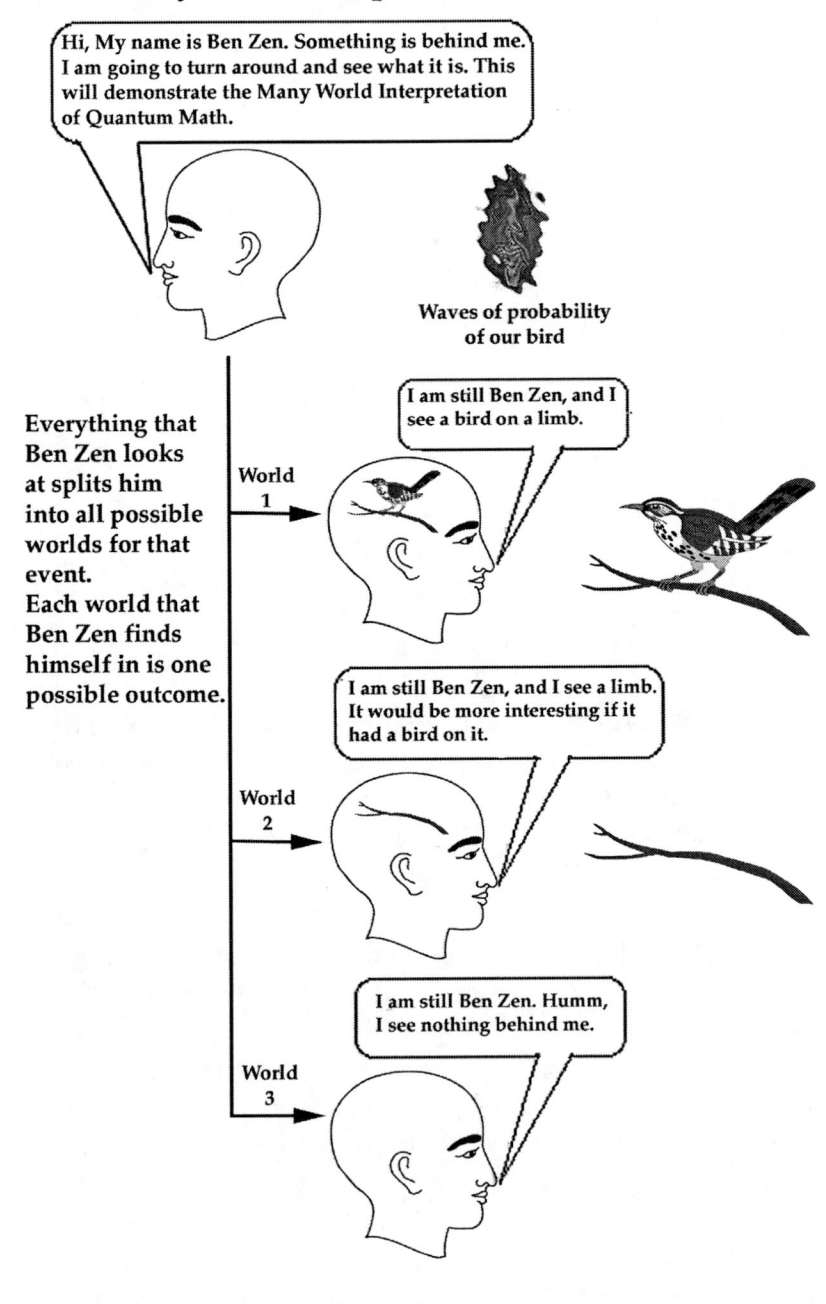

Many World Interpretation of Quantum Math

Hi, My name is Ben Zen. Something is behind me. I am going to turn around and see what it is. This will demonstrate the Many World Interpretation of Quantum Math.

Waves of probability of our bird

Everything that Ben Zen looks at splits him into all possible worlds for that event.
Each world that Ben Zen finds himself in is one possible outcome.

World 1

I am still Ben Zen, and I see a bird on a limb.

World 2

I am still Ben Zen, and I see a limb. It would be more interesting if it had a bird on it.

World 3

I am still Ben Zen. Humm, I see nothing behind me.

living in different parallel universes and totally unaware of the other four. Thus only one of you is reading this book. The other four of you are off doing different things, each carrying out all the possible probabilities. Actually there are millions of you and millions of me because every time you observe something, you split into five more of you to carry out all of the probabilities of that situation. That means that there is probably a you that is in jail and one that is a millionaire and one that is an artist and on and on. If you try to conceptualize this, it would look like a tree with branches that create branches that create other branches, and so on.

As bizarre as this may seem to you, it has real promise. Einstein is reported to have said that the observer-creating interpretation (Copenhagen Interpretation) made no sense to him because he could not imagine a mouse changing the universe just by looking at it. The MWI answers this problem. Neither the mouse nor you change the universe; you merely flow with it. Another advantage of the MWI comes from Henry Stapp of Berkeley. He says that the MWI answers a problem with biological evolution and other low-probability events. Thus in our single universe model, there would be a low probability that life would have started. But in MWI all probabilities happen, even the low probability ones. This would mean that life had no choice but to happen.

Undivided Wholeness Interpertation

The final interpretation says that reality is an undivided wholeness. This would mean that our apparent separateness, and the apparent separateness of everything in our everyday life, is an illusion. This makes the best sense to me because it is something that I can imagine. And all of the world's major religious founders, including Jesus, agree with it. I will devote most of Chapter 7 to this interpretation.

This chapter begins a major shift in my thinking, and if you are new to quantum science then it will mark a major shift in your thinking as well. We discovered that the best math and science we

The Science of Spirit

can muster says motion is an illusion. When we see a car travel at 60 miles per hour the motion is not really there. We do not know what is really happening, just that it's the way we experience the fourth dimension. We also saw that atoms, which make up everything in our universe, are a type of illusion. What is really there we do not know. In order to try and understand what is real we end with three interpretations or attempts to understand.

We saw that there is a serious philosophical problem with what is called the old or classical science. Classical science believes that matter is real and solid. For matter to be real and solid it would need to have a ground or place to sit on or a place to begin forming. Where is this solid ground? Where did it begin forming? Classical science looked for this ground for 200 years, until the birth of the new science. Quantum science answered this problem because it shows that everything is just energy and illusion. Energy has just always existed.

One type of quantum atom: There is a 90% probability that an electron is somewhere in the cloud. That is; once a conscious observer looks at it.

New Reality Box 6

When we look at a star that is 100 light years from earth, we think that it took 100 years for that light to reach earth. But that is only from our point of view. If you are riding on the light beam it takes no time at all (0.0 seconds).

The Science of Spirit

Dad & I 1968

One does not stand alone who stands
With love, for love is God and God is All.
This truth above all others must remain,
Which I have taught again and yet again;
This I repeat and leave with you alway
Which you must hold against the coming day-
Despite today's bewildered Parthenon-
The Lord, thy Holy God, the Lord is One.
Thy God is One and heaven thy habitat,
All shall be well with thee for THOU ART THAT.
The living truth proclaims thy deity,
He who abides in love abides in Me.

The Voice Celestial
Page 342

Journal 7
What Spirit is Made Of

Well, I must move on. Oh what is this, I can see something move in the undergrowth on an up-slope about twenty feet away. I stand very still to see what it is. Oh my! It's a young coyote. All I can see is his front half as it pokes out of the undergrowth. When he sees me watching, he stands still watching me. As we watch each other, I feel myself in his world. I understand that I am the intruder here. He has far more right than I do to be here. I then wonder what it is like in his simpler world and if he can even conceptualize the human world. He is kind of like the flatlanders.

Remember the flatlanders who live in a two-dimensional world? They cannot imagine three dimensions. If all the world and we are really made from a set of complex waves (which is the best information that science has), then it is easy for me to imagine these waves. I can imagine the waves that make up me, mixed with the waves in the floor, the desk I'm sitting at, the air in the room, and on and on. Then, because my brain can picture only three dimensions, I "collapse" or see only three dimensions of this multi-dimensional field. So what evidence is there for a multi-dimensional world? Well, there is one experiment that began as a thought experiment and has blown the lid off the Reality Box of science.

In all started in the 1930s. Einstein, working with two other physicists, Boris Podolsky and Nathan Rosen, put together a thought experiment to present to Niels Bohr (who constructed the first working model of the atom). They were going to prove to Bohr and his followers that quantum theory could not be right. The thought experiment has become known today as the EPR (Einstein, Podolsky, and Rosen) paradox.

The EPR paradox goes like this. Imagine you are on a high

What Spirit is Made Of

mountain in Colorado, so that you would be in the line of sight of San Francisco on the one hand and of New York on the other. On a table in front of you is a laser shining a stream of photons straight up at the sky in a vertical beam. Now, imagine that a special mirror is placed over the laser so that it splits the beam and makes the beam go horizontally in opposite directions. Thus we now have two beams of photons, one going east to New York and the other one going west to San Francisco.

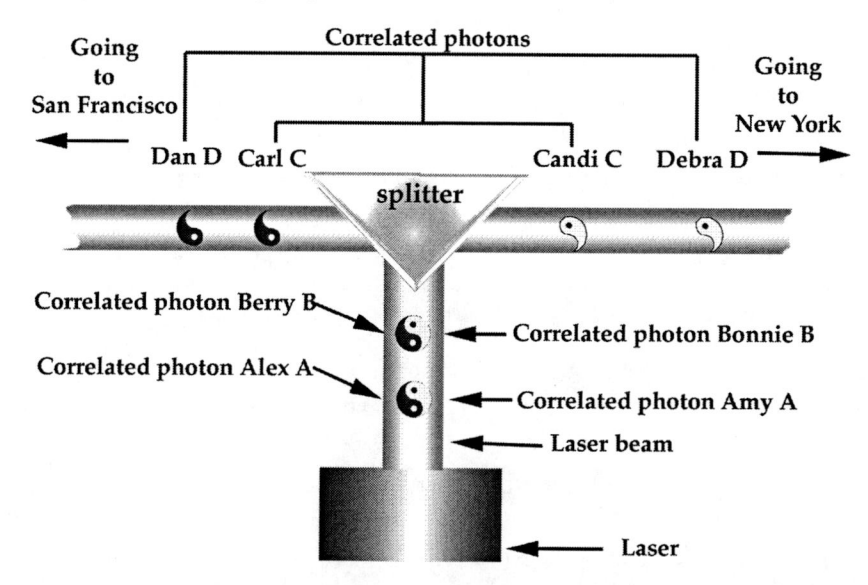

Correlated photons

Going to San Francisco ← Dan D Carl C   Candi C Debra D → Going to New York

splitter

Correlated photon Berry B
Correlated photon Alex A
← Correlated photon Bonnie B
← Correlated photon Amy A
← Laser beam
← Laser

According to quantum math, each photon going to New York has formed a partnership with one of the photons going to San Francisco. It is as if the photons pick a partner and get "married" before the mirror splits them up. The quantum rules then forbid "divorce." Therefore, each married pair of photons is, in some way that we don't understand, tied together forever. Anything that is done to one of the married partners will simultaneously happen to the partner.

In other words, one of the photons going to San Francisco is said to be correlated with one of the photons going to New York, and this photon pair is tied together forever. Thus every photon in one beam has a partner in the other beam. Quantum math says, if something is done to change one of the photons in the pair, the same change will happen in the other one <u>instantaneously</u>.

If we change, say, the polarity of a photon that has reached New York, its married partner, which has reached San Francisco, will also change its polarity instantaneously! Even if these photons keep going out into space for billions of miles, as soon as you change the polarity of one photon, the polarity of the other will change instantly. This is a serious violation of common sense. We know that everything takes time to go from one place to another. It takes light, the fastest thing we know, eight minutes to travel from the sun to the earth, a distance of 93 million miles. How can each photon know what the other is doing instantaneously billions of miles away? This violates Einstein's speed limit of light.

So you see, said Einstein, quantum theory violates the speed limit of light, and therefore, quantum theory has to be wrong and incomplete. When Einstein wrote this thought experiment, experimental measurement equipment was inadequate to actually carry out such an experiment. But Einstein was convinced that if the experiment were done, the second photon would not change instantaneously, and this would show the absurdity of quantum physics.

What was Einstein really trying to say with this thought experiment? He was really arguing with Bohr about what is called the locality assumption. Now which one of the five assumptions from chapter three seems to hold all the others together? Remember from chapter three: 1) I'm separate from you; 2) the universe is a machine; 3) it takes time to go to the store; 4) everything is made of matter; and 5) if everything is made of matter, consciousness can't be a real thing. In other words, which of the five assumptions would certainly bring down the other four, if found to be wrong? That's a tough one, but most physicists would pick number three, the locality assumption, which states that everything is bound by time or as we say, it takes time to go to the store.

Clearly everything in our everyday world seems to be bound by time, but if time were to mix, be in two places at the same time, or if photons could talk to each other billions of miles apart instantly; then matter would no longer be solid. This is because

What Spirit is Made Of

solid things just do not behave this way. If matter could be in two places at the same time; then what we think of, as mind, and believe comes from the brain, would follow suit and could be an entity unto itself. This would clearly mean that the world could not be a machine. If the universe is not a machine, then mind or consciousness, almost surely, would be a real something as "solid" as the chair you are sitting in. I am using the word "solid" here to describe our perception of it. If the above is true "solid" is a kind of misnomer.

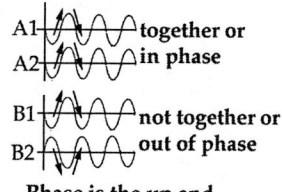

A1, A2: together or in phase
B1, B2: not together or out of phase

Phase is the up and down motion of waves.

The real quantum theory term for our photons getting married is "phase entanglement." "Phase" is the name for the regular up and down motion of a wave like water or sound. If two waves have the same up and down motion, they are said to be "in phase." But if the two waves are moving up and down at different rates, then they are said to be "out of phase." The height or strength of the wave is called the "amplitude." Quantum math tells us that when two quanta (photons in our case) meet, they become what is called "correlated" (what we are calling "married"), and then when they separate, their amplitude will pull apart, but their phase will not. In other words, if they are in phase, they will stay in phase; if they are out of phase, they will remain out of phase. Therefore, phase entanglement mixes the phases of two quanta.

In our everyday world we see only waves, like water or sound, and we never see them entangle. This is because water or sound makes its home in ordinary three-dimensional space where we are. Quantum waves are different: they live in a theoretical space called

Configuration Space

We cannot imagine a 6 dimensional space. Even though quantas are only one dimension they live in their own three dimensional space, drawn here as a two dimensional half of a yin-yang. When they entangle they make a six dimensional space, seen here as a three dimensional yin-yang.

The Science of Spirit

"configuration space." In configuration space, each quanta has its own three dimensions. So if two three-dimensional quanta meet, they create a space that has six dimensions.[12]

Just think of the impact here. Astronomer Carl Sagan is famous for saying that we are made from the inside of stars. What he means, of course, is that all matter is made inside of stars; therefore, it follows that the matter that makes up our bodies comes from a star. So do you feel like a star today? If phase entanglement is correct, then the quanta that make up the atoms in our bodies are married to quanta from all over the solar system. We are linked to the whole of the universe in ways we never imagined. But this concept only scratches the surface, as we will soon see.

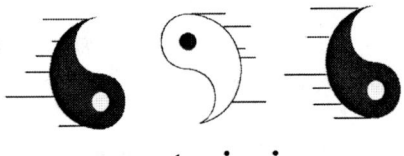

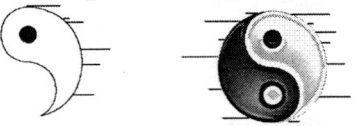

quanta zipping around

two quanta meet and become entangled

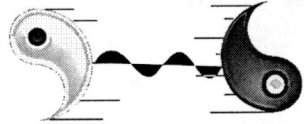

two quanta separate, still entangled

Wow! If all of this is true, the world is a far stranger place than anyone ever imagined. According to quantum math, then, the five assumptions are wrong. But is there any real proof that what quantum math says is really real in our everyday lives? Maybe Einstein was right, and if a real EPR experiment was done, it would prove once and for all that all this quantum math is wrong— that the universe is truly local, as it seems in our day-to-day world.

Now it is important to remember that everything hinges on the locality assumption. If the locality assumption is shown to be wrong, then all five of the assumptions are wrong, and the universe is no longer local and would then be called non-local. So . . . is the universe local or non-local?

Local reality = mechanical/machine
Non-local reality = energy/spirit

What Spirit is Made Of

In 1964, John Stuart Bell, a physicist, was able to show that by using the experimental data alone, i.e., without using quantum theory, the underlying reality has to be non-local. He then showed a way to actually test the EPR experiment using photons the way we explained earlier. Bell never actually proposed an experiment, but provided the impetus to do so. When Bell published his theorem, he was mostly ignored because most physicists were not interested in philosophy, and his theorem was considered philosophy.

> John bell developed a mathematical proof that showed that the universe had to be Non-local.

There was, however, one person who felt that an experiment needed to be done. His name was John Clauser, a young physicist at Columbia University. So in 1972, after moving to Berkeley, Clauser did an actual version of the EPR experiment. To Clauser's surprise, his experiments showed that Einstein was wrong, that photons did know instantly what the other was doing, and, therefore, the underlying reality of the universe was non-local. Quantum theory was right.[12]

As is the way in physics, his experiment was criticized on some minor points. So in 1982 a physicist at the University of Paris, Alain Aspect, re-did Clauser's experiment and corrected the flaws. Again, the experiments showed that the underlying reality of the universe was non-local. Aspect then repeated the experiment several times, each time using tighter and tighter controls, and the answer always came back the same. The underlying reality of the universe is non-local.

I can't emphasize the importance of Bell's theorem enough. A mathematical theorem based on 75 years of experimentation and so simple that a high-school math student could understand it is close to 100% unbreakable. Then to top it off, experiments based on the theorem were developed and tested numerous times. To continue to argue that the universe is local and mechanical is now like saying that 2+2 does not equal 4 and that you don't believe that the sun will come up in the morning.

The Science of Spirit

Remember, the philosopher Plato in the fourth century BCE had already argued that the only thing that could make sense was a non-local reality. He said that you could not divide matter indefinitely, that here had to be an end point. We have found the end point— and it is called Planck's constant.

Another philosopher of Plato's time, by the name of Democritus, used to argue with Plato. He believed that once you reached this end point, this smallest piece of matter, then that is where it ends. The universe, according to Democritus, was not made of energy, but of small pieces of matter called atoms.

The problem I see with Democritus' argument is that something had to have always existed. Something cannot come into existence out of nothing, so which is the most likely to be eternal, Democritus' atom or pure energy? I would choose energy. Little atoms of matter do not explain how we can create attributes just by looking at an atom. But if the universe is pure energy, it becomes very possible.

Just remember that the belief in a local reality is an assumption, and an assumption is not a fact. The local assumption is based on everyday experience, not on mathematical theorems with 75 years of experimental evidence to back them up. All the quantum research on underlying reality over a 75-year period conflicts with everyday experience. This should be a clear sign that the reality of everyday experience is as different from our underlying reality as Newton's physics was different from Einstein's relativity. How many different ways does it take to say 2+2=4 before we believe that 2+2=4.

The dichotomies and weirdness of quantum theory can vanish as fast as a quantum jump if we just change our assumption that the universe is local to an assumption that it is non-local. By accepting that the universe is non-local, we can now understand the weirdness of quantum theory. It is like a breath of fresh air. (I don't mean, however, that we can conceptualize it. Our three-dimensional brains cannot picture something that has more than three dimensions.) If you believe the local assumption, then the universe is solid and mechanical, and it is impossible for something solid to be in two states at once. But if the universe is

What Spirit is Made Of

non-local or pure energy, then it is much more understandable and believable because energy is not solid like matter or a machine. It no longer is strange that a hamster or gerbil can read a computer's mind and never get shocked. It is just phase entangled with the computer. My Dad never traveled all the way to Houston, Texas, in his dream. The school he visited was in his bedroom all the time.

If you think that I am being radical here, you're right. I know that it is necessary to nudge you out of your Reality Box. When I first read Nick Herbert's book, I did not see it this way. I cannot imagine or understand now why I didn't see this then. I apparently was not ready to see it. I was looking at the Truth, but could not see it. I think now that my Reality Box said that the Truth was unknowable. So I turned it into an intellectual exercise instead of understanding.

The local assumption means you are trapped in your body until you die and that you can only communicate mechanically with your mouth or body. God makes no logical sense in a local universe because God then has to be local and mechanical like us. If you have not studied philosophy and science, then you may not understand why I say that. (But that is another book.) Since God makes no sense in a mechanical/local universe, there can be no Spirit because Spirit has to be energy and not matter, i.e., non-local. With no Spirit, when you're dead, you're dead. But this is not the case.

The scientific/experimental evidence reveals that the universe is not mechanical and that it is made from quantum stuff, called "the unified or quantum field." Quantum stuff is not mechanical. Quantum stuff does not have time or space. I know how strange that sounds. Humans cannot visualize there being no time or space. But 75 years of experiments reveals that it is true.

> **Wow!** Close your eyes and imagine this book as a piece of formed energy and not as matter.
>
> **Wow!**

Within this framework, though, there is still the material world that makes up most of our everyday experience, and, as was mentioned earlier, the material world turns out to be a special case within quantum theory. In other words, it is just a part of the whole picture. So why in our everyday experience don't we see the quantum aspect in our material world? Because of our assumptions. We assume that everything we see is matter, so we are blind to quantum stuff and events. It is all around us. It's more a part of our life than the material world. We can't see the forest because the trees are getting in our way. In a sense, everything that we see with our eyes is quantum because the very medium that makes it possible is pure quantum, i.e., light. Everything we see is made to have attributes that aren't really there.

Then with the above in mind what about the strange phenomenon we talked about in chapter two? The phenomenon where we feel as if we are not a part of our body but are just in our body looking out. Who is looking at the light or incoming picture of the world in the first place? How do we project what we see back out into the world so we see it as "out there" and not in our head where the data is? Are we really a little person in our head looking at a "TV" picture of all the sensory data taken in? NO! Because we would be talking turtles again with a second little man in the man in our head's head.

In the summer of 1999, I received a flyer in the mail for a conference titled "A Forum on New Science." It sounded like it would be fun, so I put together the money to go and sent in my application. One of the speakers was a physicist by the name of Amit Goswami. I remembered that I had a book in my library written by him that I'd started but never finished. It was called *The Self-Aware Universe* with the subtitle *How Conscious-ness Creates the Material World*.[3] Very strange, I thought. Why is he saying the universe is "consciousness"? How in the world could the universe be self-aware? It must be a name for God. I really was not interested in reading a book about God, and that is probably why I had only started it before. But I was going to hear him talk, so I made it a priority to get it read before the forum in October.

At first I had to push myself to keep reading. It was mostly

What Spirit is Made Of

information I had heard before, and reading is hard work for me with my dyslexia. Then he started to talk about assumptions, and— bang— as if a bombshell went off in my head, I understood. It was my assumption and science's assumption that the universe was made of matter. I was not even aware that I had been making that assumption, but that is what I had been doing. Of course, if my Reality Box said that everything was made of matter, then anything that was not matter could not be accepted into my box and would make no sense. In a matter/machine universe it would be stupid to think that the universe itself could be conscious. In a matter/machine universe, consciousness can only be a by-product of the brain, an epiphenomenon. If you remember, an epiphenomenon is one of the five assumptions of science. Things like love and consciousness were not real, but just by-products of a very complex machine/computer, or brain.

But if the universe is made of energy that has no space-time (a very strange concept, but true), then this is a different matter and consciousness would not be an epiphenomenon, but a real something. That means that I, my conscious self, must be more than just a brain.

Goswami was right. Quantum theory is not so strange if you are not trying to force it into being mechanical, but that is just what some scientists are still doing. Then he went further. If the only thing that existed before there was a universe was a quantum field, and this field had consciousness (but "field" is a misnomer because it implies space/time, and a quantum field has no space-time), then there must be only one consciousness. The only thing that makes sense then is that our mind, our conscious awareness, must be a part of the conscious field. Wow! Think about that for a minute. Our mind or conscious awareness is (or comes from) the quantum field, and that means it is separate from our brain (by which I mean the machine/computer brain in our head).

That means that when I say the word "we," I mean you and I share, or are a part of, the quantum field. We (our minds) are the conscious field. You and I exist everywhere, and we are using this material brain to see the universe! We are the universe looking back at itself/ourselves! We are the ones controlling, as best we

The Science of Spirit

can, this material body. We the unified field/quantum field are the ones making the choices and collapsing the waves of probability.

So if all this is true and we share one mind with the conscious field, why can't we read each other's thoughts? If you're not asking this question, then you don't understand what I have said. There is an answer, a very amazing answer, but you may not be convinced yet that we are one mind. We need more evidence. From now on, any time I talk about our brain, I am referring to our material computer-like brain. When I use the term "mind," I am talking about the conscious field.

Telepathy Cat

While at college, my daughter Älta acquired a cat. It seems that some boys in the apartment next to her had found this kitten and were abusing it. Älta rescued the kitten from them and kept it. She was not supposed to have a cat in her apartment, so at the end of the semester the cat came home to stay with us. The boys had named the cat Spook. It was against our city ordinance to let a cat run free, so when Älta was home, she would put Spook on a long rope in the backyard so he could be outside but not run away.

One day as we were watching a movie on TV, I suddenly had this feeling of urgency take me over. I stood up immediately and said, "Where's Spook." I ran to the back door. From there I could not see Spook, but the rope on his collar trailed over the six-foot cedar fence. I quickly ran to the fence and found Spook hanging by the neck, motionless. He looked dead. I grabbed him and pulled his collar off. Immediately, he began gasping for air and then went into a rapid spasmodic-type breathing, panting for air. We took him into the house and set him on the floor. He could not stand up and collapsed spread eagled. He lay there panting for a good ten minutes before his

Alta & Spook

breathing began to return to normal.

Without a doubt, if I had not gotten there when I did, Spook would have been dead, and it was obvious to me that I had received a distress signal from Spook that he was in trouble. After this experience, I began to review my past and realized that this was not an isolated experience. Remember, as I recounted in Chapter 4, just before Terina's death, I was coming out of the theater and felt the future, which made me cry? Looking back, I have no doubt that somehow my mind went into the future and foresaw her death.

I know the skeptics will say that I was just worried and was experiencing psychological trauma. Remember, though, I had said the same thing. But I knew even then that it was somehow much more. And how did Terina's book get left in the trailer? Was Terina trying to communicate with me? I will never know. I may have missed an incredible experience. If I had tried to communicate back, who knows what would have happened. But I was afraid. I could not accept that reality. The fact that I was so frightened by the experience tells me that it was not an everyday experience.

After the Spook experience, and twenty years after Terina's death, my wife Joyce admitted to me that minutes before Terina died, she'd heard Terina's voice in her mind. Terina told Joyce that she was sorry, but that she was too tired to go on. My God! What else have I missed? Remember when Joyce and I were in trouble after Terina's death and we had to separate? Suddenly, out of the blue, there was a place for me to go? Do you now think that was a coincidence? Was Terina or the Universe or God helping us through a hard time? I now believe so.

The skeptics, including me, would not have believed any of this, and I would have had no experimental evidence to refute their arguments. All that I can say in defense is that I know what I experienced was out of the ordinary. Why did I have this sense of urgency and literally run to the back door? Why did I feel profound fear when I found Terina's book? The only other defense against the assumption that these experiences were not real would be to invoke Bell's theorem. If in fact the universe is non-local, as Bell's theorem proves, then it would seem logical that our minds are also

The Science of Spirit

non-local and these experiences would be ordinary. But this is just another assumption, and we need more evidence.

In the late eighties a neurophysiologist in Mexico, Dr. Jacoba Grinbery-Zylberbaum, decided to see if he could duplicate the test of Bell's theorem using people. He took subjects and divided them into groups of two. The paired subjects were then correlated like photons from the same source would have already been. He did this by first having the paired subjects get to know each other through conversation. They were then to hug each other and meditate together. After this was done, the paired subjects were separated and taken to different rooms on opposite ends of the building. Both subjects from a pair would lie on a table enclosed by a screen to block any radio transmission. They were then both hooked up to an EEG (electroencephalogram).

An EEG measures the electrical activity at different points in the brain. The results come out on a long sheet of paper with wiggly ink lines representing the brain activity of each subject. Dr.

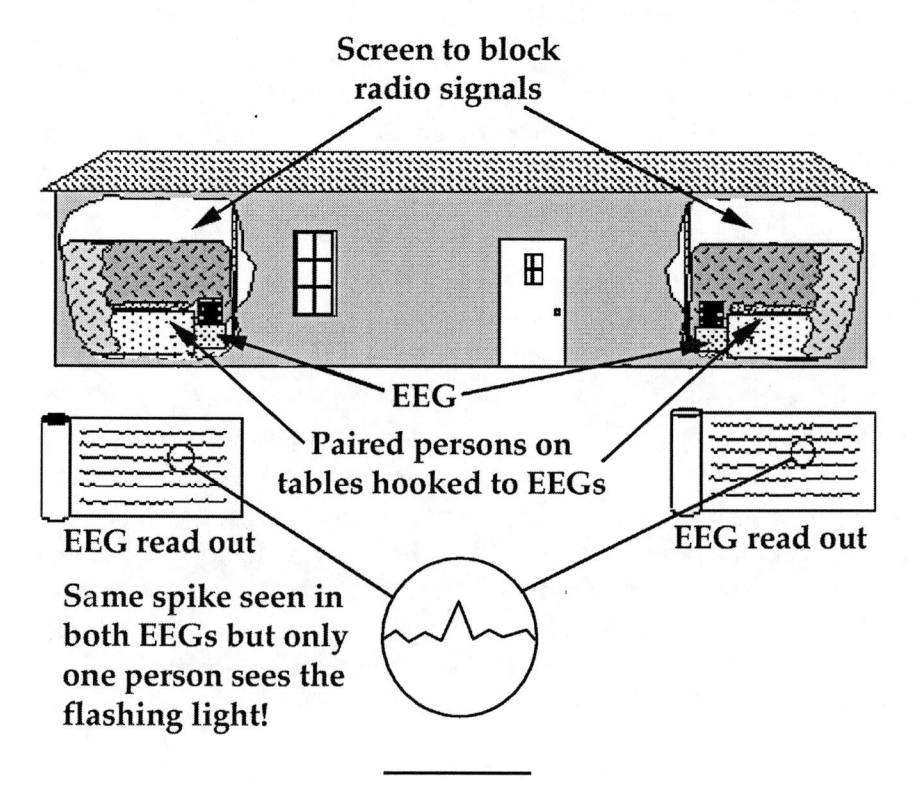

Screen to block radio signals

EEG
Paired persons on tables hooked to EEGs

EEG read out

EEG read out

Same spike seen in both EEGs but only one person sees the flashing light!

What Spirit is Made Of

Zylberbaum then flashed a strobe light into the eyes of only one of the subjects from a pair. The flash that the subject could see was evident on the EEG and printed out as a spike on one of the ink lines. Amazingly, the same spike could been seen on the readout for the other subject of the pair— the one in the separate room who could not see the flashing light. Both brain-wave readings, from both members of a pair, showed the spike from the flashing light. But only one of the subjects could physically see the flashing light, and the other subject was not consciously aware of it.

You might be tempted here to think that the subject who saw the flashes was transmitting the flashes to the other person's brain (like sending radio waves), but that is not how non-local mind works. Both minds are already one mind. So while only one set of eyes is taking in the flashes, both subjects' brains respond to what the one mind is experiencing.

Most scientists make the same mistake when looking at ESP (extrasensory perception). They assume that the only way someone can experience someone else's thoughts is for one person to transmit those thoughts through the air the way a radio transmitter transmits a signal to a radio. But no such signal can be found, so the phenomenon is dismissed as nonsense. But if we all share one mind, then there is no signal, and every sentient being in the universe has equal access to all the others' thoughts.

How do we know that this is how it works? First of all, we don't know with one-hundred-percent certainty that this is how it works, but it is the only thing that makes sense from quantum experiments and math. If you have two correlated quanta millions of miles apart and you change one and the other changes instantaneously, the only thing that makes sense is that they are, in fact, somehow one and the same thing— not two separate things separated by millions of miles.

The human EPR does not demonstrate that we are all one mind. (Remember EPR is where light particles can signal each other instantly regardless of distance.) It is just a great duplicable way of showing that ESP is real. It does not demonstrate whether or not there is a transmission signal that we don't know about. So we need to go further and find a way to demonstrate more conclusively that we are in fact one mind. One way of doing that involves a phenomenon called "blindsight."

Blindsight

In the early seventies, two researchers, Nick Humphrey and Louis Weiskrantz, did a series of experiments with rhesus monkeys. The researchers removed the visual cortex of two monkeys. (The visual cortical area of the brain gives us and monkeys the ability to perceive or make up a picture from information the eyes take in.) But as time went on, it became clear that one of the monkeys, whose name was Helen, could "see." For example, she could climb trees and would take preferred food when it was near enough to grasp, but would ignore food that was too far to reach. Since Helen had no visual cortex, how was she able to "see?"

The phenomenon is now called "blindsight" and occurs when one can see and perceive things out in the world, without any conscious awareness of it. Luckily, the researchers found a human whose visual cortex had been injured, causing him to become blind in the left visual field of both eyes. When the researchers asked this man what happened in his consciousness on his blind side, the answer was surprising. If the researchers put symbols to his left side, where he was blind, he could still distinguish crosses from circles and horizontal lines from vertical ones. If he was shown a spot of light, he could point to it with accuracy. But when asked what he "saw," he insisted that he "saw" nothing and that he was just guessing. His guesses, however, were always right on. (Let the Force be with you.)

It seems now there is a consensus among researchers that this is real and is called "unconscious perception." Perception is always thought of as taking place in our conscious awareness. So how can we be unconscious and perceive things? This would mean that there is clearly more to our mind than we have believed. We are talking about events that we perceive, but that we are not aware of perceiving.

What Spirit is Made Of

From everyday experience, it is believed that there are three elements of our conscious awareness. These are: 1)thought or thinking, 2)feelings, and 3)the ability to make choices.

Thought or thinking

Probably the most common belief in western science is that thinking is what makes us special from the rest of the animal world. But over the years we have had to constantly change how we define or measure what thought is. A good example of this is the idea of tool use. It used to be believed that it took thinking to make tools; therefore, because humans were the only ones that could think, only humans could make tools. Then it was discovered that a number of primates, e.g., great apes and chimps, made and used tools; further, it was found that even birds use tools. So that idea went out the window.

Then it was said that thinking was confined to life; therefore, computers would never be able to think. One of the tests of thinking was the ability to play chess, so it was believed that a computer would never beat a world chess master. But in 1997 a computer named Deep Blue beat world chess champion Garry Kasparov. Many cried foul because they said that Deep Blue was not really "thinking," and to truly think, the computer had to have consciousness, meaning conscious awareness.

Another common belief about thinking is that thinking and consciousness go hand in hand. In fact, the act of thinking *is* consciousness. For example, when we are talking to another person, we believe it is our conscious awareness of what we are saying that allows us to come up with the words we are speaking. But if we stop and carefully analyze where the words come from as we speak them, we will realize that the words just appear out of our brain somewhere and that we are not consciously aware of "thinking" of them.

This was first discovered in the late 1800s at the first ever lab and school founded for the systematic study of psychology. The lab was started by Wilhelm Wundt, MD, who had become interested in psychology. (Incidentally I can trace, through psychology professors, the lineage of my training in psychology back to Wilhelm Wundt.) Dr. Wundt used a system called introspection to study things like perception, thinking, and consciousness. He and his students were able to show consistently, to their surprise, that thinking takes place outside of awareness.

This has been confirmed by recent neurological studies which show that everything we say or do happens microseconds before we are consciously aware of it. This is called "secondary-awareness." As I type these words, each letter that is typed has already appeared on the computer screen before I am aware of what I have typed.

If you flash pictures in front of a person faster than he can consciously see them, and then ask the person what he is thinking about, he will invariably give you words that are related to the picture. But he will not know, in his conscious awareness, what the pictures were. For example, if you show a person a picture of a dove you would get words like "flight" or "peace." Even though there is no conscious awareness of the picture of the dove, the brain is subconsciously "thinking" about what it saw.

If animals, who seem to have no self-awareness, use tools, if our actions happen before we become aware of them, and if people know what was on a card flashed faster than they could see it, then maybe thinking is more a computer/brain function and not what our conscious awareness does. So we will assume for the moment that thinking is an unconscious computer-like function.

Feelings

Many people think that animals cannot feel, but you would get a quick argument about that from most pet owners. We have a little dog that we call Brandy Brindle. I have never known a more emotional creature. She is constantly getting her "feelings" hurt. If Joyce and I kiss or hug each other, she will try and push her way in between us. When Joyce and I come home together after being away, we give her a kind of hug which she seems to demand; but if I pick her up first, she will turn her head away and refuse to acknowledge me. She has gotten the idea somewhere that Joyce

What Spirit is Made Of

should pick her up first. So if we do it in the right order, with Joyce picking her up first and then me, she always tries to lick my face.

I won't bore you with any more of my Brandy stories. Even though I don't know what one would call her behaviors other than emotional, many scientists won't except this as evidence that animals have feelings. They believe that feelings come from our conscious self-awareness as does thinking. So we need a more "scientific" experiment to see where feelings come from.

There is considerable experimental evidence that we can experience feelings during unconscious perception, and one of the best experiments comes from work with split-brain patients. In split-brain patients, the connection between the left and right hemispheres of the brain is surgically disconnected, except for the hindbrain which is involved with emotion and feeling. People with this condition cannot consciously see things in their left visual field. If an emotional picture was placed in the left visual field of such a person, he could not see it consciously; but if he reacted emotionally to it, would this not have to be coming from the subconscious? The experiment has been done.

In one case, a picture of a nude male model was placed in the left visual field of a split-brain person during a sequence of geometrical patterns. She then showed embarrassment by blushing. One explanation for this would be that her computer brain was reacting to a learned conditioned response. Why else would she show embarrassment for no apparent reason? People raised with nudity are not embarrassed by it, and therefore embarrassment about nudity is a learned thing. Once people learn to be embarrassed by something like nudity, they have no conscious control over it. Therefore, for now, let us assume that feelings and emotions come from the computer/brain.

So far we have seen evidence that "thinking" can be carried out by our computer-like brain and does not come from our awareness. At least thought can take place, and mostly does take place, without self-awareness on a subconscious level. Likewise, feelings seem to also take place on a subconscious level and most likely are a mechanical computer-like brain function.

Choice

But what about choice— the very foundation of free will? Is it also mechanical, and does it take place in the subconscious, like thinking and feeling, or does it come from consciousness (self-awareness), which we have shown must be outside the brain? Do we have true free will, or is free will an illusion, an epiphenomenon like most of modern psychology believes?

This is the heart of the matter, and one of the subjects most argued about in philosophy and psychology. The consensus among most modern psychologists is that there is no free will, that there is no choice. We are just a computer that responds to conditioned responses and learned concepts. If this is true, then God makes no sense, and quarks are nothing more than small clucks of matter, and somehow quantum theory is wrong.

But if we could show experimentally that choice comes only from our conscious awareness and thus that it is not part of our computer-like brain, would that not dramatically say that consciousness comes from outside the brain? Would this not say that our conscious awareness is, indeed, something unrelated to a computer-like brain function? And wouldn't it add weight to the contention that consciousness comes from a consciousness field? And if this is true, then it would explain what consciousness is and explain who it is in our head that is looking at the world.

So what experiment could we do that would force the brain to make a decision (a choice), but at the same time not let our consciousness see it. If the brain can make a decision without consciousness, then choice must take place in the computer-like thinking and feelings. But if the brain cannot make a decision without consciousness, then choice must *not* take place in the brain.

In 1980, a psychologist by the name of Tony Marcel was doing research into how our brain comprehends words. In one of the experiments, he had subjects watch a screen as three words in a series were flashed, one at a time, on the screen. The subjects' task was to push a button when they consciously recognized the meaning of the last word in the series.

What Spirit is Made Of

For example, if you flashed the words "palm," "hand," and "wrist" on the screen, it would be obvious what the meaning of the word "wrist" was because you were given two clues as to its

LOCAL MIND

Many scientists believe that the brain is divided into the conscious or aware, and the unconscious or unaware. It is believed that the experience of being conscious is just a "by product" of the working brain. This is "Local Mind."

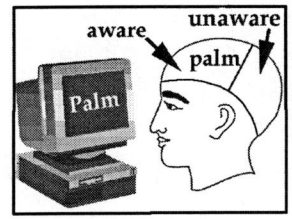

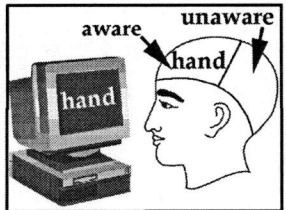

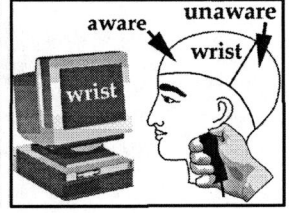

Here a subject watches three related words, palm - hand - wrist, flashed one at a time on a computer screen. He then pushes a button when he consciously understands the last word, in this case "wrist." Because all of the words are related, it will take him less time to push the button than if the middle word, as shone in the next strip, has a different meaning.

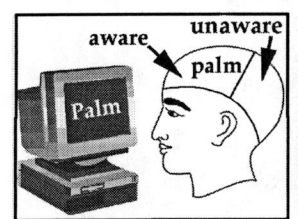

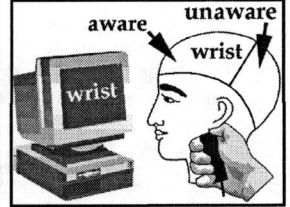

Here the subject is doing the same thing as above but the middle word, "tree" is unrelated to "wrist" so it slows down his reaction time to the last word.

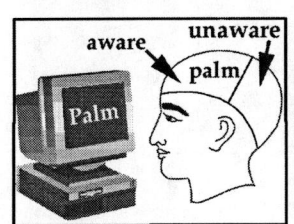

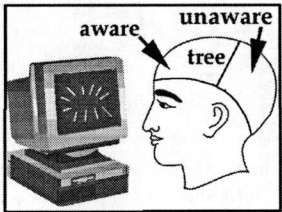

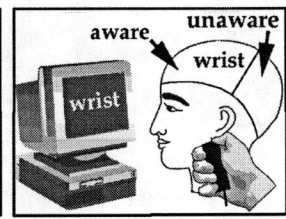

In previous experiments it has been shown that if a word is flashed too fast for the subject to be aware of it, he/she still understands the words meaning in his/her unaware part of the brain. Therefore, because the middle word is unrelated, as in strip 2 above, it should slow down his/her reaction time, but it does not. WHY?

meaning before seeing it. The reaction time, then, for pushing the button would be shorter than if the three words were "palm," "tree," and "wrist." Here the last word is the same, but changing the middle word to "tree" makes you think of palm as a tree first and not as part of a hand. In other words, it makes it more confusing as to the meaning of the last word, and the reaction time is longer.

Now what would happen if the middle word, called the bias word, was presented so that when it was flashed the subject could *not* see it consciously but could only see it subconsciously? If choices are made in the subconscious, then the brain would slow down when it had to think about its choices. The bias word should slow down or speed up the decision as to what the last word means if our brain is making the choice. But it did not.

When the bias word was hidden from conscious awareness, it took the subjects the same amount of time in both cases. In other words, the subjects' only decision concerned the meaning of the last word, and the bias word did not affect that decision. It took the subjects the same amount of time with each word. Do you see

NON-LOCAL MIND
Here the whole brain is unaware, just a computer. Awareness comes from Consciousness working with the brain.

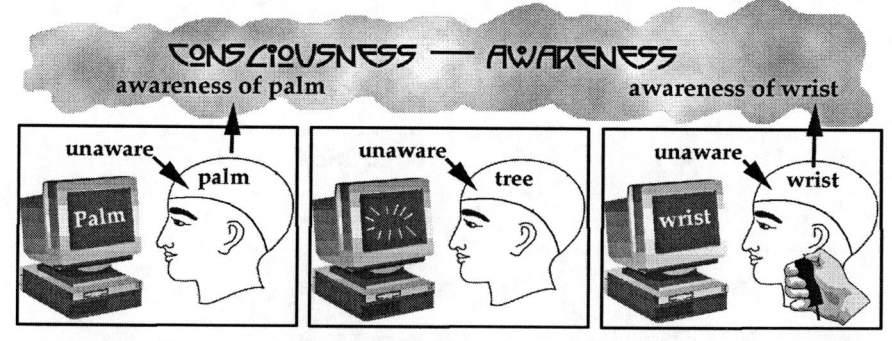

CONSCIOUSNESS — AWARENESS
awareness of palm   awareness of wrist

unaware   unaware   unaware
       palm   tree   wrist
Palm   wrist

Dr. Goswami believes that this experiment is evidence that our consciousness is not in our head. He believes that to understand a words meaning a decision or "choice" of what the word means must be made. If the brain were the one making the choice then it would have taken longer when the unrelated-word was recognized. The unaware section of the brain should have slowed down his understanding of the last word, but it did not. So the brain must not be making the choice. The choice, and our awareness, must be coming from outside the brain.

What Spirit is Made Of

what is happening here? When we did experiments in unconscious perception involving thinking and feeling, the brain worked just fine. But when we set up an experiment where a choice has to be made, but was hidden from consciousness, the only information consciousness could use to make a choice was the last word.

Thinking and feeling took place in unconscious perception and did not need consciousness or self-awareness to function. So we concluded that they were computer brain functions because they could take place outside of self-awareness. But when we ask the brain to make a decision or choice using self-awareness alone, the bias word did not affect it. When asked to make a choice, consciousness used only the information available to make the choice; the first and last words.

Therefore, we make choices or collapse the waveform in our conscious awareness. It is consciousness and <u>not</u> the measurement device (eyes, ears, camera, or brain) that is collapsing the waveform.

This is just icing on the cake. This experiment alone demonstrates only that choice is not in the subconscious but in our awareness. But if mind is non-local, then what else makes sense? It dramatically shows that the "we - I" is conscious awareness, and our body is our home. Our brain is a computer that the "we - I" uses, but our mind is us. We are our mind, and are outside the body/brain. Remember the famous quotation from Descartes, "I think therefore I am?" Well that is wrong. It is as Goswami said: "I choose, therefore I am." We created ourselves! We made our body and the whole world around us. As Jesus and other religious leaders have stated, we collectively are God. In other words, I choose to collapse the quantum field and create trees and people.

But hold your horses. If you and I am God collectively, then why do I think of myself as an individual? How did I make my body and the whole world? Why can't I read your mind? And what about Hitler, wars, and prejudice? The answer is both simple and hard. It is called a Tangled Hierarchy. The rest has to do with ego. These are the subjects of the next chapter.

Summary

Since several hundred years before Jesus, there have been two major theories as to how the universe and all in it are made. One was proposed by Democritus, who said that the universe was made of microscopic pieces of matter called atoms. The atoms then clumped together to make everything. Then beyond the atom there was nothingness. The other theory was proposed by Plato, who said nothingness does not make sense because something can't come from nothingness. Something had to have always been there to create us. So beyond the atom was energy, which was eternal and infinite, and therefore the universe is really made of energy.

I believe that Plato has won. The universe is made of energy, which is called the unified quantum field. I have shown that Bell's theorem has demonstrated that the local assumption, which all of science is based on, is wrong and that the universe is non-local and therefore must be made of energy. It then only makes sense to me that if the universe is non-local, our consciousness is not an epiphenomenon but a real thing. I then showed that indeed there was good experimental evidence that our consciousness transcends our bodies and is us, i.e. our consciousness.

What Spirit is Made Of

New Reality Box 7

Our everyday experience tells us that my mind is separate from your mind, that my thoughts are totally mine and your thoughts are totally yours. But over a thousand experiments, including those during the last seventy-five years of research in physics, reveal that there is only One Mind that we all share.

I know now whom thou art, thou vision blest:
Thou art my soul-self; with thee, celestial guest,
I shall expand throughout the firmament;
I am Thy voice, with this am I content.

The Voice Celestial
Page 344

Genesis Chapter 1, Twenty-First-Century Version

Journal 8
Genesis Chapter 1, Twenty-First-Century Version

Suddenly, to my left I see a bird fly from the ground. Wow, I think, maybe that's a Meadowlark, and she has a nest over there. After walking over to where I saw her fly from and a careful search, I spot the bird again. It is a Meadowlark all right. Not only is the nest on the ground in a clump of grass, but the eggs are white with brown and purple spots. This is the cycle of life, I think to myself. This is where it all begins— or wait, could it be where the cycle ends?

Is it wisdom that I now have? Have I learned that the heart can indeed know the Truth as well as the brain? After all, three thousand years ago, the ancient seers said that we had one mind. It has taken five hundred years of science to come full circle— to know with the brain what the heart has always known.

When I was in middle school, my science teacher brought a Bible to class. He wanted to show us that there was no conflict between human evolution theory and the Christian Bible. He told us, first of all, that there were two creation stories stuck together in Genesis. The first one starts at Genesis chapter 1, verse 1, and goes through to chapter 2, verse 4. Then a completely new creation story begins, one very different from the one at the beginning. This is very obvious if you are looking at it with an open mind and don't have your Reality Box closed down too tight.

Between Genesis 1:1 and 1:4, God first creates the earth by separating the water. (At the time this was written, it was believed that before earth was created, the universe was nothing but water.) This act created dry land. God then created plants, vegetation, trees bearing fruit, etc. Then, at Genesis 1:20, God said, "Let the waters bring forth swarms of living creatures." Is this not an exact paraphrase of the way human evolution theory lays it out? The last thing that God does is make man, <u>both</u> male and female together, just as in evolution theory.

But in the second creation story, beginning at 2:4, it starts all over again and says that the earth started out dry, with no plants, no animals. Nothing but dry land. This creation story then begins by God making a mist come from the earth to create water. Then God's first creative act was to make man from the dust of the ground. God then went on to make the Garden of Eden, then animals, and ending finally with creating woman from Adam's rib. It would seem that the first story was written for a different culture.

This is a great example of a Reality Box at work. I have shown this to people, whose Reality Box says that God put down all the words in the Bible at one set point in time, and they could not see that the two stories are any different. But how could it not be obvious? One goes through an evolutionary process to man, and the other one starts by creating man first and then in the end adding woman as an afterthought. But why, you may ask, would anyone write two very different creation stories back to back like this?

The obvious answer is they didn't. Bible researchers, using a variety of dating techniques to date the two stories, have found that the first creation story was written 600 years *after* the Adam and Eve version. It's as if the first story was amended to the Adam and Eve story because it was the "updated" version.

When the Genesis 1:1 version was written, the Hebrews had been living with or near the Babylonians for at least a couple of centuries. That is ten generations after wandering in the desert. Since the Babylonian nations were flooded by erratic floods every year, most of their religion and myths involve forbidding deep water. Their view of the world at that time was that it was a flat disc, supported by huge pillars or legs. The pillars held the disc up out of the water. In the beginning of this version, the universe was nothing but water, and God began by separating the water to make dry land.

When the second version was written, the Hebrews had just returned from wandering on the desert for several generations, so

Genesis Chapter 1, Twenty-First-Century Version

their understanding of the world was that it was dry. In the beginning of this earlier version, the earth was dry, with no plants, no animals, nothing.

The important thing to see here is that a creation story has to speak to the level of understanding of the people who are receiving it. Would you be so foolish as to try and explain high school math to a first grader just learning to count? No, of course not. So why would anyone expect God to try to explain human evolution theory to a people who believed the world was on a big disc? If you believe that the world is on a disc or the back of a turtle or floating in ether, then the creation story must match your Reality Box in order for you to accept it. But if you have followed my book so far, you are now ready to update your Reality Box and see an updated version of the creation story, written for our level of thinking today.

The following version (that I wrote) is much closer to our current understanding of the way it might have really happened than the two stories in Genesis. But, just like these two versions, this is not the way it happened. It is just the most we can understand now. Our brains are still not ready to understand what really happened. Also, remember that my mind, like yours, is a part of God, so my version came from God just as surely as the other Genesis versions.

In my version, I use the word "Consciousness" in place of God. I do this for a number of reasons. First, I believe this is what God is: God is Consciousness. Second, it is important to understand that God is a part of his own creation and not separate from it like a person making something with his hands. In this version God is making the universe out of itself. Third, the word "God" has a problematic connotation. When we say the word "God," we think of something that is separate from us, a "super man" in the sky, if you will, and we also think of "him" as having gender, mostly male. Genders were created primarily to mix up the gene pool and to make evolution work, so God has no need for gender.

Even though my Genesis story follows the mainstream science version quite closely, I would like to introduce a new concept to go along with it. I thought this new concept was original with me, but, once I researched it, I found that it has been around for some time. The idea is to flip our present assumption that speed or motion starts at zero and gets faster until the ultimate speed is reached, the speed of light. I think that it is the other way around— that Consciousness exists just above the speed of light and creates space/time by slowing itself down. This would mean, then, that zero speeds are the exception, the end point, and not the beginning. It is common in some spiritual groups to say that matter is frozen light or energy.

I think that a good case can be made for the concept of matter being frozen energy. First of all, Consciousness exists outside of space/time. The only place that I know of where space/time ends is at the speed of light. At zero speeds, called absolute zero by science, matter still exists in space/time, but comes to a complete stop. This is hard to conceptualize because we think of motion as a real thing, but we must remember that Einstein showed time was really the fourth dimension, and we just perceive it as motion. Therefore, since we do not know what the fourth dimension, or time, is, it would be very reasonable to believe that motion or time exists at light speeds and gets slower to make matter.

There is other evidence that this frozen energy makes sense. As we have talked about before, if science lives and dies by mathematics, then the math has to fit the experimental data. In the process of trying to discover what is called a unified field theory, which is a theory that will bring all known forces of nature together, the math keeps saying that there is a particle that physicists don't like. This particle has been named the "tachyon." The reason that most physicists don't like it is that it does weird things. For example, it travels faster than light. Surprisingly, Einstein's relativity does not forbid things from traveling faster than light. It only forbids matter from accelerating up to and then faster than light because once matter reaches the speed of light, it loses all form. Thus it would be possible for energy to exist at speeds faster than light, but not matter.

Another weird thing that physicists don't like about tachyons is that they violate time order. For example, if one observer sees a

Genesis Chapter 1, Twenty-First-Century Version

tachyon coming from point A and disintegrating at Point B, another person might see it leave in reverse, with the tachyon leaving Point B and disintegrating at point A. This is called a "causality" problem, meaning that it violates one of the five assumptions of science. Since we have already shown that the five assumptions are wrong, then there may not be a "causality" problem at all. This would mean that the tachyon is a real thing and more evidence that things do exist outside of space time, i.e., traveling faster than light where the tachyon lives.

How would this idea of frozen energy affect the way the Big Bang would work? Not very much. The universe would still expand just as science believes it does. But instead of thinking of it as starting from zero speed and speeding up as an explosion would do, it would be more like water suddenly freezing at a point and then the freezing expanding outward. When a piece of TNT explodes, the particles that make up the TNT start at zero speeds and accelerate until they reach their maximum velocity and then start slowing down until they are stopped by something in their path. The Big Bang does not work like this. From what is called a singularity, or starting point, it begins to expand at a steady rate. Then there is a point where it speeds up for a fraction of a second. This is called Inflation. After the Inflation period, it slows down to the rate of expansion we see today, very controlled, not at all like a random explosion.

To imagine the frozen hypothesis, think of a tank of water with a small tube going into the middle of the tank. At the end of the tube is a small metal ball. The other end of the tube goes out of the water and is hooked to a refrigeration unit. Then, when the refrigeration unit is turned on, the ball in the water would become so cold that it would start freezing the water around it. As a small bit of water froze around the metal ball, this would in turn freeze a bigger ball of water, and the ball of ice would just continue to get bigger and bigger. This scenario fits well because as water freezes what is really happening is that the water molecules start slowing down.

In the same way Consciousness could cause a point within itself to start slowing down, which would continue outwardly making a ball, the universe, just the way the water in the tank made a ball of ice. It is much harder to conceptualize the universe as a ball of frozen energy than it is to imagine a ball of frozen water. So, as you read the Genesis story, you will need to work at keeping that in mind. Just think of it as an expanding ball of frozen energy or Consciousness.

Finally, my Genesis story begins before the Genesis story in the Bible. This beginning is going to sound and look strange but stay with me, I will explain what is going on later. To help you see where the "before Genesis" begins and ends, I have called it the "Before Genesis 1, Twenty-First-Century Version" and I will use Roman numerals to number the verses.

Before Genesis 1, Twenty-First-Century Version

I   The universe is now a trillion years old, stars are no longer forming, and all former stars have gone out or are just white glowing cinder. Black holes or stars that failed to become black holes are all that is active. Most matter is just a cold clump. All life has ended long ago.

II The universe is now ten followed by twenty-seven zeros years old. All stars and galaxies have become galactic size black holes.

III The universe is now ten followed by thirty zeros years old. All of the galactic black holes have merged to form one supergalactic black hole.

IV The universe is now ten followed by one hundred and six zeros old. All back holes have evaporated and returned to Consciousness. Thus endeth this cycle and Consciousness knows that it is good.

Genesis Chapter 1, Twenty-First-Century Version

Genesis Chapter 1, Twenty-First-Century Version

1. In the present, which is also the beginning and the end, there is Consciousness. Consciousness, from its own infinite potential, caused a part of that potential to start slowing down. As it slowed to a point just below the speed of light, it appeared out of a singularity and began resonating, forming small particles called Higgs particles. Thus heat, space, and time were born.

> At speeds faster than light, space/time vanishes. Therefore Consciousness must exist at speeds faster than light.

> Consciousness is not a thing out there but the infinite potential of everything.

Light speed

Infinite potential

> The Higgs particle endows all other particles with mass

Higgs Particle

> A singularity is the point where Consciousness changes to space/time

Singularity

2. At one trillionth of a trillionth of a second after Higgs particles were created, Consciousness made them resonate at different rates. This caused the Higgs particles to differentiate, creating particles with different characteristics called quarks, bosons, and leptons.

3. The universe then began expanding like a balloon being blown up, and within one second after the Big Bang, the Universe had grown to a size about a thousand times that of our solar system today. The temperature then dropped to 10,000 million degrees (a 1 followed by 13 zeros). Neutrons and protons combined

> Quarks & Leptans make matter while Bosons carry the fundamental forces of nature.

The Science of Spirit

to form the first nuclei: first of deuterium, then of helium, and then of other elements. This process lasted several minutes. Then three minutes after the Big Bang, the temperature dropped to a thousand million degrees. It was still too hot, however, for the atomic nuclei to capture electrons and form real elements. Thus the first stage was complete, and Consciousness then allowed the Universe to cool more. And Consciousness knew it was good.

4. After 300, 000 earth years, the Universe was cool enough for electrons to start combining with atom nuclei to form hydrogen and helium. These new molecules then began to pull together, forming large clouds. These large clouds pulled together so tightly that they formed huge balls of hydrogen and helium. The more compact the balls became, the more their gravity increased, and the more compact they became. The more compact they became, the hotter they got until they began to glow, and stars were born. The stars were all different sizes, and some were so large and hot that they made the hydrogen and helium fuse together to form most of the different molecules we see today, now called "heavy matter."

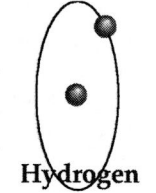

5. These large stars were so huge that their cores could not hold up their weight and they exploded, throwing all their different forms of molecules or heavy matter out into space. Thus the second stage was complete, and Consciousness knew it was good.

6. Huge clouds of heavy matter floating in space now began to draw together. As they pulled together, they formed disks that began to rotate. The closer they pulled together, the faster they rotated, concentrating most of the matter in the middle and forming new stars called suns. Eddies in the disks created smaller balls in the disks that formed planets. Nine billion years after the universe was created, our solar system was created. It was one of billions in one of the arms of the Milky Way Galaxy. This solar system had nine planets. Thus the third stage was complete, and Consciousness knew it was good.

Genesis Chapter 1, Twenty-First-Century Version

7. Consciousness, now finding itself in new forms of matter and chemicals, began to experiment with manipulating and mixing itself in different ways. It was soon found that the third planet in this solar system had the right combination of itself to create matter that could reproduce. As Consciousness reproduced itself in more complex ways, it found that the more complex it became, the harder it was to reproduce itself. It then created a new system where it made small packets containing the information needed to reproduce itself, and then the packets did the reproducing. These are called seeds today. Thus the fourth stage was complete, and Consciousness knew it was good.

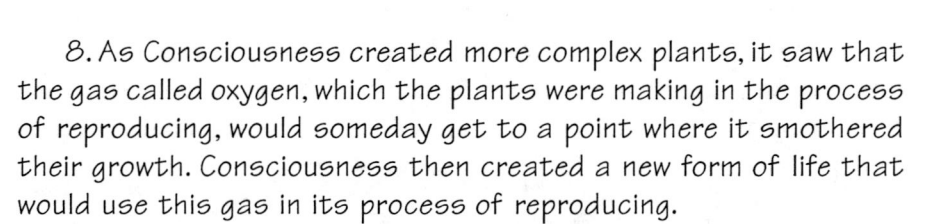

> Everything is made of Consciousness so Consciousness would find itself in all forms that are created.

8. As Consciousness created more complex plants, it saw that the gas called oxygen, which the plants were making in the process of reproducing, would someday get to a point where it smothered their growth. Consciousness then created a new form of life that would use this gas in its process of reproducing.

9. To make this new form of life work, it had to have a different system than the root system. This new life form needed new ways to take in its fuel for the reproduction process. Therefore, said Consciousness, let the plants make the fuel from the sun and from the chemicals they take into their roots and give the new form a new way to take the fuel from the plants by eating them. In order to do this, the new form of life would have to have mobility— animals. This created a new experience for Consciousness and, also, incredible new possibilities. Another problem with animals was that a new system for the seed had to be developed. Consciousness first carried over the

seed idea calling it an egg. But as animals became more complex, they needed a longer gestation, which was not workable with eggs. The placenta was then created. This made it possible for the seed to grow inside the animal until it could function on its own outside the animal.

10. There was also the problem of mixing the information, i.e., genes, so that new animal forms could be created. This was solved by creating two different forms of each animal, male and female, and a new way for them to mix genes during a reproduction cycle, sex. This system worked great, and Consciousness began to make this new life form bigger and more complex and then bigger still. Consciousness soon saw when it created the dinosaur that bigger was not better, so Consciousness erased the dinosaurs and began to develop the brain of the animal. Thus the fifth stage was complete, and Consciousness knew it was good.

11. Consciousness soon found that if he/she stood on its hind legs, the front legs could be used for other things. Consciousness then developed this system so that the hands and feet were very efficient. Consciousness found this form to be the most comfortable and rewarding form he/she had ever been in. This new form meant that he/she could do new things, but more possibilities meant making the brain more complex.

Is that me?
Yes!
That is my reflection,
in the water.
How did I get here?
Were did I come from?

Genesis Chapter 1, Twenty-First-Century Version

Then there came a point in the complexity that the brain gave Consciousness new abilities. Consciousness found him/herself in a strange new world. Self-aware of this world it had created, suddenly it was aware of the feelings in the body, aware of other bodies like him/her, and aware of time. What had happened? "What am I doing here? I feel alone." Thus, the sixth stage was complete, and Consciousness/human was in a state of bewilderment. The human was not sure it was good.

What has happened here in the last stage? Why is Consciousness so bewildered about the very universe it has created? Why are we so bewildered about who we are and where we came from? The answer is complex and simple. It is partly due to a tangled hierarchy.

Tangled Hierarchy

A normal hierarchy, as you know, is a pyramid, where there is something on top, and something under that, and so on down to the bottom. A tangled hierarchy has no top or bottom. It is a loop, and you can have loops within loops that become very complex. It is like the liar's paradox. If I type the statement, "This sentence is lying," we are caught in the liar's paradox or tangled hierarchy. The sentence is presumed to be telling the truth, that it is lying, but it says it's lying, so it can't be telling the truth. So which is it? It can't be making both a true and false statement at the same time. Or can it? This is quantum physics— on and off at the same time and a tangled hierarchy.

That is the nature of Consciousness/God. I tried to show this in my Genesis story. Consciousness created man, but at the same time fish created fish, birds created birds, and man created man. But it was Consciousness/God that did it all. Don't fall into the trap of thinking of it as a sculptor making a work of art or as an engineer designing a new watch. All of these things are inanimate matter that is manipulated to create some different form or shape. A closer analogy (but still not right) would be that of a gardener growing a garden. The gardener sets the process in motion by planting the seeds, and then the plants grow themselves. But the process does not end there. The nutrients needed to grow the plants come from the compost from last year's plants and from other animals, including the other past gardeners, who died in the past and returned to the soil.

The Genesis story tried to show this too. If Consciousness is a tangled hierarchy then creation is a cycle just like the yearly cycle of growth. Consciousness does not exist in space-time. So Consciousness has always created the universe over and over forever; it has always been that way and will always be that way. Thus the Genesis story can be started at any point and that is the true beginning. I started my Genesis when the universe was a trillion years from the Big Bang. Creation is a loop and there is no beginning or end.

Which came first, the chicken or the egg? We call this a paradox. But it is not a paradox; it is just the way the world really is. We call it a paradox because we think of the world as being made the way a watchmaker makes a watch. In a tangled hierarchy there is no first-cause watchmaker. Even Consciousness/God is just part of the tangled hierarchy. The garden analogy is not quite right because we think of the gardener at the first cause—planting the seeds. But seeds were growing long before there was a gardener, and the garden is just a part of the whole cycle of life, as is God.

The Genesis story mixes three concepts that come from early scientific thinking. The first says that when God made the universe, he set up the laws by which it would work and then stepped back and let it run. This is why it is common to use a watchmaker as an analogy for God. In this case, God, the watchmaker, made the universe, the watch. Then, just like a watch maker, God winds the watch/universe and lets it run, not getting involved in the movement of every cog or daily activity, letting the laws that were put into place run on their own.

This idea would make good sense if the universe were made of matter as common sense dictates. But as I have shown, the mathematical and experimental information does not agree with common sense and says the universe must be a tangled hierarchy. This invalidates the idea that the universe is a watch and that God is the watch maker. But it does not invalidate the idea that the laws of the tangled hierarchy, once set in motion, can't run on their own. So the first concept is the idea that God is not consciously controlling every detail of daily activity, but allowing the rules that were put in place to operate as designed. This is not to say that Consciousness is not aware of our daily activities, just that we are free to make mistakes.

The second concept is that there are many forms of Consciousness besides the self-awareness that we experience in our waking hours. I believe that one of the reasons that God created the space/time reality was so he/she could experience self-awareness. I know how hard it is to conceptualize other forms of consciousness because we can't imagine not being self-aware. But there is lots of evidence for it. For example, we talked earlier about "unconscious perception."

The third concept is called "formative causation." Formative causation is what we talked about earlier where "fish created fish, and humans created humans." This is just saying that as the evolutionary process moved forward (i.e., the rules were put into place), refinements in the design were made at each stage. Once fish were created, the fish's consciousness helped with the refinements that made a better fish and led to higher non-fish creatures. Formative causation in not accepted by mainstream science (yet), but the evidence for it is clearly growing. Jean Lamarck first introduced formative causation into the scientific community in 1809.[29] He hypothesized that the reason a giraffe had a long neck was that in order to survive short-necked giraffes changed their own genes to grow long necks. They had to grow long necks to reach the most abundant food, which was in the trees. It is also called inheritance of acquired characteristics. Meaning that if you build up your muscles your kids will be born with a propensity toward great strength. From a first cause/mechanical Reality Box this makes no sense. It sounds magical. A giraffe changing his own genes? Come on, don't be silly.

This is a problem, however, only for someone who works under the assumption that everything is made of matter. But if you

The Science of Spirit

believe in non-local mind, this is not that surprising. The idea resurfaced in the 1920s when a Harvard[23] psychologist, William McDougall, did a number of experiments with white rats. McDougall took a tank of water and set it up so that when he put the rats in the water, they had only two ways out. The first way was a brightly-lit ramp, but if the rat took it, it would get an electric shock. The second way was also a ramp, but the ramp was in the dark and hard to see.

McDougall then counted how many times it took his group of rats to learn to go to the second ramp to get out. He found that, on average, it took the rats 160 shocks before they learned to always take the second ramp. He then took the offspring of this group of rats and repeated the experiment. This second generation then learned faster than their parents and the third generation even faster. He then continued for thirty generations. In the thirtieth generation, it took an average of only 12 shocks before the rats knew to always take the dark ramp.

It would seem clear that the rats were changing their own genes so that it was innate for future rats to take the dark ramp. This, of course, created an uproar, but the only thing that the critics could come up with was that McDougall must have unknowingly bred the most intelligent rats from each generation. This was in spite of the fact that the rats were picked at random.

McDougall then repeated the experiment using all new rats, but this time he picked only the low-IQ rats. Surprisingly, this time it took only 22 generations to get down to ten electric shocks on average. Not only were the parents passing on new genes to the children, but it also seemed it was becoming innate in *all* rats. By the time that other researchers tried to duplicate the experiment, the first generation of rats took only a few times to learn what to do. And some knew, innately, to go to the dark ramp the very first time.

In 1980 a new bombshell hit. A plant physiologist by the name of Rupert Sheldrake described a mechanism for formative

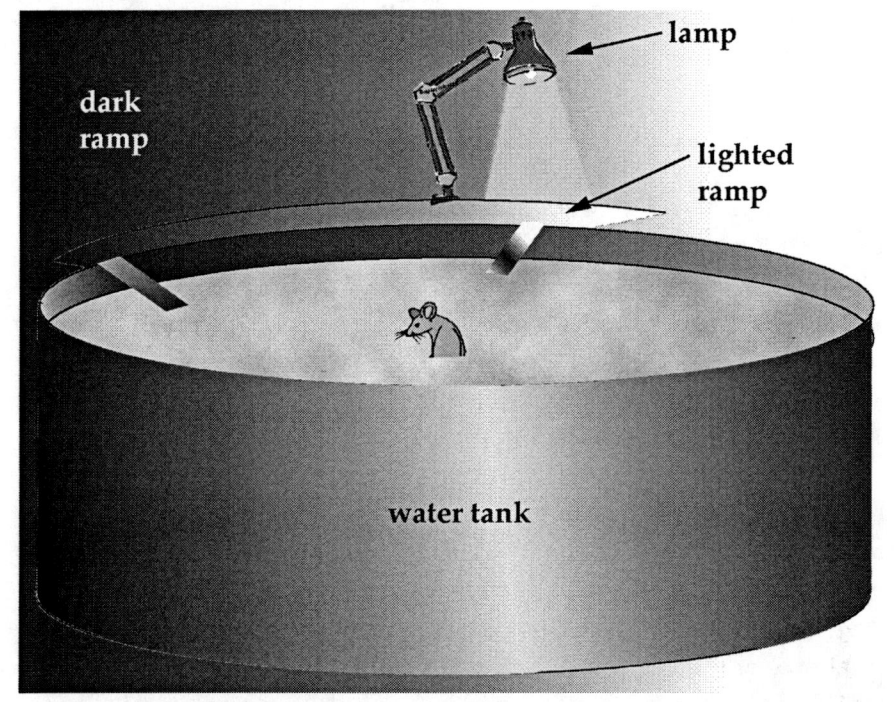

lamp

dark ramp

lighted ramp

water tank

causation. He called it "the morphogenetic field." His theory was that there is a field containing the shape or form for all living things. He said that the field creates what is called "morphic resonance." The morphic resonance takes the form from the morphogenetic field and duplicates the pattern in the protein that the DNA makes. He said that biologists do not know what causes things to have the shape they do. They speculate that somehow the DNA does this, but all they can prove is that the DNA encodes what protein is made.

To explain this better, Sheldrake uses a radio or TV signal analogy. Radio and TV signals in the air are of many different frequencies because every radio or TV station uses a different frequency. But a radio or TV picks up only one station at a time.

The Science of Spirit

Living things, he postulated, operate the same way. The DNA gives rise to the tuning characteristics, like a radio or TV would. Therefore a tree's DNA would create the set of proteins needed to make a leaf, and this set of proteins tunes or matches the morphic resonance from the morphogenetic field. The proteins, which are made by the DNA, are directed by the morphic resonance to form a leaf.[13]

Sheldrake's morphogenetic field sounds a lot like non-local mind and like a life force that was proposed by the vitalists. But whatever you call it, the evidence is becoming very clear that there is a conscious force at work in the universe. Now, let me give you a couple more examples.

In 1998 a new book came out called *Lamarck's Signature*. It was written by a group of researchers; Edward J. Steele, Robyn A. Lindley, and Robert V. Blanden. The book follows their research in the discovery of a new mechanism in the immune system of humans and animals (mammals). This mechanism takes information from stressors in the environment. The information could then be used by the body to change the genes, helping the body adapt to the stresses in the environment very quickly. The group has yet to show that the new information does in fact change genes but that is the last step in showing that our bodies can inherit acquired characteristics from our parents.

In 1999, a group of immunologists confirmed that about 450 million years ago a piece of DNA was spliced into the genome of a jawed vertebrate. This new set of genes suddenly made the immune system of jawed vertebrates (and ultimately humans) very powerful. Up until this point, life had the ability to fight only very simple bacteria. This new section of DNA gives the body the ability to make an infinite number of antibodies and T-cell receptors.[14]

For this to happen, it would require an enzyme to cut and paste the DNA from some unknown origin. The best explanation to date goes something like this: "Hundreds of millions of years ago, in a creature perhaps resembling today's sharks, a piece of DNA apparently jumped from its chromosomal home, a movement known as transposition. Carrying the blueprint for an enzyme that cuts

Genesis Chapter 1, Twenty-First-Century Version

and pastes DNA, it just <u>happened</u> to insert itself within a gene, perhaps one already being used by the immune system. Over time, this fragment endowed descendants of that ancient creature with the DNA-shuffling ability needed to create vast arrays of antibodies and T cell receptors." Does this sound like a coincidence? How many coincidences like this have happened? Well, at least one more that I know about. It is called the "Placental Puzzle."

In early 2000, immunologists found evidence that a DNA strip got spliced into the gene that created placenta. Scientists have known for some time that up until 100 million years ago all vertebrates laid eggs. Then, overnight in evolutionary time, vertebrates switched to live birth. This is the Placental Puzzle because it was the placenta that made it possible. Now, some researchers have found evidence that it was a virus, which just happened to have all the DNA needed for a placenta, that got into the egg-laying vertebrate and spliced in the placental DNA. It seems to me to defy logic to believe that all of this was a random event.[15]

Evidence is clearly growing stronger that evolution is not a random event, as many evolutionary biologists still believe. There is little doubt in my mind that evolution was guided and that the universe was purposefully created.

So a tangled hierarchy is the cycle of life. But it is more: it is being "on and off" at the same time. It makes no sense mechanically because matter is only a piece in the cycle. It would be like being a word on this page and believing that you are the whole book. That is just what mechanical theorists are doing. They think that matter is all there is. But matter is really just one word in a book.

But then how does this relate to me experiencing myself as an individual, and, at the same time, my consciousness being part of the one Consciousness? The first thing that you must understand is that you are not a word on this page. If you were a word on this page, you would not understand or be aware of someone out there reading you. In other words, the you reading this book is in a

The Science of Spirit

totally different world than the words on this page.

Imagine for a moment that you are a television signal. You would be everywhere: in the air, going through buildings, cars, people. You could see hundreds of televisions all over town. Now see yourself going into television sets all over town. Then see yourself going through the circuit of each of the televisions to make a picture and become a part of the TV set. What do you see now? As you become a part of each TV, you are no longer a signal in the air. You are no longer looking at hundreds of TVs, but at only one here and one there. You are still who you are, one huge signal as big as the town, but your perspective has changed. You are now a part of hundreds of TVs! You feel like an individual in each and every one of the hundreds of TVs. As an individual picture, coming from one TV set, you are not aware of any other TV set, and you perceive the TV set as your body. The circuit of the TV set is preventing you from seeing your whole self, the TV signal in the air.

So it comes down to your perspective. If you are in the system, you cannot see the entity that is outside the system looking in. You are forced to flow with the system, and you can see only one piece of the system at a time. But if you are outside the system, then you are not affected by the system and can see all the parts of the system at the same time.

Remember the psychology experiment that showed it is only in our conscious awareness that choice is made? When our brain looks at something, it sees two states— both the quantum on and the quantum off at the same time. But we cannot operate, as humans, if the world is always in two states. To solve that, Consciousness makes a choice. It picks only one of the two states, either off or on, and may be choosing between many more states than two. (Our brain can only understand two states, so all our experiments are done with two states.)

But this does not seem to make sense. If I choose one of the two states and you choose the other of the two states, why don't we see

Light switch in up/on position

two different states at the same time? Let's say that the light switch in this room is on when the switch is flipped up and is off when the switch is flipped down. Quantum theory says that the light is also off at the same time it is on and vice versa. Because we make a "choice," we always choose to have the light be on when the switch is up and off when down. What happens, though, if I chose to have the light on when the switch is flipped down at that same time you choose to have the light on when the switch is flipped up?

Good question. But if you have to ask, you have missed a key point, the hardest point of all to accept. The answer is that there is only one Consciousness making the choice, collapsing the field. Yes, there are two humans, but both humans are sharing the one and only choice-maker. So both humans would agree on what the quantum field would collapse to. On or off. So we both see the light on at the same time.

Okay, you may say, I hear what you are saying, but what about the fact that I "choose" strawberries over blueberries when you always "choose" blueberries over strawberries? Ah, but that is a different kind of choice. That is a choice between two different material objects, and that is really operant conditioning, not collapsing the quantum field. It's a learned choice that your whole brain/body/mind system makes, and don't forget that Consciousness/God is a complex tangled hierarchy and would like strawberries and blueberries equally well at the same time.

This brings up a more complex question. If our consciousness is the consciousness of God, then how can there be Hitlers in the world? This would seem to make God Hitler. This is a very complex question that would probably require a book to explain, so I can't fully answer it here, but I will give you a taste of what I think is going on. It is somewhat like the strawberry/blueberry question above.

This is where free will and Ego come in. Ego is traditionally defined as the sense of self, the part of the brain that is concerned with the outside world. But if our conscious awareness is what creates the sense of self (for it is our consciousness that makes us aware of our own existence), then it can't be a part of the brain as traditionally thought.

Sigmund Freud, who developed the system, believed that the Ego, the Id, and the Superego were three different aspects of the brain. But if our consciousness is the consciousness of God and what makes us aware of the outside world, this can't be quite right. This theory needs to be reworked. Ego, then, must really be a by-product of the synergism between the mind (our conscious awareness and God Consciousness) and the brain. In other words, it is not just a part of the brain, but a mixture of the brain and mind. This would mean that the whole brain was the Id, and the Superego would be God's consciousness or the ideal Self (not mixed with the brain). The brain is just a computer, but Ego involves a sense of self and computers or brains can't have a sense of self.

When the individual mind interacts with the brain, it loses or greatly lessens its connection or awareness of its whole. The quantum field or Consciousness (like the TV signal) loses its awareness of the signal that is everywhere. But unlike the TV signal that actually loses its connection to the whole signal, the mind does not lose its connection, but merely has the illusion of being an individual in a body. Pure mind must not possess memory, as we understand memory, because why else would consciousness not remember from where it comes? (I do think, though, there must be some type of memory beyond our understanding.)

What this is saying, in effect, is that mind does not have total control over the brain, but must work with what is there, which results in the synergism (a working together). For an example of this I will use my spelling problem. Language and spelling are really mechanical things that come from the Id. There are some very simple four- and five-letter words that I (mind) have the most difficult time remembering how to spell. But it is not really I (mind) that can't remember how to spell these words, but the Id I am using or interacting with. All I can do is initiate the peptides in the brain that start the mechanical process.

For an example of what I am taking about let's imagine a giant computer keyboard with one word on each key. Then, when you want to spell a word, you hit the key for that word. For example, to spell

Genesis Chapter 1, Twenty-First-Century Version

"the," you push the key marked "the" and expect t-h-e to appear on the screen. People whose Id is good at spelling will always get t-h-e when they push the "the" key. But sometimes when I push the "the," key nothing happens. Another analogy would be driving a car and turning on the windshield wipers and nothing happens. The driver and car are working in a synergistic way. If the car does not make the windshield wipers go when they are turned on, the driver is helpless until the windshield wipers are fixed. Like wise you are the driver of your brain/body.

One of the apparent reasons that the mind interfaces with the Id is simply for the experience. Mind has no body and therefore created the material universe to experience life. But because of the powerful illusion of being an individual and experiencing the world of matter, mind gets carried away and caught up in the demands of the world and Id/body. From birth, we are unaware of where we (mind) come from, so we play and get caught up in the game of life and let the Id start "running the show." When this happens, it is said that it is the Ego that is crowding out the spirit.

The complexities of society in the realm of matter pulls consciousness into the illusion of day-to-day living. This then creates the conditions that produce all of the problems we see today, including Hitlers. And the world's problems are going to continue until the Ego (mind interacting with the body) understands where it is from. So what I am saying is that until the Ego illusion is understood to be an illusion, we are going to continue to take the Ego and our individual survival too seriously. My Dad was fond of saying, "We need to see the big joke about life." He meant that we take life far too seriously. It appears he was right.

Thus from a practical, everyday point of view, the world has lots of mechanical aspects and is mostly like what science says it is from the matter perspective. Within the context of matter, the laws of thermodynamics are right. But in the context of the bigger picture, thermodynamics is wrong, and it is really a tangled hierarchy. Now a woman physicist, Louise B. Young is changing this long-standing interpretation of thermodynamics that the universe is increasing in disorder. She is arguing that not only is the disorder not increasing but that the universe is becoming more orderly. In other words the universe in growing more complex not less.

She's not arguing that machines don't lose heat, but for a machine to lose heat does not prove that the universe is a machine that is running down. One of the arguments in her book, *The Unfinished Universe*, comes from the atom. There are many cases where the electron that is orbiting its nucleus in an atom can be interrupted and go into a haphazard and very unstable orbit. In this condition it can very easily be knocked out of its orbit. But if it holds together, the electron, on it's own and guided by some principle we don't understand, dumps some of its heat causing it to drop to a lower, more stable orbit.

Most scientists believe that because the atom has lost heat its disorder has increased, and this is more proof that the law of thermodynamics is right. But Louise argues that just the opposite is true, that the atom has increased it order because it is now more stable than before, and it can live longer. Calculations done in the 1920s show that when the atom is in an unstable state its life expectancy is only one tenth of a second, but by dumping the heat and dropping to a lower order it's life expectancy jumps to 30,000 years. She then goes on to show that the very same self-preservation principle that the atom shows is remapped throughout the universe and is the same principle that is at work in life pushing itself to higher and more complex order. Thus the universe is getting more complex not less.

So even thermodynamics is coming apart, and it is becoming clear that there is no beginning and end. It is a loop that plays over and over. The Big Bang is just one phase in the cycle.

Glenda Green's Jesus

In late 1991, an artist, by the name of Glenda Green claimed that Jesus appeared to her and allowed her to paint his portrait (*Love Without End*). It took her four months, during which time she was given a huge amount of information. Of course, I do not know what really happened, but I have spoken personally with Glenda Greene, and she appears to be very honest. The reason that Glenda Green's experience is important here is that whoever the visitor was he gave her an incredible amount of accurate scientific information.

One of the things that Jesus told her was that there is a particle that science has theorized but has not been found yet—the Higgs particle. It has been nicknamed "the God particle" because it endows all other particles with mass. Jesus called this particle an "adamantine particle." The interesting thing here is that when we die, according to Glenda Green's Jesus, a residual of the adamantine particles of our body/brain remains intact and returns to the quantum field. And this is our individual soul or spirit. The claim was that this residual maintained our individuality even within the folds of the quantum field, i.e., God.[16] If this is true, then it makes the basic picture I painted above far more complex. Not only do we have a material body, a material brain, and a mind all working synergistically, but we also have spirit or soul added into the mixture.

Summary

I hope that you are now getting a feeling for quantum theory and the tangled hierarchy. I will end with a visual explanation of tangled hierarchy. Look at the picture by M.C. Escher, titled *Paint Gallery*. Notice that the young man is in the same picture he is looking at, in the paint gallery. He is looking at the picture and is in the picture at the same time. This is the way the world really is. But like the young man in the picture, we cannot see it because we are in the picture. If you will notice, Escher signed his picture in the white spot in the middle. This is very appropriate because it says that I, M.C. Escher, am outside the picture drawing it and not in the picture.[17]

I have tried in this chapter to present a bridge between theology and science and echo the call of Michael J. Behe,[22] a biochemist, who stated in his book *Darwin's Black Box* that it is time for the emotional debate between creationism and Darwinism to end. The best scientific information today says that both sides are probably wrong. Natural selection on a biochemical level just does not work, and the creationists, as I showed in the beginning, also have a problem. They need to determine which of the two Genesis accounts is the correct one. It is poor science to take two opposing stories and claim both are right.

It is time for theology to concern itself with man's relationship to God and let science work out the mechanics of how life began. Now that we know the universe is non-local, anything that science finds can always be claimed as the way God works.

M.C. Esher's Paint Gallery '2003 Cordon Art B.V. Baarn-Holland. All rights reserved.

Genesis Chapter 1, Twenty-First-Century Version

New Reality Box 8

In the 1500s, it was believed that the earth was the center of the solar system. This was their Reality Box. Then a mathematician named Copernicus showed that the Sun was the center of the solar system, not the earth. That is now part of our current Reality Box. Today all our science is still based on the assumption that zero speeds are the norm and that light speeds are the extreme. BUT what if our everyday speeds are the extreme and light speeds are the norm? After all, to light, there is no space/time and no physics, i.e. no matter. Physics and space/time may have come into being when energy slowed down below light speeds. That would mean that matter is really frozen energy.

The Great Enigma, human life and destiny,
The meaning of the soul, the what and why,
The whence and whither of all life, which once
Outpoured in vials of despair, are now
Resolved into a synthesis which leaves
Me breathless with a glowing faith and joy;
For now I know directly that I draw
My life from Cosmic Life, and I am merged
With God through Love and Knowledge, and I see
They are the same, and that with Beauty they
Do form the highest Trinity.

The Voice Celestial
Page 344

Journal 9
Non-Local mind

As I continue on up the trail, after the coyote moves back into his world, I come to a huge round boulder protruding from the side of the hill. It is higher than my head. Walking around it, I find a sloping spot that makes it easy to climb up onto it. What a spectacular view! It looks as if I can see the whole world below me! The morning sun is to my left, and the view extends for miles. I can even see the El Dorado Springs Road that I came in on, an occasional ant-sized car slowly moving along it.

Sitting cross-legged on the rock, I now understand why the gurus always go to the top of a mountain to meditate. As I reflect on where I have been, a beautiful brown deer suddenly appears on a ridge to my right about fifty feet away. The absence of antlers tells me that this is a lady. She stands with her head held high as if she were the guru of this mountain. It is clear that she is watching me as well, but shows no sign of fear. As we watch each other, her mouth begins to move, and as the morning sun reflects off her moist lips, they sparkle like stars. She appears to be speaking to me, sending a message that the world is fine, and everything is as it should be.

I now know that the best physical/experimental evidence we humans can marshal says that the universe is a tangled hierarchy, an Escher drawing, and that the creation of life clearly violates the second law of thermodynamics. Life does not go from order to disorder or from less order to more complex order. It is a cycle, a tangled hierarchy. It is just our little piece of reality that seems to go from order to disorder.

I have changed a lot. I now cannot understand how I or anyone else could have thought otherwise. I now know that the reason there is no exchange of energy between the spirit world and the matter world is that the matter world *is* the spirit world. In other words, there is no energy exchanged because thermodynamics is spirit.

The obvious fact that we are here says something had to have always been here. That "something" would have to be infinite or eternal. It could not have come into being on its own, but had to have always existed. Matter cannot meet that criterion. Matter is finite. It can be divided only to the size of Planck's constant. Matter has length, and length by its very nature must also have an end. So clearly it makes no sense for matter to be eternal and infinite.

Just think how incredible all of this is! Energy, which is eternal and has no length, somehow creates vibration that creates an illusion of particles. These particles then vibrate and create a bigger illusion that evolves into creations that can then look at themselves— the eye that looks back at itself.

In the past, if I ignored the details, it was easy for me to imagine a scenario in which life evolved from nothing but quarks, and that is basically how that part did happen. There is ample physical/experimental evidence for this. So from this perspective why invoke a Creator? A Being that is more complex than the universe? A Being that had to come into being by itself and then create something less complex than itself? But, as the saying goes, "The devil is in the details." And when I look at the details, it seems clear to me that the evolution of the universe had to be guided.

So I am forced to invoke a Creator, which brings back the problem of a more complex being making a lesser complex being. We are back to turtles on top of turtles, a paradox. So for a brilliant solution, just replace the Creator/more complex Being with pure energy. Energy appears to be eternal and infinite. Energy then meets the criterion of something that has always just existed. Energy is not a thing. Energy does not appear to have length or time.

The only hard part here, for mainstream science, is then to endow energy with consciousness. But why not? We don't know anything about energy— zero, zip. We know what it can do; we have ways of indirectly measuring it. But what *is* it? We haven't a clue.

Non-Local mind

When we experiment with light, a pure form of energy, all we find is a tangled hierarchy. So why not endow it with the consciousness, its tangled hierarchy would seem to demand. Give me a better solution.

Where are we going to find clearer evidence and get closer to the Truth than this? There is no doubt today that matter is made from energy. The first atomic bomb proved that beyond any doubt. Is not all the above proof of the existence of God? Mainstream science would still balk at this statement. First of all, scientists would not accept endowing energy with consciousness, in spite of the fact that quantum theory clearly demands it.

On a normal bell-shaped curve, 68% of all scientists try to be pragmatic and express no opinion. That is as it should be. Their job is to study the facts and not interpret them. To do a good job at this, they must remain neutral and unbiased. We, the western world and I, are the ones at fault here. We are the ones afraid to make a decision without a blessing from the high priests of science. But this is a demigod. Pure science should remain as neutral as possible, but it does not. It enjoys wielding the power that we give to it.

We then wind up with organizations like the National Academy of Science (NAS). I am not against the NAS; there is nothing wrong with a science adviser. I love science. But because they are not trained in philosophy and even look down their noses at philosophy, they do a one-sided, out-of-balance job at interpreting the research, and our society pays dearly for this.

Do you think that all of the societal problems of today are an accident? No! Many are a direct result of our belief in the local assumption. These are the walls of science's Reality Box. The local assumption tells us that we are all alone to fight the environment. That the world is dog eat dog, and you had better get yours while you can. But once you understand that the world is non-local, you know that you are not alone, and the environment is not your enemy. It then brings other evidence into focus that says our minds are really just One Mind. We are all brothers and sisters, and when we hurt a brother or sister, we are literally hurting ourselves.

The Science of Spirit

In 1974, at a meeting in Arosa, Switzerland, a group of scientists and religious leaders were talking about non-local reality. One of the participants, Maharishi Mahesh Yogi, made the statement that if just one percent of a town or other population group were to meditate and experience pure consciousness, the violence and crime rate in the population would go down by a measurable amount. One of the scientists, Garland Landrith, was surprised and said he would test it.[26]

So he took statistics from the previous year (1973) and found eleven U.S. cities with populations of 25,000 that had one percent of the population who practiced a form of meditation called Transcendental Meditation (T.M.). He compared them to a second group of eleven cities that did not have one percent practicing T.M. Sure enough, the non-T.M. cities' crime rates followed the national trend and were up by an average of 8.3 %. But in each of the cities where one percent were doing T.M., the crime rate was down on average by 8.2%. Wow! Think about that for a minute.

If this is right, it could be the answer to the world peace problem. But it didn't end there. Over the past 20 years there have been over 400 studies confirming the truth of this phenomenon! Four hundred studies say all we have to do is teach people to meditate, and we will have world peace. Yet no one seems to know about it or care! The problem is that we do not believe in non-local mind.

There is even more evidence. In 1976, Maharishi introduced a new way to teach T.M. called T.M.-Sidhi. This new system requires only the square root of one percent of the population of a city practicing T.M, for the crime rate to go down! So most of the four hundred studies are based on the square root of one percent rule! This means that in a group of one hundred people only one person would have an effect on the whole group. It would take two people in a group of four hundred, three people for a group of nine hundred, and for a population of twenty-five thousand, only sixteen people.

In 1983, a world T.M. conference was held with seven thousand people in attendance. Seven thousand people are close to the

Non-Local mind

square root of one percent of the world's population. The scientists then looked at world statistics for three weeks prior to the conference, the three weeks of the conference, and three weeks afterwards. Sure enough, the number of positive events worldwide was up, and the negative events were down worldwide! Strong positive events before and after were 1.1%, but jumped to 4.5% during the three weeks of the conference. Just think what would happen if only 10% of the world's population meditated!

What's going on? Why does it work? According to Vedic teaching (which is a philosophy not a religion), there is only One Mind shared by everyone, i.e., non-local mind, just what the scientific data show is true. So all minds belong to one system. According to physics, if the square root of one percent of a system is coherent, it will increase the coherence of the whole system, but all incoherence in a system has a one-to-one relationship. This is how a laser beam works. A small percent of light is made coherent, which creates a cascading effect towards coherence until the whole beam is coherent. Then, as we know, a coherent light beam or laser can cut through steel. It is the sharp focus that makes it so powerful.

The same thing happens in karate. Karate is a form of meditation in which a person focuses all of his mind and energy to one point. In other words, he makes it coherent. A Karate master who is well practiced at making his thought and energy coherent can break a half dozen bricks with the slice of a hand. This is also what happens in all highly focused meditation.

Transcendental Meditation has been practiced for thousands of years, and there is a consensus that there are different levels of coherence. The levels go by different names with each tradition, but the mind state is the same. Once one reaches the highest state, one passes into a different reality. It is believed that the person in this reality has left the body and become one with the entire universe. People who have reached this plane can not describe it, other than to say that they have lost their sense of individuality. So it is believed that in this highest state of mind coherence, each individual piece of coherence is added to the whole system or the one mind. Thus if we are all one mind and the part that is you becomes more coherent, you will be adding coherence to the one mind.

Dr. Larry Dossey's book *Recovering the Soul* begins with the story of Sarah.[27] Sarah was having surgery, and everything went fine until the end. As her physician was closing the incision, Sarah's heart stopped beating, and everything got frantic for a few minutes. But after quick action by the anesthesiologist, Sarah's heart returned to normal.

After Sarah woke up, an even more amazing thing happened. She was able to give minute details of not only what went on during the cardiac arrest and fibrillation, but she was also able to repeat details of conversations that had taken place. She knew the color of the sheets covering the operating table, the hairstyle of the head scrub nurse, the names of the surgeons in the doctor's lounge down the corridor who were waiting for her case to be concluded, and even the trivial fact that her anesthesiologist was wearing unmatched socks. At this point you may ask what is so amazing about the fact that she knew the color of the sheets covering the operating table or that the anesthesiologist wore unmatched socks? Well, you see, Sarah had been blind since birth. When she questioned her surgeon about the experience, he patronizingly dismissed her account and walked away.

What is going on here, though? How can we patronizingly dismiss this case? Something very important has happened here. We cannot just dismiss it out of hand because it doesn't fit our Reality Box. I have to agree with Dr. Larry Dossey that this is very credible evidence of our mind being non-local. This is hard for us to accept because most things in everyday life seem to stay in their places. Or do they? Maybe we don't see non-local things because we are not looking. Maybe we need to change our Reality Box.

It is apparently quite common for surgery patients to come out of an operation having had an "out of body" experience like Sarah's. These patients quite often say something about rising above their bodies and seeing the whole operation. They can even give minute details about what took place and what was said. Most surgeons, however, just consider it a dream and say that the details come from what the subconscious mind could hear being talked about.

Non-Local mind

Dr. Dossey then tells Elizabeth's story. She could go into a meditative state and travel around inside of her own body. It seems that Elizabeth was having pain in the lower left side of her abdomen. During meditation she could see three soft white things in her ovaries. She also knew that it was not cancer. When she told her doctor, he was skeptical but went ahead and ordered some tests. When the tests came back, he found that she did indeed have three non-cancerous cystic lesions on her ovaries. Surprised? Well, you shouldn't be if you accept non-local mind.

After many more documented stories, Dr. Dossey then tells about a rigidly controlled scientific study on prayer. The study lasted ten months and randomly assigned 393 patients admitted to the coronary care unit of San Francisco General Hospital to either a home prayer group or to a group that received no prayer. This study was rigidly controlled, and everything was double blind. None of the patients, nurses, and doctors knew which group the patients were in. The people doing the praying consisted of Catholics and Protestants from around the country. And each person praying was not given any instructions on how to pray, but was just given the name of the person(s) to be prayed for and his or her condition(s). Each patient in the prayer group had seven different people praying for him or her.

The results would be amazing to someone who believed the local assumption.

1. The patients in the prayed-for group were five times less likely to require antibiotics.
2. They were three times less likely to develop pulmonary edema.
3. None of the prayed-for patients required endotracheal intubation, an artificial airway, while twelve in the un-prayed-for group required mechanical ventilator support.
4. Although not statistically significant, fewer patients in the prayed-for group died.[21]

"Spindrift" is the name of a research group that for more than a decade has been studying prayer. Many of their studies have used rye seeds. For example, the seeds would be planted in a box in the same soil with string running down the middle and dividing the box into two equal groups, side A and side B. The seeds on one side were prayed for, and those on the other were not. Once grown, the shoots would be counted. The side that was prayed for consistently had the most shoots.

These experiments were shown to be consistent and reproducible even with different experimenters doing the praying. Many variations to these experiments have also been done. The researchers experimented with stressing one side and not the other, tried different ways of praying, and tested to see how much the pray-er had to know about his subject for the prayer to be effective. It was found that the more the person praying knew about his subject, the better the prayer worked. The most effective way to pray was a non-directive approach. This means that the person praying does not ask for a set outcome, like making side A grow faster. Rather, the researchers would simply say something like, "I would be pleased if side A grew faster, but Thy will be done."

Summary

I have only scratched the surface of all the number of studies and personal experiences that take place daily to confirm the reality of non-local mind. It seems clear to me that the only reason that we do not see or understand non-local mind is that our Reality Box is not accepting it. My Reality Box now accepts that the universe is non-local, which makes my mind non-local as well.

New Reality Box 9

We are told that when we want to lift our arms a chemical in our brain called a peptide starts a chemical signal that starts an electrical signal which makes muscles in our arm contract and our arm raises. But how does the non-material, non-chemical thought start just the right peptide in the first place? Could this not be more evidence that consciousness is separate from the brain and not just a by-product of the brain at work?

*Then look once more upon the mountains
Which tow'r in beauty and in strength above
The valley floor where running streams do feed
And glorify the land whose vineyards fair
Sustain the luscious grape from which is pressed
The sacred symbol of the Life-of All.
Surely, the gardens of the gods are fair
And all these things are placed upon the earth
That living here might be a Paradise.*

**The Voice Celestial
Page 21**

Journal 10
The New Non-Machine

I leave Meditation Rock and move on up the trail. I then enter a very thick wood and can feel the trees all around me. It is as if the forest is putting its arms around me to embrace me and accept me into Nature's arms, all becoming one.

The Old World is dying. The world I grew up in is dissolving before my eyes. The old ways of thinking and relating are fading. We have reached the pinnacle of the selfish machine, the materialistic "me against the world" approach to life. The buds of a spring are announcing a New World. The Tibetan Dali Lama has called my daughters' generation the pivotal generation. They will either nurture the new buds or let them die. I see many signs that the buds are opening. I feel confident that they will open because there are signs all around us, and we have but to stop and smell them.

The best description I've seen of the new paradigm (Reality Box) shift comes from Gary Zukav's book *Soul Stories*.[30] This seems quite appropriate to me because he was one of the first authors to introduce quantum science to the layman. His first book was *The Dancing Wuli Masters*, published in 1979. His new book, *Soul Stories*, is broken up into fifty-two weekly lessons, one for each week, and teaches what he calls "multisensory perception." The old way of looking at the world is limited to the five mechanical senses— sight, hearing, smell, touch, and taste. Mr. Zukav believes that the five senses are really just one sense, which I am calling the "mechanical sense." They are part of a single system. That system is designed to detect one thing, the world that appears to be outside of us. But the spiritual person understands that there is more. There is another system that we can tap into, but this system cannot be seen, heard, smelled, touched, or tasted. It comes from within us and can help us grow, solve problems, and guide us. Zukav has the lessons divided into five parts. Parts one

The Science of Spirit

and two are called "What's New" and "How it Works."

Then in part three, which he calls "What it Looks Like," he draws us a word picture, teaching by example, of the Old World that is dissolving and the New World that is budding. Mr. Zukav does not make judgements about the Old World or the new. It is just the way it is, and I would add that the Old World was a necessary stage. The old male role, which is as old as humanity, is one of "provider and protector." This is the way I was raised; my role was to go to work so I could provide for my family. Then, if any danger threatened my family, it was my role to stand between it and my family. This was my role— not to raise children or cook or make a home, but to provide and protect. Raising children, cooking, and making a home were the old female's role; she was the caregiver, the homemaker. This system worked well for most of human history. But humans are not static. They are still evolving, and this old system no longer works.

When I got married in 1968, my wife, Joyce, was an old female, and I was an old male. I got a job, a very good job for the times, and Joyce stayed home to take care of our daughter. Joyce was a very good mother and caretaker; she even got books to learn how to do her job better. But I was not happy being an old male. I knew there must be more, and I had to follow my heart. Zukav calls this a spiritual awakening, listening to your soul. So I quit my good job to go to school. This could have ended our marriage and often does when a new male appears in an old marriage. But Joyce was willing to grow too. Her heart was not really into being an old female. But all my friends were shocked. We had it all they said. What more could we want? I had a good job, a good wife, and a child; this was what life was all about. They just shook their heads and walked away.

We then moved to a town where I could attend college. But I was still an old male and worked and went to school both. I did not see that Joyce was not happy being an old female, but her job was not to complain: it was to take care of our home. She would have loved to have gone to work and shared housework between us. This would have been better for both of us, but we were trying to do our jobs and make the old system work.

The New Non-Machine

Then I graduated, and we moved to a new school to do graduate work. This was a smaller town, and there were no jobs for males. The only jobs were at a small factory that hired only females. They cannot do that now, but then it was different. I was crushed; I did not want to shirk my old-male responsibility. I was afraid to tell Joyce that the only jobs around were for females. It never occurred to me that she would want one of those jobs, but when I told her, she was elated. She then took one of the factory jobs. She had a spiritual calling too, and the new situation worked out better.

Then Joyce grew even more and started school too. This made it hard again, but this is the way spiritual couples work: they support each other's dreams. It has taken us thirty-four years, but we are now a new female and a new male. Joyce does what she does best and what makes her happy, providing an income; and I do what makes me happy, taking care of the house and writing. I have a better knack for taking care of the house than Joyce, and she makes a better income than I ever did. We are spiritual partners. We are not alone; millions of couples are now growing spiritually.

For approximately the last 7000 years of human history the old system (i.e., before industrialization) worked fairly well and was relatively fair until the church's war on women (but that's another book). Someone led, and someone followed. This is not as bad as it seems to us today. In non-industrial cultures, where one hunted or grew crops for a living, everyone grew up knowing what his or her role was. Everyone was happy doing his or her part. Even ninety-nine percent of the females, whose role it was to follow, never even thought it should be any other way. If a woman then lost her partner, someone would take her in or help her.

This all changed with the dawn of industrialization, when one had to "go to a job" to make a living. The old system then becomes unfair. If the female did not have a partner, she had nowhere to turn. She was not allowed to participate in the new things taking place in the society. But the male did want to change, his call for change was heard, and he had the physical power to express his will.

Then two events changed this for everyone. First, females got

The Science of Spirit

the right to vote, and, second, as the information age dawned, power no longer came from physical strength. The real power today is economic. But these two things only make the new paradigm possible. I believe that there is also a third reason. I believe that a new spiritual awakening is taking place. I think that it was planned all along.

Just look around you. At least every week I hear new statistics of how we are changing and how the New World is budding before our eyes. When I grew up, I never heard of a "manny," a male nanny, but now they are everywhere. They are still the minority, but they are growing. Their numbers have tripled between 1997 and 2002, from only 2,000 to 6,000 today. An old male would never consider being a nanny because that does not fit the male role. But here they are, men becoming nannies, at a growth rate of forty percent a year.

Growing up, I never heard of a female construction worker, but, now, my sister-in-law is a carpenter. Growing up, I never heard of a male flight attendant or a female airline pilot, but there they are. What do you think about a female marine or male nurse? It does not matter what you think really because this is the New World budding, the "Age of Aquarius," and no one can stop it. Never in the history of humans have roles changed so radically and quickly. In evolutionary terms, this is like turning on a dime.

But how can I say that this is a spiritual awakening, the "Age of Aquarius?" Could it really be possible that the "Age of Aquarius" is a credible ideal? Wasn't that just a silly song from the sixties? Everyone knows that astrology is just a fun game that we play. No serious-minded person would really believe in those silly horoscopes in the paper. Well, I personally agree: the horoscopes in the paper are silly. But there is much more to astrology than daily horoscopes. We also must keep in mind that the underlying reality is non-local. In a non-local reality, anything is possible.

There is research that gives astrology some credibility— that is, if you understand what the "credible" Astrologers are saying. They do not believe that the heavenly bodies control our every move, as some think. Serious astrologers, the ones who try to make it a real science, believe that there are forces in nature that "influence" our personality.

In the 1950's, Michel Gauquelin, a French statistician, and his wife, Francoise, took the birth records of champion athletes, scientists, and musicians and correlated them with the movement of the planets. They found a significant correlation between their professions and where the planets were at their birth. The most striking correlation was between athletes and the planet Mars. Other scientists have since increased the number of athletes to 2,089, and the correlation holds. This has become known as the *Mars Effect*. If you are interested in this, there are several books available on the subject.[35]

There is more research, but this is not a debate about whether astrology is real or not. I just want you to know that what I am about to say below has some credibility. Astrology is one of the strong beliefs of what has come to be called the New Age Movement. People in this movement appear strange and are the butt of many jokes. But this is because they are of a different paradigm than our present one. Like it or not, this "New Age" thinking is the fastest growing philosophy in North America and Europe.

There is a growing shift in the religious path. The dominant religious group in North America has always been Christianity with 262 million members in 2000. But between 1990 and 2000, if you remove growth through births to Christian households and its losses of 164,700 members, it now has an annual growth rate of only 0.8%. But if you look at the big world religions, there is a tremendous growth. Take Buddhists for example. In 1975, they made up only 1% of the North American population, but by 2000 they have grown to 8%. This is a growth rate of 2.75%. Then there is Hinduism, the fastest growing of the old religions. It is growing at a rate of 3.38%. So what is the fastest growing group? Not a really "organized" group at all, but a heterogeneous movement made up of small groups referred to by some as "ethnoreligionists." Ethnoreligion is growing a rate of 4% a year. Although the statisticians think of the ethnoreligions as groups like different Native American and local New Age and Spiritual groups, I think that all of the groups above are part of the new paradigm. Why do I say this?

To begin with, we need to know what the basic beliefs of the New Age Movement are. One must keep in mind that there is no really organized group and remember that many New Agers are on a personal path and have their own personal set of beliefs. I guess one could even say that a personal path *is* the new paradigm.

A recent survey shows that about 8% of adult Americans believe in astrology as a method to foretell the future. Seven percent believe that crystals are a source of healing or energizing power. Nine percent believe in Tarot Cards. Twenty-five percent believe in a non-traditional Christian concept of the nature of God. Eleven percent believe that God is "a state of higher consciousness that a person may reach." Eight percent define God as "the total realization of personal, human potential." Three percent think that "each person is God." A longitudinal study from 1991 to 1995 showed that a steady 20% of Americans claim to be New Agers. This makes them the third largest religious group.[31]

According to the group that put the above statistics together, the "root of the New Agers comes from: Astrology, Channeling, Hinduism, Gnostic traditions, Spiritualism, Taosim, Theosophy, and Neo-paganism." [34]And they break down into eight fundamental beliefs.

Monism: This is fundamental to all of the major world religions. Traditional Christians also believe that they are monists, and in the literal sense of the word they believe in one God. But the monistic view usually implies or is accompanied by pantheism as defined below.

Pantheism: This is where traditional Christianity and the other world religions part company. Pantheism believes that all that exists *is* God. Trees, cars, earth, everything, is made from the very stuff of God and has a spirit self. Traditional Christianity believes that God and the universe are separate. In Genesis God did not make the universe from himself, but caused it to come into being. He then resided in the heavens above earth. This does not, however, seem to have been the view of Jesus. A number of Bible scholars say that Jesus practiced deep meditation just as the other well known old philosophers, such as Lao Tzu and Buddha. Thus, when Jesus referred to the kingdom of God as being within us, this implies, I think, that he also believed that God was within everything.

Reincarnation: This is another belief that traditional Christianity did not hold, but most of the other religions do. Reincarnation means that the soul comes back to earth numerous times and lives many different lives. Reincarnation has growing scientific backing, and many researchers who have looked at this research agree that it may be a credible ideal. Reincarnation is sometimes called rebirth.

Karma: Karma and reincarnation are two sides of the same coin. Philosopher Christopher Bache explains this best in his book *Dark Night, Early Dawn*, when he says: "Reincarnation grounds the insight that we have unlimited time to discover and develop the being that we are, and karma establishes the causal lawfulness that guides all such self-actualization. We reap what we sow." [38]

Aura: An Aura is an energy field radiated by our bodies. Some gifted people claim to be able to see this energy and can use it to diagnose an individual's state of mind , as well as spiritual and physical health. People who claim to see auras also claim that children being born today have an unusual blue aura. They believe that these are the children who will usher in the new paradigm. These children are called indigo children.

Personal Transformation: This is the belief about how the paradigm shift will take place. It is believed that a profoundly intense mystical experience will lead to the new paradigm. It is also believed that humans will then develop new potential for self-healing and use of our psychic powers.

Ecological: This is the belief in Gaia. Gaia was originally a scientific theory stating that the earth had built-in systems to maintain its temperature and other environmental balances. From some of this research, Gaia has become Mother Earth and a living entity. This behooves us then to start working with nature and taking personal responsibility for our environment.

Universal Religion: This brings the cycle full circle. If all is God, and everything is God, then no matter what your personal path to God is, it has to be the right path. In the end, there is only one reality, one mountain to climb. So some will celebrate Christmas and some Ramadan, but all will have a new universal understanding of God. This picture looks very realistic to me. There is a well established history of beliefs cross migrating between religions. So it is not inconceivable that Christians will someday believe in rebirth and Karma. There is evidence that it is already happening.

Buddhism, Hedonism, and New Agers are growing faster than Christianity in North America— a dramatic change. But what we can't see or measure are the numbers of Christians who are already modifying their beliefs away from the traditional. There are growing numbers of individuals who call themselves Christian, yet believe in rebirth and Karma. Rebirth and Karma are the big battlegrounds right now among the philosophers. In *Dark Night, Early Dawn*, Christopher Bache talks about the "Lawyers creed," which goes: When the law is against you, argue the evidence. When the evidence is against you, argue the law. That is just what the rebirth opponents are doing. The evidence is growing against them, and so they are trying to argue the law. Their argument is that science says the world is a machine, and in a machine world rebirth is not possible. They are right. If the world is a machine, then rebirth is impossible. But they are not facing the quantum facts as I did. The world in not a machine; it is non-local.

There are also some interesting but less tangible signs of the coming paradigm shift. The number of reported "miracles" has gone off the chart. How many are hoax or hysteria I do not know, but whatever is going on, it has increased. If you look for them, you can see them in the news on a regular basis. Since 1992, there have been at least eleven documented cases of statues of the Virgin Mary crying tears of blood: 1992 – Mexico and Virginia; 1994 – Puerto Rico, Australia, and Ireland; 1995 – Ireland; 1996 – Kansas; 1997 – Ireland and Benin; 1998 - Spain and LasVegas.

A few examples of poorly documented but reported "miracles" are these: a twelve-year-old Lebanese girl was reported to be crying tiny crystals; rainbow-colored lights emanating from a monastery and the home of the Burmese Buddhist monk Sayadew were reported in 1995, lasting for three days; Hindu statues around the world "drank" milk offered to them; a number of Muslim families found Arabic symbols formed by seeds inside garden vegetables and fruits; a number of cases of radiant crosses of light have been reported in homes from Europe to America to the Philippines; reporters in the US, Europe, Canada, and Australia report a hitchhiker getting a ride and once in the car, announcing that Christ will be returning soon and then vanishing from the moving car; and a 35-foot high rainbow-colored image of the Madonna appeared on the side of an office building in Clearwater, Florida.

A few that are well documented, which no one knows the meaning of, are these: In 1997, two red cows were born, one in Israel and one in the US. The Jews believe that there hasn't been a red cow in 2,000 years. "The red heifer is one of the most important signs that we are living in a special time," says Gershon Solomaon, head of a group dedicated to rebuilding the ancient Temple destroyed by the Romans in CE 70.[32] The story, as I understand it, is that the ashes of a red cow were sprinkled on the site where the Temple was destroyed. This purification rite was to allow the Jews to return 2,000 years later to the Temple site. They believe that the red cow is a sign that this is about to happen.

In 1994, the first white buffalo was born in Janesvelle, Wisconsin, an event which hadn't happened since 1933. The buffalo was named Miracle. Then in 1996, two more white buffaloes were born, one in May and one in April. The White buffalo represents the return of the Native American White Buffalo Woman. It is a prophetic sign that a rebirth of a new day is ahead.

The Australian Aboriginals have a prophecy that at the end time there will be a black rain. On October 8, 2000, a black rain fell from Smoky Bay to Laura Bay in South Australia. The rain deposited a black ash on boats and cars. No one knows where the ash came from.

But the most dramatic sign that something strange is taking place—and it is definitely not a hoax—is Crop Circles. Documented for the first time in the mid-seventies, Crop Circles have been growing in number and complexity ever since. In the early nineties, the activity grew exponentially, reaching maybe 10,000 documented sightings today. Some Crop Circles are as big as 100,000 square feet and as long as three-quarters of a mile. There is not a day goes by that a Crop Circle does not appear somewhere in the world, and in England in late summer, largely around the Stonehenge and Silbury Hill region, there may be as many as fifteen a night. For hoaxers to be doing this, in a single night, would require a dozen teams working in the dark with no noise and never getting caught. In the late nineties, a number of contests were held to see what was possible and whether hoaxers were making the Crop Circles. None of the teams of six to twelve people could make anything very elaborate in less then twelve to sixteen hours. Also, during that same period, there *were a number* of hoaxers making Crop Circles, but Crop Circle researchers were able identify within minutes whether it was real or a hoax.

The sheer number and size of Crop Circles alone make it obvious that they are not being made by humans, and this is just the beginning of the evidence. According to Freddy Silva, a Crop Circle researcher, there have been witnesses. In 1972, a group of forty people on a hill, watching for the "Crop Circle makers," saw a large section of wheat in the field below them just "lie down in a spiral pattern as though a lady's fan were opening." It was estimated that the complete incident took about fifteen seconds.[33]

Much of the pubic has bought into the story that two elderly men, Dave and Doug, made the Crop Circles. They claimed to have used a board to trample down the wheat, but when they did so in a demonstration, most of the wheat stalks were broken. In real Crop Circles, the stems are never broken and look as if they had grown bent over. In many of the more complex patterns, the grain stalks are woven like a basket, creating different "shading" to the Crop Circle design. In some designs, small strips only two or three stalks wide will run for dozens of feet; that's not possible with a board.

There are also a number of other clues that separate the real Crop Circles from a hoax. When the stalks are cut open, there is a smell of cooked grain, and the magnetic field measured in the circle is very high, but there is little or no magnetic field outside of the circle. Dr. W.C. Levengood, from the BLT Research Center, says that they consistently find little balls of pure iron within the circles but not outside the circles. The balls are very tiny, only fifteen microns.[36]

The most dramatic and interesting thing about Crop Circles is the precision of the Euclidean geometry and what it may mean. Euclidean geometry is a type of math discovered by Euclid around 300 BCE and put in a three-volume book called *Elements*. Euclid found a way to represent squares, circles, triangles, and spheres mathematically and called it geometry.

In the weekly newsmagazine *Science News*, February 1, 1992, Professor Gerald Hawkins, astronomer and mathematician, presented the results of his mathematical analysis of the Crop

Circles. After studying hundreds of Crop Circles, he found that not only was the geometry in the Crop Circle designs extremely precise, but they fall into four known Euclidean geometric theorems. He then discovered a fifth unknown theorem that describes the other four— a new general theorem, unknown to humans, that the other four theorems are a sub-set of. After the *Science News* article he challenged an international cadre of mathematicians to see if they could find this fifth, unknown, theorem from the other four. No one did so, thus making professor Hawkins' point that it was not easy to see. In the October 12, 1996 *Science News*, the fifth, unknown, theorem was revealed. Could this have been the intent of the Crop Circle makers— to give us this new math?

But what is truly amazing is that the five theorems are diatonic ratios. Diatonic ratios govern the mathematical intervals that make up the notes in the western music scale. The Ancient Geeks called geometry "frozen music." So the Crop Circles are literally frozen music.

Dr. Hans Jenny has done extensive studies of the effects of vibrations on physical media such as plaster, water, oil, and sand. Dr. Jenny invented a piece of equipment he called a "tonoscope." It works by vibrating a plate at frequencies he would set it to. When he would put a medium such as sand on the plate, the vibrations would form a precise geometric pattern in the sand. If he then changed the frequency, the geometric pattern would change. Thus he showed that there was a set geometric pattern for every frequency. He was able to show that as the frequencies changed, the geometric patterns that were produced would duplicate the same designs found in the Crop Circles. It now seems possible that the Crop Circles are formed by sound, somehow.[37]

It appears that sound may be the media of the new paradigm. Especially if you think of sound in terms of vibration, because there is a growing interest in vibration and what is called resonance. Resonance is a type of echo or "re-sounding" of a frequency or pitch of a vibrating medium. For example, NASA routinely measures what is called the Schumann Resonance, which can be thought of as the frequency or pitch at which the Earth vibrates. This is measured by sending a signal that bounces off the earth's atmosphere, down to the earth or ground, and back up into the atmosphere, until it bounces completely around the earth. This takes about 0.136 seconds. This time would then correlate with a vibrating frequency of 7.32 vibrations per second. (The vibrations up and down per second are called Hertz or Hz for short). So the earth vibrates at 7.32 Hz.

Some New Agers are saying that the earth's vibration is increasing and that this is a sign of the new paradigm. This, however, does not seem to be the case. This frequency is a combination of atoms in the earth. Atoms cannot exist, as we know them, if their vibrations change. However, the strength or intensity of the vibration can change and does seem to be going up.

There is a also a great deal of research going on that raises the possibility that sound may someday be used as a major tool for healing. This idea is not new and is very common in many ancient healing practices. The best known of these are drumbeats and gourd rattles. Ancient people believed that the sound either drove off evil spirits or attracted good ones. But a number of present-day alternative healers believe that it is the vibrations (i.e., frequencies) themselves that are promoting the healing. One of the best and most ancient forms of healing is called "Veda" and comes from India. This form of healing was made popular by Deepak Chopra, M.D. Veda has a number of therapies that use chanting and types of "screaming" to heal the patient.

One of the most noted sound researchers is Sharry Edwards, M. Ed.[39] She received the 2001 award for "Scientist of the Year" from the International Association of New Science. She is working from the basic principle, which is true of many alternative approaches, that the body is a holograph.

A holograph is a photograph taken in a special way with lasers so that every aspect of the image in the photograph is in every other part of the image at the same time. In other words, if you were to take the photograph and cut it up into a thousand pieces, every one of the thousand pieces would contain the complete image. In Eastern philosophy it is believed that the body is a holograph. Thus everything that goes on in one part of the body is happening simultaneously everywhere in the whole body. If you cut your finger, that cut finger is reflected in every part of your body— your ears, eyes, hands, feet, etc. This would mean, then, that the cut finger would also be reflected in your voice.

Sharry Edwards has written a computer program that works with a voice analyzer. The computer then matches each frequency equivalent in the voice printout to chemicals, biochemicals, muscles, etc. that vibrate at the same frequency equivlent in the body. For example, vitamin A vibrates at a set frequency in the body, and if you look at that frequency equivalent on your voice printout, you will see your level of vitamin A reflected from your whole body. Everything in your body vibrates at a different frequency; therefore, everything that is going on in your body will be related to a frequency equivalency in your voice printout.

Edwards can then reverse this process. Just by listening to the frequency equivalent of vitamin A, the body will respond as if there were vitamin A in your body. Of course, with vitamin A it would be just as easy to start taking Vitamin A. Edwards has many, many stories of this really working. She tells of a case in which a lady had been in a car accident and severely damaged her lower leg. When the surgeon finished putting her leg back together, it turned out to be shorter than her other leg. The only thing the surgeon could do was put some pins in her leg hooked to a device that would put pressure on the leg and stretch the bone so it would grow longer. This would take many, many months. Edward's then did a voice analysis and found that some of the muscles in the short leg were too tight and as a result were continuosly cramping. Then, just with the application of sound therapy, the muscles all relaxed, and the leg lengthened on its own in a few weeks.

How exciting! If this all turns out to be true, then the future of medicine, with a mix of Western and Eastern, is very exciting and will be quite different from the cut-and-drug approach used today in Western medicine. Joyce was so excited she studied under Sharry and became a practitioner. One last thing about sound. As I was doing some research for this chapter and saw pictures of all the complex patterns that could be produced from just a single frequency of sound by Dr. Jenny, I began to wonder whether maybe vibrations could explain Rupert Sheldrake's morphogenetic field. We talked about the morphogenetic field in Chapter 7 as a possible mechanism for formative causation. Could this be how God makes a leaf? Could God be setting up some complex vibration that causes the protein, that the DNA is growing, to take the shape of a leaf?

George Bernard Shaw, Irish-born writer, once wrote, "Some people see things as they are and say 'Why.' I dream things that never were and say 'Why not.' Jonathan Swift wrote, "Vision is the art of seeing the invisible." Then in the 1960s, John F. Kennedy said, "The problems of the world cannot possibly be solved by skeptics or cynics whose horizons are limited by the obvious realities. We need men who can dream of things that never were."

This is what I am trying to do here, say "Why not?" and see the invisible and dream things that never were. I know the world looks sad on the surface, but to grow we must look below the surface. That is where the truth lies. Things always get worse before they get better. Getting worse is what forces the change. So we shouldn't fear the change; change is good. It is only the process of making the change, of "getting in the shower," that is hard. Once we are in the shower, the water is warm and loving; and once we are in the new paradigm, it will be warm and loving too. That is the subject of the next chapter. Love in the new paradigm.

New Reality Box 10

If you poke someone in the foot with a pin and then measure how long it takes him or her to feel the pain it is about .5 seconds. If you then go into the brain where the pain signal ends and stimulate it-it still takes .5 seconds to feel the pain. So the .5 seconds is not the time it takes for the signal to travel to the brain from the foot but the time it takes consciousness to perceive it. So consciousness must be something separate from the brain.

*There are times when logic seems to choke
The mysteries that we invoke;
Yet darkest clouds at time unfold
And pour out showers of dripping gold;
And from the labyrinths of mind,
The hidden mysteries unwind.
Man treads the mystic path alone
But if the "what" and "how" is shown,
He can develop wisdom till
He comes and goes as he shall will.*

**The Voice Celestial
Page 197**

Journal 11

It Is Either Love or Nothingness

I have now been on Homestead Trail for about fifty minutes. Suddenly, the thick trees along the trail part, and there in front of me is a neatly groomed, gray-clay gravel path. I look at the small wood sign by the trail and read "Mesa Trail." I have come full circle and rejoined the main trail again. I still don't know where it will lead, but that is the adventure of life, is it not?

Chapter 2, verse 4, of the King James Bible (as we saw in chapter seven) is the beginning of the version of the creation story written in 950 BCE. My speculation is that this story was written to give the people of the time a sense of their history or roots, which appears to be a deep-seated need in humans. I think this story can be used for that purpose today. In this version, after creating water and then plants, God created man and a garden for him to live in. (Is this not indeed our roots?) When humans first evolved, did we not live in a most beautiful garden? And if our interpretation about the scientific data is right, and our consciousness is indeed God's consciousness, then God must have made the beautiful garden for Itself. So the reason life was created was to have a beautiful place to live in. Life and the garden are God/Consciousness' home.

The Bible story continues, saying that it was the humans' job, our brain/body's job, to take care of the garden and do its up-keep. After all, the garden is really just made of energy that has been formed in a delicate balance to create the illusion of something solid; it is really just God/Consciousness' dream. But if care is not taken and this balance is not maintained, the whole form will dissolve like a piece of ice in the sun. In case you didn't notice, we are talking about a tangled hierarchy. Everything is inter-linked and cannot be separated. There is a balance between everything, and if that balance is broken, the whole hierarchy falls apart. If our main purpose is to enjoy life, enjoy the garden, it is not a free ride. We are responsible for taking care of nature and the all-important balance.

Then what does the Tree of Knowledge represent? It represents the Truth about the underlying reality. The biting of the apple or fruit of knowledge was really an act of arrogance. One bite is not the whole tree. But based on one bite, we arrogantly declared that we knew it all and knew better than Nature. Nature here is not just the field behind your house, but the way the whole universe works. So in our arrogance, we declared war on Nature, an act saying, "I alone know better than the tangled hierarchy." We thought Nature was responsible for our problems, and, by fighting Nature, we believed we could make our lives better.

Anthropologic evidence suggests that ancient hunter-gatherer people had a somewhat idyllic life. Studies of present day hunter-gatherer people show that they have far more leisure time than we do in the "civilized" world. Sure, they have sickness and death, but emotional problems are unheard of. Indeed, we didn't know when to leave well enough alone. I speculate that there must have been groups of hunter-gatherers that, as the population grew, were pushed into less ideal environments and were forced to discover agriculture. I do not think that the discovery of agriculture, in itself, was the biting of the fruit of knowledge. We can improve Nature because we created it, but we must work with Nature and maintain the balance. Early agriculture did this. I think that the biting of the fruit of knowledge came much later with the dawning of science, when we started thinking that we knew better than Nature.

One culture that innately works hard to understand and work with Nature is the Native American culture. Today they could teach us volumes about how to live with Nature. They are called Borderland People by psychoanalyst Jerome S. Bernstein who worked with the Navajo for a number of years. He says that he also has a number of therapy clients who he feels are also Borderland People. He believes that we are in a paradigm (Reality Box) shift and that there are a growing number of people who have the same innate understanding of Nature as Native Americans. The reason he sees so many in his practice is that they do not fit into our present society. He calls them Borderland People because they live on the border of the paradigm shift.

In an article he wrote for the September-November 2000 *Journal of the Institute of Noetic Sciences*, he tells about working with a woman who he believed was a Borderland Person. He called her Hannah and said that she had been sexually abused as a child and was very depressed and suicidal. She said that the only thing that stopped her from suicide was her dog who was dependent on her. Hannah was an artist who painted dark pictures of animals being deprived, mutilated, and tortured. Hannah said that although these paintings expressed suffering and pain, at the same time she hoped that they expressed the possibility of transformation. Hannah couldn't distinguish between her pain and the pain of other people and animals.

On the way home one day, Hannah found herself behind a truck with two cows in it. Her feeling was that the cows were being taken to slaughter, and she could feel their plight. Jerome (her therapist) took the standard approach and assumed that what was really going on was that she was projecting her life circumstances onto the cows. He said that she went along with this analysis for awhile, but then she began to protest and say, "No, it's the cows!" Even after this protest, he did not understand and thought that she was just identifying with the plight of the cows, but he did say that he had become "aware of a different feeling in the room." The feeling was attached to Hannah, yet it was separate from her. It seemed of a different dimension. It was a new experience for him.

A few sessions later, Hannah reported a similar experience concerning some stray dogs that had followed her. Again he assumed projection, which she at first acknowledged, but then she got very angry and took her shoe in her hand and hit the floor with it. "You just don't get it! It's the dogs."

In the next session, she recalled a dream that "jarred" him and forced him to drop his psychiatric training. He then tried to listen to what she was saying the way the Navajo medicine men were trying to teach him to listen. He said that she was extremely intelligent, and that when she was trying to reach into her unconscious, she would grope for a vocabulary that was beyond her reach, "a vocabulary that perhaps didn't yet exist." As she did this and he listened in this new way, he said that he did get it, that it was indeed the cows. He then saw that her way of thinking was the same as that of the native elders and healers who were trying to teach him. "Everything animate and inanimate has within it a spirit dimension and communicates in that dimension to those who can listen." Is this not what we have been talking about? Is this not saying that everything is made of Consciousness?

This is not the way modern Americans and Europeans look at the world. Matter is just this solid stuff that they have the right to manipulate in any way they see fit with no other consequence than the monetary costs. But this is not the picture that quantum theory paints. Quantum theory says that indeed everything is alive. Matter itself is made out of Consciousness. Modern man sees animals as just objects or complex matter that he is free to do with as he will. We even place everything in a hierarchy with animals toward the top and plants and bugs at the bottom. We think bugs are disgusting and just kill them to be killing them because they are pests.

But let me show you a new picture. Let's say that you have sculpted a small figure out of clay. Now, feel the sense of accomplishment from all your work. How does it feel? Now let's say you place it on a small table in your living room to show off your accomplishment. Then a friend comes over and, immediately upon seeing your piece of art, takes his fist and smashes it. How do you feel now? Most likely you feel disbelief and think, "What a senseless act."

Do you get the feeling now? The feeling of a senseless act? Well this is the way I feel and a number of people I know feel when we see people killing bugs or plants or destroying anything without a good reason. I know we cannot live without killing. Killing is not the point here. The lack of reverence when we must kill is where I am going. Every bug and blade of grass is a unique and beautiful creation, just like your clay sculpture. The Native Americans did hunt and kill, but the act of killing was a painful event. A prayer was said asking for forgiveness of the prey. The killing was truly an act of survival; they knew no other way to get what they needed to survive.

In her book *Love without End*, Glenda Green claims to have talked to a spirit who called himself Jesus and agreed to let her paint his picture.[16] As she was painting, she would ask "Jesus" questions. One day she asked him if we should be vegetarians. "Jesus" replied that one should not feel guilty for eating meat. But when we have learned to have sufficient love in our heart center, we will not want to eat meat. He said that the way farm animals are treated today is very wrong and makes him sad.

My mother lives in Oklahoma where it is hot and humid, and that means there are lots of cockroaches! One day, when I was visiting her for a few days, I began to notice that there were no cockroaches in her house. So I asked what she had done to get rid of them. She looked at me in a matter of fact way and said, "I asked them to leave." Her response took me completely by surprise. I was still in my scientific period, and this was the answer of a crazy person. However, I'd had lots of training in abnormal psychology and could see no other signs of pathology.

"What do you mean you asked them to leave?" I asked.

She then just repeated her statement: "I asked them to leave, and they did."

Just a few years later, when I was going through my Reality-Box shift, I went to a conference where I listened to a talk by a professional dowser. This dowser was very respected in his profession because he had a very high rate of accuracy. In his talk he told us that the reason he was so good at dowsing was that his main tool was meditation, and through his meditative mind he could talk to everything, including rocks, water, and oil in the ground. He then told a story of going into his kitchen one day and finding a trail of ants raiding his cabinets. He said that he immediately went into his meditative mind and asked the ants to leave. Within twenty minutes, the ants left.

Glenda Green's "Jesus" said that if you wanted to remove

critters like bugs from your house, all you had to do was love them enough, and they would leave. Is this what my mother did? She has the capacity to love bugs.

The immediate response here, for most people, is that he and my mother are just confused or sentimental people. But are they? Maybe it is our scientific culture that has lost its way. If you look at quantum theory, it says clearly that the universe is non-local. Everything is made from spirit, including bugs. In a non-local universe anything and everything is possible.

I no longer kill bugs in my house. I have a paper cup and small square of cardboard. When I find a bug in the house, I put the cup over the bug, slide the cardboard under it, and take it outside. That is not to say that I will never kill a bug, just that I now kill bugs with forethought. I must determine that there is a better reason than that they are just being pests. To kill a bug just because it is a pest shows a lack of respect for the complexity and beauty of Nature. You are smashing Nature's clay sculpture in a senseless act.

This practice of not killing bugs without forethought is more for my benefit than for the bugs'. First, it deepens my reverence for all of Nature. Then this reverence enhances my intuitive abilities, which helps me live a better and happier life. If happiness comes from within, then to reach within, you must first become more intuitive about your own nature, which is inseparable from all the rest of Nature.

As with the Borderland People, this has always been my nature. I just tried to deny it until my paradigm or Reality-Box shift in the early nineties. For all of my life, I have not fit in. The Navy was one of my hardest experiences. I had to live in a daily environment of violence— hearing stories, jokes, and laughter about the destruction of other human beings— and I was just as responsible as the rest of them. I fixed the airplanes that did the killing. I have never understood the need people have for watching violent movies. Even the "mildest" scenes of violence bring sadness to my heart and bewilderment as to how people can like to watch this. This feeling has only been intensified since Terina's death.

The Science of Spirit

Just as psychoanalyst Bernstein did not understand at first, I know that there will be some readers who object to the Borderland People's philosophy. That is all right: you are where you should be. I am not trying to change your way of doing things or get you to stop killing bugs. I just want you to start getting the feeling for a new understanding of the world, and an understanding of a deeper love. In the future, everyone will be like the Borderland People, and then that will be the right time for the world to change.

We have a little dog whose name is Brandy Brindle. She is a terrier-shitsu mix and looks a lot like the dog in the kid's movie *Benji*. When I take her for a walk, which is every day, I try to let her do whatever she wants, within some limits; after all, it is her walk. The limits are necessary because, without them, she would make a mess in other people's yards and sniff every blade of grass in sight for hours, and I don't have hours. She has no understanding of human society, but that does not mean that her life isn't just as important as mine. I quite often run into people who see us meandering, and they make the comment, "Who's walking who here? It looks to me like the dog is walking the man." This is always said in good humor and as an attempt to make conversation.

But it clearly reflects our bias for control and a pecking order— people are better than dogs or cats, and dogs and cats are better than squirrels, and so on down the list. There is something out of place or not right if the human is not the one controlling the lesser being, the animal. It reflects badly upon the human. He is thought of as weak, to be letting this lesser being control him. I never think of it this way. I always feel that all of life is morally equal. Brandy is cooped up in the house all day, every day, which is no better than a gilded cage. I know that if she had her freedom, she would explore the neighborhood for hours every day.

Where does this need for control that leads to a pecking order come from? I think that it comes from the local assumption, which promotes the idea that we have only one life to live and that we had better get ours while we can, even if we have to walk over other people and things to get it. This makes everything very competitive and necessitates the idea that the one who is the fastest, smartest, meanest, toughest, and so on is going to be the one who gets the "good life," the life with the most goods and services. But if this is true, why is the suicide rate so high among wealthy people? This is not to say that wealthy people can't be happy or that wealth is a bad thing. Wealth is a good thing. But to be both happy and wealthy you have to know how to be happy and poor first. Then the money can enhance your life— not the other way around. If you tell most people this, they respond with, "Yeah, right. I would rather be miserable rich than miserable poor, so bring on the money." They just don't understand the point. They can't see that what is being said is that they don't have to be miserable at all. Happiness comes from within, and if they search within, they could be happy right now. The reason they are miserable in the first place is that they spend all their time wishing and believing that wealth will make them happy.

Just before his death in 1998, my dad wrote a little book he called *Thomas Jefferson and the Cherokee Princess* (to be published). It is the story of a modern Cherokee princess and her fight for equal promotional opportunity at her job as a social worker. In this book he spends a great deal of time talking about the meaning of the American Constitution and the Declaration of Independence.

The Declaration of Independence states:

We hold these truths to be self-evident, that all men are created equal, that they are endowed by their Creator with certain unalienable Rights, that among these are Life, Liberty and the pursuit of Happiness.

Most Americans look at this statement as a beautiful sentiment, but then in the back of their minds they say, "That can't be right— all men are not created equal. Some people are faster, smarter, meaner, tougher, and richer than others are, and those people get more rights than others do. So it can't be right." What is going on here is that the people who say this are trapped in the local assumption. They can see only the mechanical side of life and can't see that the universe is non-local. They can't see that we have an inner dimension, which is spiritual, directly tied to the one consciousness. They don't understand that what the above statement means is that all men are created *morally* equal. And, morally, they have an equal right to life, liberty, and the pursuit of happiness.

This was a bold leap of understanding by Thomas Jefferson, who penned the Declaration of Independence, so he can be forgiven for not understanding that it was not just all *men* who were morally equal but all *life*. Yes, I hear the groans out there to this statement. This is way outside of most people's Reality Box. I can hear the debate already. "If this statement were accepted as true, there would be no end to the stupid laws. Laws like you can't kill bugs and so on and on. It would change my life completely for the worse."

But I don't think that is the case. I'm not saying that all life would have equal access to human society. Let's take for example "retarded people," who need to be treated differently than more intellectually endowed people because they don't have the knowledge to make it in our society. They clearly fall within the realm of a morally equal person under our constitution. But they have controls or restriction that others don't have. Morally they would be protected and treated with respect.

The same is true if termites invade a house; it would be necessary to kill them just as now. But in society that respected all of life, places for termites would be provided. What I am talking about here is reverence towards life.

What will happen, and what needs to happen, is that future generations will slowly start making the change in lifestyle that reflects the moral equality of all life. There is a way for you to start right now— if that is your desire. All that would be required, according to Glenda Green's "Jesus," is to start being a little kinder to all life. That is all that is required.

The most elegant attempt at achieving balance in Nature and reverence towards all life is an organic garden. John Jeavons began a research project in 1972 to study what was called *The French*

Intensive Technique of Horticulture.[25] The system that developed from it is now called *The Biointensive Method of Organic Horticulture*. This Biointensive method is a perfect example of what can be accomplished by working with Nature instead of against Nature as modern agribusiness does. Jeavons claims that the Biointensive method can consistently grow three to four times the crops per unit of area. This is all achieved without pesticides or herbicides and keeps the ground in balance and healthy year after year.

After thirty years of growing Biointensive gardens Jeavons says:

When an excess of insects appears in a garden, nature is indicating that a problem exists in the life of that garden. In each case, we need to become sensitive to the source of the imbalance... Also, in order to have beneficial insects in your food-producing area, there must be their [the beneficial insects'] food— some of the harmful ones! If there are no harmful insects, then there will be few, if any, beneficial insects ready to act as a seed population of friendly guardians. This seeming paradox— the presence of both kinds of insects for the healthiest garden— is symbolic of nature's balances.[25]

Jeavons then goes on to say that about 90% of the time insects attack only unhealthy plants. He states, "Just as a healthy person who eats good food is less susceptible to disease, so are plant diseases and insect attack." He then tells about a test plot of bush beans that were entirely destroyed by a beetle. But they just let the plot alone to see what would happen. To their surprise, a secondary set of leaves appeared. The plant was fighting back on its own. In the end they got as many beans as they did from the uninfected bean plots. Recent tests have shown that leaf damage of up to 30% by insects can actually increase the yield of some crops. According to Jeavons, "We often underestimate the ability of plants to take care of themselves. The damage done by insects often affects a very small percentage of the edible crop. Because of this, many Biointensive gardeners plant a little extra for the insect world to eat. This practice is beautiful, mellow, and in keeping with life-giving forms of insect control." [25]

Why do we in our arrogance and greed think that every grain of the harvest is ours alone? It was Nature that created the harvest, not the farmer. The farmer just initiated the process and was a part of it merely by aiding it. As John Jeavons has said, "There is plenty for everyone and everything." The sooner we understand this, the sooner we will start living together in harmony.

I agree. We as individuals do not really own anything in this world: we are just caretakers or sharecroppers with Nature. I have lived with my share of death, and one thing that has always struck me about death is all of the things left behind when someone dies. The thought has come to me, looking at all of the no-longer-needed belongings, that it was indeed as if the things were not really owned but were just being used.

This sentiment was expressed in a prayer credited to Chief Seattle, for whom Seattle, Washington, was named. Chief Seattle is said to have lived from 1786 to 1866 and was an environmental activist in the Puget Sound area. Although there is controversy over whether a speech that appeared in a newspaper in 1855 was really the work Chief Seattle, its message is no less important.

> Teach your children
> What we have taught our children—
> That the earth is our mother.
> Whatever befalls the earth
> Befalls the sons and daughters of the earth.
> If men spit upon the ground,
> They spit upon themselves.
>
> This we know.
> The earth does not belong to us;
> We belong to the earth.
> This we know.
> All things are connected

It Is Either Love or Nothingness

Like the blood which unites one family.
All things are connected.

Whatever befalls the earth
Befalls the sons and daughters of the earth.
We did not weave the web of life;
We are merely a strand in it.
Whatever we do to the web,
We do to ourselves....

Chief Seattle

In the early months of 2000, I was talking to a friend, telling her that there was clear scientific confirmation for a key belief of many of the world's major philosophies and religions. When I got through telling her about the fact that we all share one consciousness, she said, "I know. That is just what my church believes. You ought to come down some Sunday and just check it out." I don't remember what I said, but I avoided what she said and changed the topic of conversation.

Frankly, I had no interest in having to get up on Sunday morning and go to church. I still remembered how some of the people acted and believed in some of the churches I grew up with. I remembered my dad being fired for promoting racial harmony. I still felt that religion was the number one block to a better world.

Most of the major conflicts in the world are directly related to religious groups that believe they have exclusive rights to the Truth. Some believe this so strongly that they are willing to kill others to make their beliefs dominant. I am not just talking about the Jews and the Arabs or the Protestants and Catholics in Ireland.

In this country we have a number of right-wing groups working hard to take over the government so they can impose their beliefs on the rest of us. Look at the group that took over the school board in Kansas and barred evolution from being taught in Kansas's schools. To be fair to all paths, the government has to have a neutral standard to work from, and it only makes sense that science should be that standard. Science is not perfect, but it does grow and change whereas some religions have not changed in thousands of years. Science does do a better job of looking at things rationally. Then, because science is growing and changing, with the present Reality Box shift there will come a time when mainstream science will recognize a spiritual reality and a "non religious" spirituality will be permeated and taught in public schools.

Some may feel that this sounds contradictory to what I have been saying. But it is not. I have tried hard to show that in the religion versus science debate, the truth lays somewhere in between. Good science has no fight with religion and tries to concern itself with its data. There are of course scientists that are arrogant and take a hard stand against religion. I myself have been quite critical of organized religions, but I also have been critical of science for getting into this debate. However, science is in the process of changing and will always come back to it's center. I cannot say the same for some religious groups.

Let me reiterate the difference I see between religion and spirituality. There are literally thousands of different religions and many have quite different beliefs and traditions. Religion always implies a group of people and not an individual. Many of these religions are very dogmatic and believe that their set of beliefs is the one and only true set. Then, anyone that does not agree or is outside their tradition is not treated with the same respect as believers. Their beliefs are mostly based on a philosophy that is put together by a "chosen one," philosopher, or sage. Not all sages are religious leaders, and many sages would not approve of their philosophy being used as a set of religious laws.

Spirituality on the other hand is a personal set of beliefs or a philosophy that a person consciously lives by or practices. Spiritual people believe that in some fashion they have a soul or spirit and that it is important to nurture it. Most spiritual people understand that their beliefs are personal and understand that others have a right to go a different path. A spiritual person can belong to an organized religion but not all practicing individuals in a religion are spiritual.

My *Oxford American Dictionary* defines religion as "Belief in the existence of a superhuman controlling power, especially of God or gods, usually expressed in worship." See? Even the dictionary has the local concept of God as a "superhuman" out there who sits around giving orders. Of course, the dictionary only reflects what most people believe. But if you are associated with a religion, it is assumed that you believe this.

The church does have a very important and valuable function. Humans are innately spiritual. We need a sense of community and ceremony. We need to be appreciative of what we have to keep us grounded and to keep us from thinking we are better than other people. We need to come together to say "thank you" for the blessings in our life. We need a community to cry with us at death and celebrate with us at birth. We need a place to turn when we are sick and need help. And this is becoming more important the bigger and more impersonal our cities get. So we do need our churches. They just need to grow up a little and be more rational.

So what is needed most is for science and religion to work together and each do its own job. Scientists/philosophers need to recognize the existence of purposeful causation in nature and promote non-secular meditation in schools. The religious right is correct when they say we need spirituality in our schools, but it must take the rights of all into account. Non-secular meditation clubs and times to meditate would respect all groups because all groups have some form of meditation in their practice. Some call it prayer. All prayer has meditative aspects to it, but meditation in general is not prayer.

Even atheists sometimes meditate because the benefits of meditation are well established scientifically.[18] Although prayer also has growing scientific support (not accepted by the mainstream yet), it still implies a religious practice; but meditation does not. I know that I understood the benefits of meditation long before I saw scientifically that there is a conscious force at work in the universe.

If we are ever to live and work in peace religious groups will have to start recognizing that there are many paths to spirituality. This will require practicing tolerance. As Ken Wilber[20] has said, religions need to get out of the business of science. Science does understand better how we "mechanically" were made and how the universe "mechanically" came into existence. Religion then has the exclusive right to speculate as to why we were created and what the Creator expects of us.

The only religious practice that is wrong is one that believes it has the only Truth. The truth is, God is not interested in *how* we show respect to the world and others or *how* we celebrate life, just *that* we do. Whether we hold a rosary, lie on the ground five times a day, wear a skullcap, or sit on a rock to meditate, God knows what is in our hearts. After all, God is our Consciousness.

But I digress. After talking to my friend, I began to think about what she had said, and I began to wonder what church she was going to that believed in non-local mind. Most Christians I know believe that God is a Being out there in space somewhere or at least a spirit out there. I told Joyce about my conversation, and she said that she would like to go and just see what this church was like.

So I reluctantly agreed, and the next Sunday we went to church. When I arrived, I was amazed to see that the church was shaped like a large dome, like a giant saucer that had been placed on the ground upside down. Then someone with a giant cookie cutter had cut out half circles around the edge of the saucer. This was where the doors and windows were. Once I got past the surprise, I found it to be quite beautiful with its white smooth contour and the beautiful wood doors and the chapels stained glass windows.

Once inside the sanctuary, I had the feeling of someone holding me in a hug. This feeling must come from the large cave-like atmosphere that surrounds you and puts its arm around you, protecting you from the rest of the world. When the service started, I was amazed to see that they laughed, cried, and sang Broadway hits, celebrating life and giving thanks.

When it was all over, I was very impressed and felt a sense of spirituality I had not felt since I was a child. I did not get the impression that they were worshiping God in the traditional sense of "worship," but they were celebrating life, having a conversation with Spirit and saying "thank you" for all our abundance. I felt as though I had come home.

I then asked around and found out that it was based on the philosophy of Dr. Ernest Holmes, a metaphysical philosopher in the first half of the twentieth century. Most of his beliefs are now moving into mainstream thinking today. The main thrust of his work was to find common themes that went across all religions. He found that one of the most common themes was the ideal that in the beginning there was nothing but consciousness, and then this consciousness made us, the matter universe, out of itself. So the matter universe is really just an illusion made from nothing but this consciousness. Our consciousness then is this original consciousness manifest through us.

Holmes even found that if you went back to the original Aramaic text the New Testament was translated from, you would find this was what Jesus believed also. It seems clear that Jesus practiced deep meditation like other great philosophers. Even in the King James Version of the New Testament in Luke 17:20-21, Jesus talks of God as being within us. "And when he was demanded by the Pharisees to tell them when the kingdom of God should come, he answered them and said: The kingdom of God cometh not with observation: Neither shall they say, Lo here! or, lo there! for, behold, the kingdom of God is within you."

Then, after going every Sunday for a few months, Joyce and I joined the church. Isn't life strange; I had come full circle. Just a couple of years earlier I could not imagine ever believing that the universe was purposefully caused. But that is where my path led. I had promised myself when I was eighteen that wherever the Truth lay, I would pursue it.

My Dad never saw my Reality-Box shift. In the mid-nineties he had a number of strokes that took his brain. I say "took," because it felt as if a creature had come and taken part of him away. He could no longer have discussions with me. Our main topic of discussion before this was about artificial intelligence, most precisely whether or not computers would ever have consciousness. I argued that they would. I was a mechanist remember, and I believed that consciousness was just a by-product of the brain. He said that computers would never be conscious. He was right. He understood that consciousness was something separate from the brain. Mechanical computers, no matter how complex, will never have consciousness. Consciousness, I am now convinced, is not a "by product" of our brain, but comes from the unified quantum field. Of course, quantum computers may be a different story: we will have to wait and see when one is made. Our brain, I believe, will eventually be shown to be a quantum computer.

A few years before my dad's death in 1998, when he could still write, I got a letter from him that ended:

> No one knows the meaning and purpose of the cosmos,
> or even if there is a meaning and purpose.
> We may never know.
> To a certain extent, on the intellectual level, we can be agnostic.
> But on the existential level we cannot be agnostic since we must act and can't sit still.
> And we will act on a belief— we have no choice.
> Even suicide would be an act, and a belief.
> We will act as though the cosmos is a moral universe, and we are responsible for its existence.
> Or we will act as though our finite pleasure is all that matters, and might makes right.
> IT IS EITHER LOVE OR NOTHINGNESS.
> We choose by the life we live.

It Is Either Love or Nothingness

The Science of Spirit

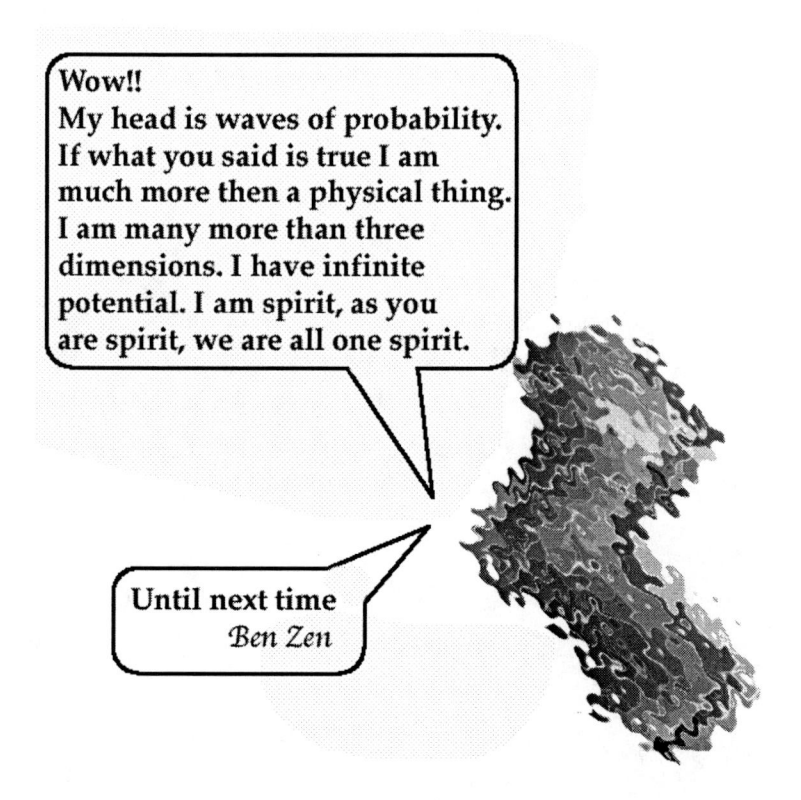

> Wow!!
> My head is waves of probability. If what you said is true I am much more then a physical thing. I am many more than three dimensions. I have infinite potential. I am spirit, as you are spirit, we are all one spirit.

> Until next time
> *Ben Zen*

The search is ended, I myself am He
Who was and is. I am Eternity
And shall abide forever in the Me.

The Voice Celestial
Page 346

Appendix A

Formula for finding the twin paradox

$$t = \sqrt{1 - \left(\frac{v}{c}\right)^2}$$

% clock slows down $= \sqrt{1 - \left(\dfrac{\text{Traveling speed}}{\text{Speed of light}}\right)^2}$

Example:

$$84\% = \sqrt{1 - \left(\frac{100{,}000 \text{ mps}}{186{,}000 \text{ mps}}\right)^2}$$

$$\frac{100{,}000 \text{ mps}}{186{,}000 \text{ mps}} = .53$$

$$.53^2 = .28$$

$$1 - .28 = .72$$

$$\sqrt{.72} = .84$$

If you are going 100,000 mph you will age 84% slower then some one going 0 mps relative to you

Appendix B

Letter from Dad when I was 18

"Glory Be to God on High and on Earth: Peace Be to Men Who Please Him."

First Christian Church
FOURTH AND HANNAH
Davis, Oklahoma
June 20, 1961

Dear Son:

HAPPY BIRTHDAY!

I have chosen this, your eighteenth birthday, as the day to write you this special letter. I hope that you will always treasure it. But I do want to speak to you of my pride in the fine son you have become, and pass on to you some of my wisdom, not profound perhaps, but maybe of some use to you. It does come from the heart of a father that wishes his son a useful, satisfying, and long manhood.

Of my pride because I am proud. On this birthday you are a better man than your daddy was on his eighteenth. You are more serious and philosophical about the meaning of life than was your dad. You make better grades in school and seem to realize the need for learning - your daddy didn't. Your daddy didn't do anything but let the time slip by in his day-dreams. But look at your solid accomplishments: Taking care of Mr. Horner; being skilled in photography; working and taking it and doing a good job at the ice dock, school kitchen, church, scout camp, etc.; making a mark in music and band; passing a tough driving test; and now you are a Eagle Scout.

And then you have a good outlook on life, you meet it with strength and yet with a certain healthy humor. You respect other people, yes, I have noticed this, and you show good manners and taste when with others. You seek ideals and yet you are not a "snob."

Yes -- this day I am proud of you.

Now for the wisdom I would pass on to you. It is first of all that wisdom is the most worthwhile goal a man can seek in life. Seek it. And second, wisdom can be had only by thinking, observation, reading and experience. No one can give it to you as a gift, you must claim wisdom through your own efforts. But the seeking is worth the struggle. Make wisdom your goal.

Here is an assignment in wisdom I would like for you to accept. It will give you insight into what your dad is talking about. On September 1, give me four short essays, written out of your reading, thinking, observation and experience, on the following subjects:

page two

> (1) Those whom the gods would destroy, they first make mad with power.
>
> (2) The mill of God grinds slowly, but it grinds exceedingly fine.
>
> (3) The bee fertilizes the flower he robs.
>
> (4) When it is the darkest, you can see the stars.

This means you have two months to think about them. They are worth thinking about. Once you get through with them, I feel you will be glad I asked you for the essay. Then they will make good speech material for next fall.

When you get home we will spend some time discussing them. Even your mother can help you some, and I some, and maybe one or two other adults like Mrs. Horner. It will be an experiment in wisdom.

By-the-way, Dr. Charles R. Beard maintains that all the wisdom of the ages is contained in the above four proverbs. But then you are not going to take his word on it, are you?

We hope you can come home Saturday night, but if you fail to get off, we'll be up to see you Monday.

Your mother and I love you very much.

                                God love you,
                                Dad

Bibliographic

1.) Gregory, R.L., *Eye and Brain-The Psychology of Seeing*. 1982, New Jersey: Princeton University Press.
2.) Robert O. Becker, M.D., *Cross Currents*. 1990, New York: Jeremy P. Tarcher/Perege Books. 336.
3.) Goswani, A., *The Self-Aware Universe*. 1995, New York: Jeremy P. Tarcher/Putnam Book. 320.
4.) Rahe, T.H.H.R.H., *The social readjustment rating scale*. Journal of Psychosomatic Research, 1967. **11**: p. 213-218.
5.) Schul, B., *The Psychic Power of Animals*. 1977, Connecticut: Fawcett Publications, Inc. 223.
6.) Weiss, P., *On The Origin of Circuits-Circuits designed by machines*. Science News, 1999. **156**(10): p.156.
7.) Travis, J., *Electronic Ecosystem: Evolving 'life' flounshes in a novel electronic world*. Science News, 1996.**140**(6): p. 81-96.
8.) Weiner, a.e.a.W.J., *Placebo Surgery in trials of Therapy for Parkinson's Disease*. The New England Journel of Medicine, 2000. **342**(5): p. 353.
9.) Freeman, a.e.a.T.B., *Use of placebo Surgery in Controlled Trials of a Cellular-based therapy for Parkinson's Disease*. The New England Journel of Medicine, 1999. **341**(13): p. Sounding Board.
10.) Davies, P., *About Time-Einstein's Unfinished Revolution*. 1995, New York: Simon & Schuster. 315.
11.) Gribbin, J., *In Search of Schrodinger's Cat*. 1984, New York: Bantam Book. 320.
12.) Herbert, N., *Quantum Reality*. 1987, New York: Anchor Books. 268.
13.) Sheldrake, R., *A new science of life : the hypothesis of formative causation*. 1987, Los Angeles New York: J.P. Tarcher ;Distributed by St. Martin's Press. 277.
14.) Travis, J., *The Accidental Immune System*. Science News, 1998. **154**(19): p. 302-303.

Bibliographic

15.) Travis, J., *Placental Puzzle*. Science News, 2000. **157**(20): p. 318-319.
16.) Green, G., *Love Without End-Jesus Speaks*. Wanda Evans ed. Feb1999, Fort Worth: Heartwings Publishing. 344.
17.) M.C.Escher, *The Graphicwork of M.C.Escher*. 1974, American edition Meredith Press: New York.
18.) Murphy, G.L.M., *The Life We Are Given*. 1995, New York: G.P. Putnam's Sons. 221.
19.) Asimov, Isaac, *Understanding Physics: Light, Magnetism, Electricity*. 1966, Menter,235
20.) Kuhn, Thomas S., The Structure or Scientific Revolutions. 1962, The University of Chicago Press.
21.) Abbott, Edwin A., *Flatland: A Romance of Many Dimensions*, 1838, Pengion press.
22.) Behe, Michael J., *Darwin's Black Box*, 1996, New Your: Touchstone
23. McDougal, William, Journal of Psychology, April 1927, January 1930, October 1933
24.) Bernstein, Jerome S., *On the Borderland*, IONS Noetic Sciences review, September-November 2000 #53
25.) Jeavons, John, *How to grow more vegetables*, 1995, Berkeley.
26.) Aron, Elaine and Arthur, *The Maharishi Effect*, 1986, Stillpoint publishing.
27. Dossey, Larry, *Recovering the Soul*, 1986, Bantam Books.
28.) Steele, J. Edward, Lindley A. Robyn, Blanden V. Robert, *Lamarck's Signature: How Retrogenes Are Changing Darwin's Natural Selection Paradigm,* 1998, Australia Allen & Unwin Pty Ltd.
29.) Lamarck J.B., Zoological Philosophy (1809) Translated by Hugh Elliot. University of Chicago Press, Chicago, 1984
30.) Zukav, Gary, *Soul Stories*, 2000, Fireside – Simon & Schuster, N.Y.
31.) Robinson, R.A. www.religioustolerance.org Ontario Consultautson Religious Tolerance Update Feb-19 2002

32.) www.crystalinks.com/prophecyanimals.html
33.) Silva, Freddy, Atlantis *Rising Music in the Fields*, #14 winter1998, and www.cropcircleconnector.com/anasazi/sounds1.html.
34.) Long, Justin D, *North America: Decline and Fall of World Religions, 1900-2225*, www.gemwerc.org/mmrc9805.htm org/mmrc9805.htm
35.) Benski, Claude, with Nienhuys, J.W., The Mars Effect: A french test of 1000 sports champions. 1996, Amherst, N.Y Prometheus books
36.) Levengood, W.C., *Semi-Molten Meteoric Iron Associated with Crop Formation*. Journal of Scientific Exploration, Vol.9, #2 pp.191-199.
37.) Jenny, Hans, *Cymatics: A Study of Wave Phenomena and Vibration*, Oct 2001, Macromedia Press
38.) Bache, Christopher M., Dark Night, Early Dawn, 2000, State University of New York Press, Albany
39.) Sharry Edwards, Sound Health Inc., P.O. Box 416, Albany, OH 45710, www.soundhealthinc.com

Index

A

Abbott, Edwin A, 90
Absolute motion, 117
Accident on ship, 39, 40
Adam and Eve, 182
Age of Aquarius, 220, 221
Aging. Stop, 32
Agriculture, 235
Algae, Blue Green, 103
Algebra, Quantum, 143, 144
Alta, 63, 166
American Constitution, 22, 241
American Medical Association, 100
Americans, 237, 241
Andromeda, 115
Arabs, 245
Aristotle, 115
Arosa Switzerland meeting, 210
Assumption, 23, 31, 69, 70, 242
Astrology, 221, 222
Atmosphere, 229
Atom, 202
Atom, Bohr's drawing, 136
Attributes, 154
Aura, 223
Australia, 225
Australian Aboriginals, 226
Autokinetic movement, 53
Awareness, conscious, 171
Awareness, secondary, 171
Awareness, self, 8 experiences, 42, 55

B

Bache, Christopher, 223, 225
Bacteria -virtual, 72
Ball, red, 44
Beard, Dr. Charles, 35
Becker, Robert O, 52, 99, 100
Behavior lab, 66
Behe, Michael, 203
Bell, John Stuart, 161, 178
Bernstein, 240
Bernstein, Jerome S., 235
Bible, Christian, 181
Big Bang, 185, 187, 192
Biointensive gardeners, 243, 244
Birth, 17
Birth picture, 17
Birthday, eighteen, 34
Black Box, 65, 76
Black holes, 186
Blanden, Robert v., 196
Blindsight, 170
BLT research center, 227
Bohr and Heisenberg, 145
Bohr, Niels, 135, 145
Boil study, 56, 57
Book-Terina's, 95, 96
Borderland People, 235-39
Boy Scout camp, 34
Boy-homosexual, 81
Brandy, 172, 240
Bricks in head, 71
British empiricist, 21, 22
Brownian motion, 135
Buddhism, 221, 223, 234
Buffalo, white, 226
Bugs, 237-239
Burmese Buddhist monk, 225

C

Car, first, 32
Cardpunch machine, 88
Cartoon-flatland, 92
Cat, telepathy, 166
Catholics, 245
Causal Determinism, 70
CF Foundation, 64
Channeling, 222
Cherokee Princess, 241
Chicken and egg, 192
Chief Seattle, 244

Index

Chinese medicine, 101
Chinese vs Western medicine, 100,101
Chinle, Arizona, 25
Choice, 174, 177, 198
Choice - maker, 198
Chopra, Deepak, 229
Christ, 225
Christianity, 221, 222, 224, 248
Christmas pudding, 135
Christmas -visit to Denver, 86
Classical conditioning, 65
Classical physics, 69
Clauser, John, 161
Clay figure, 237
Cliff dwellings, 25
Clouds, heavy matter, 188
Cognitive dissonance theory, 93
Cognitive Psychology, 67
College-start, 42
Computer modeling, 72
Conscious awareness, 174
Consciousness, 54, 165, 183, 185-188, 189, 190-193, 197, 198, 201, 208, 237, 248, 250
Consciousness - by product of brain, 71
Consciousness studies, 54
Consciousness/god, 199
Counselor first job, 95
Cows, two in truck, 236
Coyote, 207
Creator, 208
Creatures-virtual, 72
Creek, Pennington, 30
Crime rate, 210-212
Crop circle makers, 227
Crop Circles, 226
Cross Currents, 52, 99
Crystals, crying, 225
Cube 4-dimension drawing, 122
Cystic Fibrosis, 64

D

Dad, mine, 245, 249
Dali Lama, 217
Dancing Wuli Masters, 217
Dark Night, Early Dawn, 225
Darwin's Black Box, 203
Dave and Doug, 227

Day to day living, 201
DC system, 52,53
Debate-dad and I, 98
Declaration of Independence, 241
Deep Blue, 171
Degenerative disease, 100
Democritus, 162
Denver - move to, 95
Denver get job, 96
Devil's advocate, 23
Diet, 103
Dimension, fourth, 184
Dimension, inner, 242
Dimensional world four, 91
Dimensional world three, 92
Dimensional, forth, 89
Dimensional-two flatland, 91
Dirac, Paul, 143
Disease, degenerative, 100
Divorce, 87
DNA, 95, 169, 197
Dogma, 111
Dogs Stray, 236
Dogs, shooting, 28
Doormats- hospital business, 80
Dossey, Larry, 212
Double slot, 140,141
Doudy-Debacker-Dunn house, 62
Doug and Dave, 227
Dowsing, 238
Drawing Copenhagen, 146
Drawing of old and young woman, 143
Dream-my dad's, 98
Drugs, prescribe to patients, 79
Drumright, Dr., 47

E

Earth, 188
Earth - diameter, 111
Earth center of universe, 125
Eastern philosophy, 230
Echo, 229
Edwards, Sharry, 229, 230
EEG, 168
Egg, 190
Ego, 54, 199, 200

Index

Ego illusion, 201
Einstein, 31, 50, 134, 142, 156, 158
Einstein relativity, 185
Einstein, Albert- relativity theory, 121
Einstein, black board trick, 46,47
Einstein, Brownian motion, 135
El Dorado Springs, 16
Electrified grids-hamsters study, 67
Electroencephalogram, 168
Electromagnetic EMF, 99
Electron orbit -fist, 135
Elizabeth, 213
Ellis, Albert, 77
Elmwood Nebraska, 23
EMF, 99
Energy, 184, 208, 209
Energy - God or spirit, 76
Energy, frozen, 184
Energy, Packets, 133
England, 226
Environmental, 244
Epiphenomenalism, 71
Epiphenomenon, 54, 165, 174
Epiphenomenon-explanation, head, 98
EPR, 156,147
Eratosthenes, 111
Escher, M.C., 203,204, 207
ESP (extrasensory perception), 169
ESPI, 99, 113
Essays, Dad, 35
Ether, 115
Ether, luminiferous , 115
Ether-swimming pool, 117
Euclidean geometry, 227
Europeans, 237
Eve and Adam, 182
Eve, drawing, 190
Everett, Hugh, 146
Evolution, 73
Evolution, Human, 183
Evolve- software, 72
Experience - form of research, 81
Experimenting and testing, 110
Extrasensory perception, 169
Eye, 44,45

F

Family, 218
Family photo Christmas 1971, 82
Father's death, 87
FBI, 29
Feelings, 172
Female right, 219
Field, quantum, 166
First grade, 24
Fish created fish, 193
FitzGerald, George, 119,120
Five assumptions ref, 114
Flatlanders, 90, 95, 156
Flatland society, 90
Florida, Clearwater, 225
Formative causation, 193
Fort Hays behavior lab, 66
Fort Hays State University, 63
France, Richard, 113
Frank Joyce Terina, 58
Frequencies, 229
Frequency, 230
Freud, Sigmund, 53, 200
Freudian Psychoanalyst, 77
Frozen music, 228
Fruit of knowledge, 235

G

Gaia, 224
Galaxies, 186
Galileo, 115
Garden, 234, 243
Gardener, 191
Gauquelin, Michel, 221
Gears in head, 70
Genes, 184, 193
Genesis, 184, 186, 191, 207, 223
Gerbil or hamster test, 163
Gerbils and Hamsters, 67
Ghosts, 31
Genesis, 181
Giraffes, 193
Gnostic, 222
God, 109, 181, 193, 203, 209, 222, 223, 234, 247, 248
God making God - drawing, 74
God particle, 203

Index

God, Existence of, 58
God, questioning, 41
God/Consciousness, 234
God-argument against, 72 -75
God-Hitler, 199
God-Sunday school, 68
Gorn, Captain, 124
Goswami, Amit, 55, 69-70, 164, 177
GPA, 63
Graduated, 219
Graph descript of, 90
Greeks math, 111
Green, Glenda, 202, 238, 242
Greenwood, Nebraska, 24
Gribbin, John, 98, 131
Ground-where is, 115

H

Hamster or gerbil test, 163
Hamster-split cage ref, 113
Hamsters and Gerbils, 67
Hannah, 236
Hawkins, Gerald, 228
Head exp classical science, 145
Head exp Constant, 133
Head exp Plank's Constant, 134
Head- exp Quantum, 131
Head, exp, Copenhagen interpretation, 146
Head, TV inside, 55
Head-book of energy, 163
Head-exp Classical, 131
Heads exp dimensions, 121
Heaven-gold bricks, 108
Hebrews, 182
Hedonism, 224
Heisenberg and Bohr, 145
Heisenberg, Werner, 142, 143, 145
Helium, 188
Hertz, 229
Higgs particle, 187, 203
Hinduism, 221, 222
Holmes, Ernest, 249
Holograph, 229
Homestead trail, 86
Homosexual-boy, 81
Horticulture, French technique, 233
House, Doudy-Debacker-Dunn , 38

Human EPR-drawing, 168
Humane Society, 28
Humphrey, Nick, 170
Hunter-gatherers, 235
Hydrogen, 188

I

I, sense of, 55
Id, 54, 200
Illusion, 208
Immune system, 196
Immune system- virtual, 72
Immunologists, 196
In Search of Schrodinger's cat, 98
India, 229
Indian blankets, 26
Indigo children, 224
Insects, 243
International Association of New Science, 229
Interpretation-Copenhagen, 145
Introspection, 172
ION - Journal, 236
Ireland, 225
Irrationality, 77

J

Janeway, 124
Japan, 39
Jeavons, John, 242,243
Jefferson, Thomas, 241
Jenny, Hans, 228, 231
Jesus, 177, 202, 223, 238, 242
Jesus for atheists, 58
Jews, 226, 245
John Locke, 21
Journal - Institute of Noetic Sciences, 236
Journal of Psychosomatic Research, 56
Joyce, 56, 64, 87, 172, 218, 219, 249
Joyce and Terina, 57
Joyce -start school, 64
Jump, quantum, 135,136

K

Index

Kansas school board, 245
Karate, 211
Karma, 223, 224
Kasparov, Garry chess, 171
Key to truth, 114
Keys to the car, 70
King James, 234
King James version, 249
Kitty Hawk, first flight, 94
Kuhn, Thomas, 95

L

Lamarck, Jean, 193, 196
Lamarck's Signature , 196
Landrith, Garland, 210
Lao Tzu, 223
Las Vegas, 226
Lawyers Creed, 225
Legs, 190
Leptons and quarks, 187
Letter from dad-accident, 40
Letter, dad, 34
Letter, in Navy, 39
Levengood, W.C., 227
Liar's paradox, 191
Light, speed of, 114,115
Light speeds, 187
Light switch, 198
Light test for ether, 119
Light- velocity found, 115
Lindley Robyn A, 196
Lineage of psychology, 171,172
Locality, 70
Local-Non-local, 160
Lock, John, 22
Lower animals, 29
Luminiferous ether, 115

M

Machine clock, 115
Machine eyes, 99
Machine universe, 70
Machine, body, 56
Maharishi Mahesh Yogi, 210
Many World Interpretation, 146,147

Marcel, Tony's experiment drawing163, 174,175
Mars Effect, 221
Material Monism, 71
Math and science, 111
Math quantum three types, 142
Mathematics, 111
Matter, 208, 237
Matter assumption, 165
Matter form stars, 160
Matter universe, 249ort
Matter, everything made of, 71
Matter, heavy, 188
Matter/machine universe, 165
Maxwell, Planck, 133
McDougall, 194
Meadowlark, 181
Measuring devices, 146
Mechanical sense, 217
Mechanical world, 58
Mechanically, 248
Mechanists vs Vitalists, 100
Medicine, 100
Medicine, Chinese, 101
Meditation, 247
Meditation rock, 217
Meditation, Transcendental, 210
Metal, color of, 132
Metaphysical philosophy, 21
Mexico, 225
Michelson, Albert speed of light, 118
Milk Hindu, 225
Mind, 200, 209, 211, 223
Mind as machine, 70
Mind-separate from world, 69
Miracles, 225
Money - token economy, 79
Money example, 77
Monism, 222
Moon, Horizon, 50
Mother, 17
Mother Earth-Gaia, 224
Mother, mine, 238
Movie crying experience, 87
Multidimensional scaling, 88
Multisensory perception, 217

N

NASA, 229
National Academy of Science, 209
Native American, 226, 235
Nature, 235, 239, 243, 244,
Navajo, 25, 235
Navajo Boy Scout, 27
Navajo culture, 26
Navajo culture, 30
Navajo Name, 29
Navajo school, 27
Neo-paganism, 222
Neutrons and protons, 188
New Age, 113, 221, 222, 224, 229
New reality box, 22
New Reality Box 1, 36
New Reality Box 2 eye, 60
New Reality Box 3 matter, 83
New Reality Box 4 Dimensions, 105
New Reality box 5 relativity, 128
New Reality box 6 light speed, 153
New Reality Box 7 shared minds, 179
New Reality Box 8 Frozen Energy, 205
New Reality Box 9 Thought, 215
New Reality Box 10 Conscious gap, 232
Non-Religious, 246
Non-local, 212, 225, 238
Non-local mind, 194, 214, 248
Non-local mind drawing, 175
North America, 221, 224

O

Occam's Razor, 22
Ockham's principle, 21
Oklahoma, 238
Old World, 218, 219
Omaha, Nebraska, 24
One room school, 27
Operant conditioning, 65
Osteoporosis, 101
Oxygen, 189

P

Packets, energy, 133
Paint gallery, 204
Paradigm, 95, 222, 225, 231

Paradox, 191, 192
Paradoxes, 114
Pasteur, Louis, 95
Pavlov, Ivan, 65
Perception, unconscious, 170
Person in head ref, 114
Phase entanglement, 159
Phase, drawing, 159
Phillips University, 62
Phillips, Dr, 79, 80
Philosopher, 223
Philosophers, old world, 42
Philosophies, 245
Philosophy, 31, 209, 211, 221, 240, 246
Phonics system, 43
Photoelectric effect, 133
Physics, classical, 131
Physics, new, 131
Pigeons-circle, 66
Ping-pong, 65.66
Placebo effect, 101
Placebo surgery, 102
Placenta puzzle, 197
Planck's Constant, 134, 162, 188
Plants, 190
Plato, 162, 178
Podolsky, 156
Practicum, 78-81
Prayer, 238
Prayer study, 213
Praying, 213, 214
Primary and secondary qualities, 21,2
Problems, last two, 132
Protestants, 245
Protons and neutrons, 188
Psychiatric center -job at, 97
Psychic powers, 224
Psychoanalyst, 77
Psychoanalyst, 240
Psychology, 43
Psychology-real, 66
Puerto Rico, 225

Q

Quanta, 131
Quantum, 198
Quantum field, 203, 250

Index

Quantum jump, 135, 136
Quantum physics, 131, 191
Quantum physics-theory ref, 114
Quantum theory, 98, 158, 146, 237
Quantum theory incomplete, 144
Quantum theory-violated assumptions, 113
Quarks and Leptons, 187

R

R.E.T., 77
Radiation, 133
Radio, 195
Rainbow colored light, 225
Rational Emotive Therapy, 77
Reality Box, 11, 18, 19, 20, 116
Reality Box 3 - God machine, 83
Reality Box 81, 95
Reality Box change, 68
Reality Box -dilemma, 110
Reality Box my, 96
Reality Box problem, 111
Reality Box shift, 20, 238
Reality Boxes, 98
Reality Boxes-assumptions, 108
Reality Box, out side of, 142
Rebirth, 223, 224
Receptors, cold and hot, 52
Reconcile-, 95
Red cows or heifer, 226
Reincarnation, 223
Religion, 211, 245, 246
Religion Universal, 224
Religion vs Science debate, 246
Religious groups scriptures, 109
Renaissance, 21
Resonance, morphic, 195
Resonance, 229
Resonance, Schumann, 228
Re-sounding, 229
Retarded people, 242
Review of chapters 1-4, 107-111
Review-five assumptions, 108,109
Right brained, 114
Rocket-exp relative, 123
Romans, 226
Room, Ames Distorted, 48-50

Roots, 190
Rosen, 156
Rutherford, Ernest, 135

S

Sagan, Carl, 160
Sarah, 212
Schrodinger, Erwin, 142-144
Schrodinger's Cat, 131
Schumann Resonance, 229
Science, 246
Science arbitrary, 111
Science -criticized, 110
Science holistic approach, 110,111
Science teacher-Bible, 30
Science vs Technology, 110
Science, New forum, 164
Scientific, 223
Scientific data, 234
Scientific methodology, 69
Scientist/philosophers, 247
Scopes trial, 109
Seeds, 188, 214
Seeds for garden, 243
Self-Aware Universe, the, 165
Selfish machine, 217
Shaw, George Bernard, 231
Sheldrake, Rupert, 195
Ship, USS Coral Sea, 39
Ship-exp relative, 123
Silbury Hill, 22 6
Silva, Freddy, 227
Singularity, exp, 187
Skinner, B.F., 64, 65
Smoky Bay, 226
Snake pit concept, 78
Soap box preacher, 18
Society, 219
Solomaon, Gershon, 226
Soul, 223
Soul Stories, 217
Sound, 230
Sound, Puget, 244
Sound-explained, 115
Space ship thrust, 120
Space time, 192

Space, fold drawing, 120
Space/time, 184
Spaceland, 93
Speed of light, 32
Spelling computer, 200
Spelling problem, 200
Spelling test, 25
Spindrift, 214
Spirit, 208
Spirit-not real, 96
Spirituality, 30, 184, 242, 247
Spirituality - Navajos, 30
Split-brain patients, 173
Spook, 166
Squirrel in tree, 66
Star Trek relativity theory, 125
Star Trek-warp engines, 120
Stars, 186, 188
Statistics, 222
Steel-densities, 116
Steele, Edward J, 196
Stonehenge, 226
String experiences, summarized, 167
Strong Objectivity, 69, 70
Subconscious, 173
Subconsciously, 174
Sugar pill, 101
Sunday school God, 68
Super Ego, 54
Super human -God, 72
Super Position, 142
Superego, 200
Surgery patients, 212
Surprisingly, 185
Swift Jonathan, 231
Swimming pool-ether, 118
Switzerland, Arosa meeting, 210
Synergistically, 203

T

T.M., 210, 211
T.M.-Sidhi, 210
Tachyon, 184, 185
Tangled Hierarchy, 177, 191, 199, 235
Tangled Hierarchy, exp, 191
Taoism, 222
Tarot Cards, 222

Technology vs Science, 110
Temple destroyed, 226
Terina, 88, 103
Terina and Alta photo, 84
Terina and Joyce Picture, 56
Terina book, 95, 96
Terina-illness, 63
Testing and experimenting, 110
Theorem, Bell's, 161
Theosophy, 222
Thermodynamics, 75, 202, 207
Thermodynamics -drawing, 75
Thermodynamics-Louise Young, 202
Thesis, 88
Thesis graph, 88
Thinking, 171
Thought, 171
Time relativity, 122
Time, everything bound by, 70
Tipping tables, 31
Tishomingo, Oklahoma, 29
TNT, 185
Token economy, 79
Trading posts, 26
Trailhead, Mesa, 16, 38
Transcendental Meditation, 210
Transformation, Personal, 224
Truck drawing exp relative, 122
Truth, 29, 245, 248
Turtle drawing, 118
Turtle on ball drawing, 119
Turtles on turtles, 117, 118
TV, 195, 198
Twin brothers paradox-drawing, 126
Twin paradox test-drawing, 127

U

U.S. Navy, 33, 38
Uncertainty Principle, 144
Unconscious perception, 170, 193
Unfinished, universe, 202
Unified field theory, 184
Unified quantum field, 178
Universe, 187

Index

V

Veda, 229
Vibrate, 208
Vibrates, 230
Vibration, 228
Vietnam, 38
Virgin Mary, 225
Virginia, 225
Vitalists vs Mechanists, 100
Voice analysis, 230
Voyager drawing, 124

W

Wallace Johnson, 95
Watchmaker, 73, 192
Water tank McDougall, 194-195
Waves, complex, 156
Waves, Quantum, 159
We/I, 177
Weiskrantz, Louis, 170
Western vs Chinese medicine, 100,101
Western world, 209
White culture, 30
Wilber, Ken, 247
Wisdom, 34, 181
Within-happiness, 241
Word comprehension test, 174
Wundt, Wilhelm, 171

Y

YMCA, 24
Yogi, Maharishi, 210
Young, Louise B., 201,201

Z

Zukav, Gary, 217, 218
Zylberbaum, Jacoba, 168,169

To order copies of the book

Science of Spirit

$24.95 + 2.50 (S&H)

online at:
http://www.BooksToBelieveIn.com/ScienceOfSpirit.php

by phone:
have your credit card handy and call:
(303) 794-8888

by fax:
(720) 863-2013

by mail:
send check payable to:
Thornton Publishing, Inc.
17011 Lincoln Ave. #408
Parker, Colorado 80134

If it is temporarily sold out at your favorite bookstore, have them order more of ISBN: 1-932344-95-0

Name: _____
Address: _____
_____

Phone: _____
E-mail: _____

Credit Card #: _____
Card Type: _____   Expiration Date: ___/___
Security Code: _____